# THE DYNAMICS
# OF RUSSIAN
# POLITICS

# The Dynamics of Russian Politics

## A SHORT HISTORY

### BARBARA B. GREEN

PRAEGER

Westport, Connecticut
London

The Library of Congress has cataloged the hardcover edition as follows:

Green, Barbara B.
 The dynamics of Russian politics : a short history / Barbara B.
Green.
  p. cm.—(Contributions in political science, ISSN 0147–1066
; no. 337)
 Includes bibliographical references and index.
 ISBN 0–313–28886–0 (alk. paper)
 1. Russia—Politics and government. 2. Soviet Union—Politics and
government. 3. Communism—Soviet Union. I. Title. II. Series.
DK61.G74  1994
947—dc20    93–28042

British Library Cataloguing in Publication Data is available.

A hardcover edition of *The Dynamics of Russian Politics*
is available from the Greenwood Press imprint of
Greenwood Publishing Group, Inc. (Contributions in Political Science,
Number 337; ISBN: 0–313–28886–0).

Library of Congress Catalog Card Number: 93–28042
ISBN: 0–275–94828–5 (pbk.)

First published in 1994

Praeger Publishers, 88 Post Road West, Westport, CT 06881
An imprint of Greenwood Publishing Group, Inc.

Printed in the United States of America

The paper used in this book complies with the
Permanent Paper Standard issued by the National
Information Standards Organization (Z39.48–1984).

10 9 8 7 6 5 4 3 2

# CONTENTS

# PREFACE

This book addresses fundamental questions about the nature of political, economic, and social development in Russia. It examines and evaluates the capacity of Russia's political system to deal with problems of late modernization, including the problems of establishing and maintaining political order, economic growth, and legitimacy. The book emphasizes dynamic relationships and changes over time. This approach addresses underlying issues rather than transitory changes in government structure and seeks to evaluate the possibility of transformation to an effective democratic political system.

It is the contention of the author that contemporary political development can only be understood in a broad historical context. The first two chapters go back to the Tsarist empire to examine how control was established over the center and periphery, the nature of the economy and society, the inability of the system to meet challenges of modernization, problems of inefficiency and corruption, loss of control over the periphery, the rise of revolutionary movements, and the collapse of the Tsarist system.

The book then traces how control was reestablished over the center and the periphery in the Lenin years, the consolidation of power by Stalin, his transformation of the economy, the impact on the periphery, the centralization of control, and the establishment of the totalitarian state. The book discusses the impact of the Khrushchev era of experimentation, de-Stalinization, and dissent, a period which shaped the reformers of the Gorbachev period. The book then turns to a consideration of the subsequent search for political stability and order under Brezhnev, leading to the period of stagnation marked by growing economic crisis and corruption.

The major portion of the book focuses on the Gorbachev and Yeltsin years. Chapter 9 considers Gorbachev's initial efforts to consolidate power and bring about in-system reform through *glasnost*. *Glasnost*, intended as a means of improving the system by encouraging criticism of corruption and inefficiency, brought the legitimacy of the whole Soviet ideology into question. Chapter 10 explores Gorbachev's shift of power from the party to the government and its impact on the legitimacy of the system and the ability of the leadership to maintain control of the system. Chapter 11 considers the growing economic crisis, the failure of the system to deliver on its economic promises, the effort to reform the system, and the growing recognition of the impossibility of resolving the crisis without transforming the system. Chapter 12 explores the dissolution of the Soviet Union with particular emphasis on the Baltics and Transcaucasia. The unwillingness or inability to use the force necessary to hold the system together is attributed to the loss of legitimacy.

The last four chapters consider the fundamental question of whether Russia faces transformation or collapse, recognizing that transformation could be toward dictatorship or democracy. Chapter 13 considers the political structure, emerging political coalitions, and the political struggle between Yeltsin and the legislature. Chapter 14 covers the problems of economic transformation including an evaluation of the political consequences of "shock therapy." Chapter 15 discusses the tenuous Commonwealth of Independent States and Russia's relations with other former Soviet republics. It then considers problems within the Russian Federation itself and the growing loss of control over the periphery. The final chapter assesses prospects for a democratic transformation of Russia.

This book is an outgrowth of lecture courses and seminars I have given at Cleveland State University. I am indebted to my students whose comments and questions have helped me to clarify my own thinking. I am pleased to thank Mark Hogan for his valuable technical assistance. My appreciation goes to the editors of Greenwood Press for helping to make this project a reality. I am deeply grateful for the help and encouragement I received from my colleague at Cleveland State, Louis Barbato. Finally, I want to thank my daughter and son, Nancy and Richard, to whom this book is dedicated.

# THE DYNAMICS
# OF RUSSIAN
# POLITICS

*Chapter 1*

# THE ESTABLISHMENT OF
# EMPIRE: THE TSARIST CYCLE

The autocratic Tsarist system with its official state creed bears enough of a resemblance to the Soviet system to make it evident that the Soviet system was not solely a product of communism. Certain factors in Russia's past have predisposed it to act as it has. The Tsarist and Soviet systems faced similar problems, which they tried to solve in similar ways. This does not imply that the Soviet system was a direct continuation of the Tsarist regime or that it was influenced *only* by its past. Rather, it means that one cannot understand fully the problems faced by the Soviet and post-Soviet systems without some understanding of Tsarist Russia and its empire.

The first task of any political system is to establish control over the center to ensure its survival. This chapter traces how the original Russian state was established and how the government penetrated society. It then focuses on the conquering of empire and the process by which the regime attempted to establish control over the periphery. Finally, it discusses the economy and social groups. The chapter carries us up to Russia's disastrous defeat in the Crimean War.

## THE TSARIST EMPIRE: ESTABLISHMENT OF CONTROL
## OVER THE CENTER

Modern-day Russians, Ukrainians, and Byelorussians trace their origins to the Kievan state (862–1200), which had close ties with the Byzantine Empire. Kiev received Orthodox Christianity from Byzantium in the late tenth century. Although the cultural influence of Byzantium and Orthodox Christianity continued to influence Russia, Russian political development does not find its roots in the Kievan state. It is in Moscow that the Russian state was first developed as a centralized autocratic system.

A small fortified outpost, Moscow rose to become the capital of the first centralized Russian state. Moscow princes paid tribute to the Tatars for two centuries, but still managed to expand territorially, assert Moscow's political importance, and take advantage of internal Tatar disputes. The two centuries of the Tatar Yoke, however, had lasting significance for Russian development in that it broke Russia's ties with Western civilization, cutting Russia off from contact with European developments, both technological and cultural.

Ivan the Great (1462–1505) liberated Russia from the Tatars and greatly expanded the territory of Muscovy. He attempted to transform and modernize the society over which he ruled. He was most notable for centralizing political power at the expense of the minor princes and landed nobility (*boyars*). The nobility's land tenure became dependent upon service to the sovereign as Ivan moved to eliminate competing centers of power. The Orthodox faith became the official creed. Although the church and state were mutually supportive, the church was subordinate to the sovereign. Moscow saw itself as the center of Christianity, the successor to Rome and Constantinople—the concept of Moscow as the Third Rome was born. The state had a mission—to spread the true faith. The belief in Russia's divine mission became an integral part of the Russian tradition.

Ivan the Terrible (1533–84), the first Moscow ruler to be crowned Tsar of All Russia, built on the absolutist state created by his predecessors. Convinced of the necessity of centralizing power in order to survive, he carried out a relentless struggle against the *boyars*. He created the *oprichnina*, a terrorist army used to destroy real and potential opponents of his power. William Henry Chamberlin writes that

there was no legal restraint on what the *oprichniki* [members of the *oprichnina*] could do. . . . The result of this policy was to break the inherited power and prestige of the old nobility and to transfer much of the land . . . to a new class, selected by the Tsar for his personal terrorist service and completely dependent on him for favor and advancement.[1]

Peasants were increasingly enserfed, tied to the soil. They were bound to their masters who were, in turn, subject to the will of the Tsar.

Ivan's death in 1584 was soon followed by civil war and chaos. Boris Godunov had himself elected Tsar when Ivan's son died without designating an heir; however, the legitimacy of his rule was questioned by rivals. When the country suffered three years of disastrous famine, his position became increasingly untenable. The *boyars'* power had been so weakened that they were unable to take advantage of the situation to limit the autocracy and create the beginning of a constitutional government. Instead, with Boris's sudden death, the country was plunged into the Time of Troubles (1605–13), a period of anarchy, chaos, and starvation. As bands of armed peasants roamed the countryside looting and burning, foreign enemies took advantage of Russia's weakened state. Swedes and Poles seized Russian territory. The Troubles are often attributed to the lack of a workable succession, a problem that continued to plague Russia. But clearly they are also evidence of the fact that, although the sovereign had centralized power through terror and fear, the system lacked flexibility to respond to critical problems. What had appeared to be a strong centralized state melted away, leaving a Hobbesian war of all against all.

Russians may fear centralism and autocracy, but they fear the consequences of anarchy and chaos more. The danger of a return to the Hobbesian state of nature continued to haunt Russians, who feared that it might be the only alternative to autocratic government. In the early seventeenth century, order was finally restored by a Russian army that drove the Poles out of Moscow. Michael Romanov, who founded the dynasty that lasted until the 1917 revolutions, was chosen Tsar by the *zemsky sobor* (land assembly). Under his rule and that of his early successors, centralized autocratic power was reestablished and strengthened. Peasant riots and rebellions were put down ruthlessly. All centers of power that could limit the power of the Tsar were weakened. Both the *zemsky sobor*, which included representatives of several classes, and the Boyar Duma, a consultative body, lost most of their limited powers. The institution of precedence, which had permitted individuals to occupy state positions based on birth, was abolished. The Tsar now had a free hand in making official appointments. With the aid of Western mercenaries, Michael reorganized and strengthened the army, which he used to bolster the power of the throne. Although the Church remained strong, it was subordinate to the power of the state.

The power of the Tsar was finally institutionalized by Peter the Great (1682–1725), who founded the Russian Empire. Peter is well known, of course, for modernizing and Westernizing Russia, but it must be recognized that this modernization was technical and instrumental. There was no intent to introduce liberal ideas or to limit the power of the autocracy. On the contrary, Peter had every intention of strengthening centralized power and using the power of the autocracy to force Russia to modernize. He was aware that his efforts would be resisted by the *boyars*, who did not want to see their status threatened. Peter acted as if he had taken instruction from Machiavelli, who, in Book VI of *The Prince*, tells us that force and violence cannot be avoided in the creation or reformation of a state: "For the reformer has enemies in all those who profit by the old order, and only lukewarm defenders in all those who profit by the new order."[2] Machiavelli is talking not simply about a change of rulers but about a political and social revolution that creates a people and its fundamental social institutions. It is precisely such a revolution that Peter tried to bring about. Indeed, Westernization itself served to strengthen his hand against the *boyars*. He forced the *boyars* and then the lesser gentry and officials to shave their beards and adopt European dress and then eliminated the Russian title of *boyar*. This severed the nobility's connection with tradition and thereby weakened its claim to legitimacy. Nobles became increasingly dependent upon the Tsar for their status and privileges. The very founding of St. Petersburg as his new capital symbolized the breaking of ties with the past.

Peter was no longer basing his right to rule on the ancient traditions inherited from Muscovy. Tradition was something to discard and overcome. Peter instead based his legitimacy on future-oriented reforms that penetrated into, and altered, many aspects of Russian life. Peter, in Machiavelli's words, "introduced new orders."

Peter established a regular army, founded a navy, and built up a merchant fleet. He encouraged the building of factories, drafting peasants to work in them and on public works. In fact, almost all his subjects were drafted to work for the state in one capacity or another. Enserfed peasants served masters who themselves served the state. Taxation was increased to provide funds for modernization. Although the Church had never been an independent base of power, Peter limited its influence by allowing the office of patriarch to lapse. To ensure its subservience, he established the Holy Synod under a lay procurator to manage church affairs. He also established a terroristic political police, realizing that those who stood to lose under the new system would resist unless deterred by fear.

Under Peter's successors in the eighteenth century, the aristocracy was gradually freed of its service obligations while it retained its privileges. Under Catherine the Great (1762–96) nobles were freed from taxes and their estates became their permanent property. As the landed aristocracy was given increased power, the conditions of the peasantry worsened. Although Catherine dabbled with the ideas of the French Enlightenment, they were never permitted to weaken the power of the autocracy or modify the noble-serf relationship.

Russia never really experienced the effects of the French Revolution. Young Russian noble soldiers returning from the Napoleonic Wars demanded reforms but were repressed. The unsuccessful Decembrist uprising in St. Petersburg in 1825 was an attempt by educated Russian officers to establish constitutional government. The new Tsar, Nicholas I (1825–55), smashed the revolution and moved to reinforce the power of the autocracy. He established the Third Section, which functioned as a secret police force. Government was militarized with the appointment of army generals to head ministries. All were required to support "Orthodoxy, Autocracy, and Nationalism," the slogan of Nicholas's empire. When Nicholas bungled the Crimean War, it became evident that the regime was not only autocratic but inefficient, corrupt, and stupid. The most autocratic ruler in Europe proved incapable of defending Russia. Although the Tsarist system was to survive another sixty years, its very legitimacy was shaken in the aftermath of the Crimean War.

## THE TSARIST EMPIRE: CONTROL OVER THE PERIPHERY

The Tsarist Empire expanded to establish control over a vast colonial empire contiguous to the center. Richard Pipes points out that "Russia, somewhat like the United States, found outlets for expansive tendencies along its own borders instead of overseas."[3] The problem of where national consolidation ended and where colonial expansion began continues to be a central issue of Russian politics. The Russian core itself, as we have seen, was formed as Muscovy grew from a small principality to become the capital of a centralized state. After Ivan the Terrible captured the Tatar Khanates of Kazan and Astrakhan in the mid-sixteenth century, Turks and Finns were included in Russia.

In the seventeenth century, Russia expanded into Siberia, and Russians began to colonize the territory. When Orthodox Ukrainians rebelled against the Catholic Poles in 1648, they sought help from Orthodox Moscow. Russia accepted union with Ukraine in 1654 and soon established a protectorate over it. Many Russians today find it impossible to reconcile themselves to a Russia without Ukraine since the union between the two predates the establishment of the Russian Empire under Peter the Great. To the Russians, but not the Ukrainians, Ukraine is part of the central core.

After the victorious Northern War against Sweden in 1721, Russia acquired Estonia and part of present-day Latvia. As a result of the Polish partitions of 1772–96, the western part of the Ukraine, Byelorussia, and some Lithuanian ethnic lands were incorporated into the Russian Empire. Russia gained control over Latvia at the end of the eighteenth century. The partitions brought about 1 million Jews into the empire, where few had lived before. Jews were restricted to the Pale of Settlement in the northwest and southwest parts of the empire.

Further European expansion took place in the nineteenth century. Finland was annexed from Sweden in 1809 and eastern Bessarabia (Moldavia) from Turkey in 1812. Central Poland came under Russian control through the Congress of Vienna in 1815. Both Finland and Poland were initially granted extensive autonomy. After the Russians had to exert a major military effort to put down the Polish rebellion of 1830, the Poles were deprived of their constitution and most of their autonomy.

Russia expanded its frontiers at the expense of Turkey and Persia beginning in the eighteenth century. Catherine the Great annexed the northern shore of the Black Sea, and the Crimea was taken in 1783. The Transcaucasus came under Russian control as well. Georgia initially asked the Russians for protection against the Turks in 1782. In 1801, Russia annexed eastern Georgia and incorporated the rest after wars with Turkey. Azerbaijan was ceded by Persia in 1813 and the Russians conquered Persian Armenia in 1828. Consolidation of control over the Caucasus took another forty years of warfare.

By the middle of the nineteenth century, Russia was a vast empire with an enormous wealth of natural resources. While ethnic Russians occupied the center of the empire, the peripheral regions were peopled by diverse nationalities and ethnic groups at varying stages of economic, political, and cultural development. Thus the minority nationalities were far from the center of power, making control difficult, particularly in a country with poorly developed communication and transportation systems. Disintegration at the periphery was a constant danger. But rather than concentrating capabilities on controlling and integrating the borderlands, the Tsar spent his resources in defending reaction in the West, where he became known as the "Gendarme of Europe," and in attempting to expand into southeastern Europe. The latter effort led to the Crimean War, which put the survival of the empire at risk.

## THE TSARIST EMPIRE: THE ECONOMY AND SOCIETY

The adoption of Christianity from Byzantium as the official state religion in 988 and the subsequent cultural influence of the Byzantines had lasting influence on Russian development. The years under the Tatar Yoke also strongly affected the country's future. As noted, Russia was cut off from contact with general European developments. Not only did Russia not experience the Renaissance and Reformation, but Tatar rule became a model for autocratic rule.

Ivan the Great centralized political control and prevented the growth of independent economic power, which might serve as a base to limit or challenge his power. Land was awarded for military service, and holding it was dependent upon continued service to the sovereign. He had enormous control over the lives and property of his subjects. Under Ivan the Terrible and Boris Godunov, peasants were bound to the soil while *boyars* were suppressed. Everything was done to prevent the development of a civil society.

The establishment of the Russian Empire under Peter the Great was accompanied by more complex social development. We have noted that Peter established a regular army, founded the Russian navy, and built up a merchant fleet. Although these were clearly intended to serve the needs of the empire, they did form groups that might in time develop needs and interests of their own. Peter attempted to build his power on a heavy industrial base. The condition of the peasants worsened as they were drafted to work in factories and on public works. More and more peasants were enserfed. Although the *boyars* and lesser gentry had enormous power over their serfs, they were unable to limit the power of the Tsar. Master and peasant both served the state. Peter sponsored the publication of Russia's first newspaper, books were translated into Russian, and education was encouraged. This created an enormous rift between the gentry and the peasants, who began to inhabit different cultural worlds. While the gentry became at least superficially Westernized, the peasants continued to follow the ways of their ancestors, following old customs and traditions.

The eighteenth century saw a widening of the rift between the Europeanized gentry, officials, and intellectuals, on one hand, and the mass of illiterate peasants, on the other. Under Catherine the Great, the members of the gentry were freed of service obligations and the paying of taxes while they were made responsible for collecting taxes from the peasants, drafting peasants into the army, and policing the countryside. They were now given their estates as permanent private property—they could buy and sell both the land and the serfs. The conditions of the serfs worsened while the gentry prospered. Catherine brought European architects to St. Petersburg, bought European paintings, and founded the Hermitage Museum. She opened the window to Western philosophers, such as Voltaire, Montesquieu, and the Encyclopedists, who influenced the new intellectual class. When she became frightened by the peasant rebellion led by Yemelyan Pugachev, she called a halt to the intellectual ferment.

The population was overwhelmingly rural at the beginning of the nineteenth century, with only slightly over 4 percent town dwellers. Only the gentry, which accounted for about 1 percent of the population, was Westernized. Its privileges had grown while it ceased to perform meaningful service to the state. It found itself in the dangerous position of a social parasite. The country was economically backward compared with the West. Communications were poor; there were few railroads or paved roads. This lack of roads continued to plague Russia throughout the Soviet period. Merle Fainsod points out that mid-eighteenth-century Russian industry was not hopelessly backward compared with that of Western Europe.[4] But a great lag developed in the late eighteenth and early nineteenth centuries, as Russia failed to introduce new technology. Although Russia boasted strong mining and iron industries, these stagnated in the early nineteenth century. By the 1840s grain was the chief export.

The Napoleonic Wars led to an increase in support for the empire but exposed Russian soldiers to European life, to a society without serfdom. Returning officers were infected with ideas of liberty. The Russia they found upon their return was autocratic, corrupt, incompetent, and repressive. Their experience was not unlike that of returning World War II soldiers who, like Aleksandr Solzhenitsyn, were exiled to Siberian labor camps. In this earlier case, the young officers staged the Decembrist revolt, which was smashed by Nicholas. Nicholas's regime embraced increasing reaction as he tried to stifle liberal ideas. As the autocracy worsened, so did the corruption and incompetence.

Despite Nicholas's efforts to suppress independent ideas, the nineteenth century was an era of remarkable cultural blossoming. In literature, this was the era of Pushkin, Gogol, Turgenev, Lermontov. Music and science also flourished. Intellectual circles, particularly in Moscow, formed to debate the issues of the day. The educated classes increased in number, though the great mass of the people were still illiterate peasants. Many members of the nobility and gentry experienced a cultural awakening. Although most supported the autocracy as the best means of preserving their privileges, some called for modernization in order to increase government efficiency, while some even supported economic and social reform. By the 1840s the core controversy emerged between Westernizers, who urged Russia to assimilate Western culture and values, and the Slavophils, who advocated preservation of Russia's unique cultural heritage. This conflict, in one form or another, remains a central issue of Russian development.

## NOTES

1. William Henry Chamberlin, "The Soviet Union Cannot Escape Russian History," in *The Soviet Crucible*, ed. Samuel Hendel, 5th ed. (North Scituate, Mass.: Duxbury Press, 1980), 7.

2. Niccolo Machiavelli, *The Prince and the Discourses* (New York: The Modern Library, 1950), 19–23.

3. Richard Pipes, *The Formation of the Soviet Union* (Cambridge: Harvard University Press, 1954), 1.

4. Merle Fainsod, *How Russia Is Ruled*, rev. ed. (Cambridge: Harvard University Press, 1963), 20–21.

*Chapter 2*

# REVOLUTION AND DISINTEGRATION OF EMPIRE

## CHALLENGES OF MODERNIZATION

The major challenge to mid-nineteenth-century Russia was modernization and industrial development. Russia lagged considerably behind the West. Its problems parallel in many ways those of present-day Russia. Russia had failed to modernize its industry and introduce technological advances in production, while the West forged ahead. Industries in which it had once led the world, such as pig iron production, stagnated. Much of its backwardness was attributable to the nature of its labor force. Factories were heavily dependent upon illiterate serf labor until the Emancipation of 1861. Although the Emancipation freed up serf labor, which was a necessary precondition for economic development, the country lacked both an adequate banking and credit system and a stable currency.[1]

The 1890s were a period of economic takeoff in which the state played a central role: Russian finances were reorganized, and the currency was stabilized; commercial banks and joint stock companies were organized; capital flowed into railroads and banking while foreign investment grew. The textile industry was modernized with the assistance of foreign businessmen and technicians. New coal, steel, and petroleum industries developed; Russia produced more oil than the rest of the world combined in 1898–1901. The annual growth rate for industrial production was 8 percent. The percentage of industrial workers was small, although it had increased at a rapid rate since Emancipation. Industrial growth was supported by an active government policy that guided overall development. Nevertheless, Merle Fainsod concludes that "despite striking gains . . . Russia lagged far behind the most advanced industrial nations of the West."[2]

Agriculture has been called the Achilles' heel of the Soviet regime, but it was also the weakest point under Tsardom. Agricultural technology was primitive and periodic famines ravished the countryside. There was no tradition of an independent landowning peasantry. Despite the Emancipation of 1861, until 1906 peasants were tied to the *mir* (peasant commune), which practiced outdated agricultural techniques. Crop yields were low and there was enormous land-hunger. In Ukraine a prosperous class of independent farmers developed after Emancipation, but elsewhere the peasantry was desperately poor. Peasants were governed by different laws and subject to different obligations than were other classes. There was little opportunity for education, and social mobility was severely limited. Because of the peasants' discontent, disillusion, and desperate circumstances, radicals looked to the peasant as the source of revolution.

The industrial working class was formed when the Emancipation made about 4 million peasants landless. They moved to urban areas in search of a livelihood as the country industrialized. Most retained ties with their villages, but over time some broke their ties and began to develop some class consciousness. Labor exploitation was at its worst in the 1870s and 1880s. Workers were subject to long hours, low wages, and horrendous working conditions. The government was unwilling to tolerate even moderate trade unionism, which led factory workers to respond to revolutionary appeals. Trade unions were finally legalized after the Revolution of 1905. The concentration of industry in huge enterprises in Moscow, St. Petersburg, and a few other areas facilitated labor organization.

The bourgeoisie was weak. Much development, particularly in oil extraction and mining, was in the hands of foreign investors. The rest was either directly in the hands of the government or intertwined with it and dependent upon government guidance and intervention. There was no independent entrepreneurial class with an economic base that could be used to limit the power of the state. Barrington Moore has said, "no bourgeois, no democracy."[3] In Russia there was neither.

Russia seems to have epitomized the dualistic nature of the economies of underdeveloped states, with what Gerald Heeger calls "an expanding modern sector and a stagnant, often deteriorating traditional sector." Heeger argues that, as the gap between the two widens, overall economic expansion is defeated, and this raises "the possibility of serious economic and political challenges to the political system."[4]

## INABILITY TO MEET CHALLENGES OF MODERNIZATION

Reforms might have seemed inevitable to anyone witnessing the inability of the regime to organize its defense in the Crimean War or to meet the changing demands emanating from an increasingly industrialized society, but concessions were made only reluctantly, under pressure, and withdrawn or modified when that pressure was removed.

The accession of Alexander II in 1855 gave hope of reform. Although Alexander was by no means a liberal, he recognized the necessity of reforming the system if it was to survive. He loosened controls over society, allowing increasing freedom. The reforms, however, led to disillusionment, demands for further concessions, and agitation. This, in turn, led to reassertions of control, further disillusionment, and more radical agitation. Alexis de Tocqueville in *The Old Regime and the French Revolution* tells us: "The most perilous moment for a bad government is when it seeks to mend its ways. Only consummate statecraft can enable a king to save his throne when, after a long spell of oppressive rule he sets to improving the lot of his subjects." Although Alexander saved his throne, he did not save his life, and the survival of the regime became increasingly problematic.

Alexander II is, of course, best known for the Emancipation of the Serfs in 1861. This was carried out from above, largely to forestall the possibility of revolution from below, and met strong opposition from many serf owners. Serfs received only that land they had cultivated for their own subsistence, but not the land they had worked for their owners. Peasants felt cheated. The landlords were immediately compensated by the government, while the peasants were saddled with large redemption payments. Furthermore, the Emancipation did not result in individual peasant ownership of the land. Instead, control of the land was put in the hands of the *mir*, which divided the land among the peasants according to the size of the peasant families, with periodic redistribution. No peasant could leave the village without the consent of the *mir*, which was reluctant to grant such permission as it was responsible collectively for the redemption payments, army recruitment, and tax collection. Peasants were still subject to legal discrimination.

In the aftermath of the Emancipation, the peasants' standard of living actually fell. The average size of peasant allotments shrank as the population increased and rural poverty worsened. Some peasants in search of work moved to cities, where they were exposed to revolutionary agitation. Since they had not broken their ties to the villages to which they periodically returned, the revolutionary ideas spread to rural areas. Those who stayed in the cities were to form the base of an urban industrial work force.

Local government reforms had great potential for modifying the system and providing the experience of self-government. In 1864, *zemstvos*, local assemblies for rural self-government, were introduced. Although these were dominated by the nobles, they did permit some self-government and made important contributions to health, social services, education, and sanitation. Within two years of their introduction, however, their powers were curtailed significantly. Doctors, lawyers, teachers, and members of the gentry devoted to reform found the path increasingly blocked.

The judicial reforms of 1864 provided for greater independence of the courts and for procedural guarantees, including trial by jury. A professional bar was created to improve the competence and independence of judges. But as significant as these reforms were, their operation depended upon the goodwill of the Tsar. In 1881, a system of extraordinary courts not subject to these guarantees was established.

The reforms were opposed by many nobles who wanted a share of government power in exchange for their loss of privilege. There was also opposition from the radical intelligentsia, who wanted more thoroughgoing changes. When even these mild reforms from above were taken back by the Tsar, Russian revolutionary activity became widespread.

Following the assassination of Alexander II by revolutionary terrorists, the country was plunged into reaction under Alexander III (1881–94). More land was sold to peasants, redemption payments were lowered, and the head tax abolished. Nevertheless, the amount of land available to the peasants could not keep pace with the increase in the peasant population. The size of peasant allotments shrank, and peasant discontent heightened. The *zemstvos* were weakened. The position of Land Captain, appointed by the Ministry of the Interior from among the local nobility, was established to supervise the peasantry. There was some labor legislation to regulate conditions of labor, but the nascent working class suffered from appalling conditions. Russification policies were increased in an effort to control the periphery, but these policies served to alienate minorities. Discrimination against Jews was strengthened and they were barred from government service. Intellectuals were subjected to increasingly repressive policies. Universities were reorganized and education was put under tighter government control. Educational opportunities for peasants were restricted. Censorship was strengthened. Intensified police pressure was directed at revolutionary movements.

The government, seeking a class upon which it could depend, determined to win the support of the nobility by granting it special privileges and exemptions. It thus relied upon a class that had been made largely irrelevant by the changing economic structure. Reliance upon this dying class further alienated other classes whose roles were of increasing importance to the economy. The bourgeoisie and intelligentsia were gaining economic and social power but were barred from political influence.

Nicholas II (1894–1917) continued the effort to build support among the nobility while insisting on the maintenance of autocratic power. Peasant disorders broke out in 1902, followed by raids on landlords and burnings of manor houses. Accumulated social discontent and frustration exploded after Russia's humiliating defeat in the Russo-Japanese War (1904–5). The rot uncovered by the Crimean loss was further exposed by Russia's performance against the Japanese.

The unpopular war led to increasing discontent at home. When, in January 1905, Father Gapon, a priest, led unarmed workers to the Winter Palace in St. Petersburg to petition the Tsar, they were fired upon. This event, Bloody Sunday, precipitated the Revolution of 1905. This revolution was a combination of peasant rebellion, strikes, riots, and mutinies in the army and navy. Workers organized *soviets* (councils) controlled largely by Social Democrats. The Soviet of Workers' Deputies, in which Leon Trotsky played the central role, was established in St. Petersburg to coordinate revolutionary activity. A general strike spread from St. Petersburg across the empire. There was a collapse of authority beginning at the center and spreading to the periphery.

The revolution was put down by the end of the year through a combination of concessions and military force. The October Manifesto promised universal suffrage, civil liberties, and the creation of a national parliament, the Duma. Once the tide of revolution ebbed, the promises were partially withdrawn. The vote was neither equal nor direct: the upper classes were overrepresented. The Tsar had sole power to initiate legislation, and he retained exclusive control over the executive branch and over foreign policy. He appointed half of the members of the upper house, which could veto decisions of the Duma. The Tsar himself could both veto decisions of the Duma and dissolve it. Still, for the first time, legal political parties had a role in politics, and for the first time there were constitutional limits on the power of the Tsar. It might have seemed as if Tsarist Russia was at last on its way toward establishment of constitutional democracy.

Hope for the evolution of constitutional government was increasingly frustrated. After revolutionary pressures died down, the Tsar became impatient with limits on his authority. He dissolved the first two Dumas and then changed the electoral laws to give greater representation to landowners and cut down the representation of the peasantry. Minority nationalities had a lesser role. The third Duma, which was more conservative, lasted its full term. The fourth, elected in 1912, was dominated by conservative nationalists. But even they were soon pushed into opposition by the ineptitude and corruption of the government.

Efforts were made to suppress independent political activity and prevent the development of a complex civil society. Censorship was strengthened and control over universities was tightened. The Okhrana, the Tsar's secret police, infiltrated and disrupted organizations that might have served as the basis for independent political life.

The Tsar's appointment of Peter Stolypin, an intelligent conservative, as Prime Minister could have led to the most significant alteration in the social structure of the country since the Emancipation. Stolypin introduced agrarian reforms in an effort to encourage individual peasant ownership and create a new class of small landowners who would have a stake in the system and thus serve as a bulwark against revolution. If this approach had been followed at the time of the Emancipation, not only might Russia's severe agricultural problems been overcome, but the development of an economically independent class of farmers might have modified the entire political system. Now there was not sufficient time, since the outbreak of world war interrupted any peaceful progress.

## CONTROL OVER THE PERIPHERY

The central issue of empire was no longer one of expansion, but rather one of penetration and control over the periphery. Territorial expansion was pretty much halted by the early 1880s. Russia had begun its expansion into Central Asia before the Crimean War, establishing control over Kazakhstan in 1850. Conquest of the independent khanates in Tashkent, Bukhara and Samarkand, and Turkmenistan followed later in the nineteenth century. Lands were also annexed from China, and the port of Vladivostok was established in 1860 to serve this territory. In 1875, Russia obtained Sakhalin Island.

The Russian Empire now formed a vast, contiguous territory of more than 8.6 million square miles, covering one-sixth of the world's land surface, comprising more than 100 different nationalities and ethnic groups.[5] The vast size and diversity of the empire made control over the periphery a constant challenge. In an effort to increase control of the borderlands, Alexander III introduced a systematic policy of Russification and minority repression. Finland lost many of its rights, and Ukrainian and Polish cultural activity was curtailed. Discrimination against Jews intensi- fied, and the government instigated, or at least failed to control, a wave of pogroms.

National consciousness among the European peoples of the empire rose in the nineteenth century as part of the general increase in intellectual ferment. Cultural nationalism led to increasing resentment against Russian rule, which denied peoples the use of their own languages, myths, and histories. By about 1900, political nationalism was a significant movement in the European areas of the empire. The Tsarist regime refused to make any concessions to the strivings of the national minorities, who became increasingly disaffected.

The nationalist movements in the borderlands did not seek inde- pendence from the empire before 1917. Rather, they wanted increasing autonomy, the right to educate their children in their native languages, the right to maintain their own traditions, and increasing democracy and social reform.

## REVOLUTIONARY MOVEMENTS

Revolutionary ideas began to grow after the mid-nineteenth century, particularly among the intelligentsia, who were increasingly critical of the government. The period saw the growth of newspapers and magazines, which provided vehicles for them to transmit their ideas.

The Narodnik, or Populist, movement centered on the peasantry. Its organization, Land and Freedom (Zemlya i Volya), considered industriali- zation and proletarianization as dangers to avoid. The students, teachers, and educated professionals of the Going to the People movement believed they had an obligation to go to the rural villages and awaken the peasant masses. They were shaken when they were greeted with hostility by these peasants. The gulf between the intelligentsia and peasantry was far wider than they had imagined. Their activities were also met by government repression, including imprisonment and exile. The consequence was to radicalize the intelligentsia.

In the mid-1870s, Land and Freedom increasingly relied on terror. In 1879, the organization split into two differently oriented groups, People's Will (Narodnaya Volya) and Black Repartition (Chernyi Peredel). People's Will made an important organizational contribution to what ultimately became Bolshevism. It advocated a tightly disciplined party of professional revolutionaries and tried to establish a network of secret organizations to infiltrate the government and army. Following the assassination of Alexander II in 1881, People's Will was shattered by police repression, its remnants driven underground. The Socialist Revolutionary Party, founded in 1902, revived the Narodnik traditions and focused its activities on the peasantry. It played a major role in future political developments, gaining the backing of the peasants in this overwhelmingly peasant country.

Black Repartition, in contrast to People's Will, opposed terrorism and instead advocated propaganda and agitation. Georgi Plekhanov, one of the leaders of Black Repartition, became disillusioned with the peasantry's potential as a revolutionary force. In 1883 he established Emancipation of Labor, the first Russian Marxist organization. Plekhanov, who became known as the Father of Russian Marxism, argued that peasants are basically conservative, not revolutionary, and that the industrial proletariat was the coming revolutionary force. His disillusion with the revolutionary potential of the peasants imbued the Russian Marxist movement with a distrust of the peasantry. Plekhanov argued that industrial development in Russia was inevitable. Russia would need to go through a capitalist stage of development before it could reach socialism, although it might be possible through conscious action to shorten that stage. He also emphasized the need for propaganda to bring consciousness to the workers. In 1898 this organization became the Russian Social Democratic Labor Party (RSDLP), which would split into the Bolsheviks and Mensheviks.

Marx argued that progress is toward material equality and the historical effort to produce that equality takes the form of the class struggle. There have always been two classes struggling against each other: nobles against serfs under feudalism, the bourgeoisie against the proletariat under capitalism. The state has always been the tool of the dominant class to suppress the subordinate class. In the final stage of development, all will be freed, classes will disappear, and the state will wither away. To get to the final stage, society must progress through feudalism to capitalism and then to socialism. Each system must develop all its potentialities before it is ready to be replaced.

Capitalism is essential. Its task is to create the industrial base to make socialism possible. But advanced industrialism is incompatible with capitalism. Capitalism produces periodic crises of overproduction. These destroy the weaker capitalists and plunge the entire society into misery. The capitalist, to survive, cuts wages to the minimum subsistence level and prolongs hours. The worker has no choice but to work on the capitalist's terms. There are increasing numbers of unemployed, the reserve army of the proletariat, ready to take his job. The periodic crises increase in severity. The final crisis spells the destruction of the capitalist economy.

Capitalism has failed to solve the problem of distribution, and by concentrating the means of production into larger and larger units, it has made the very idea of private property absurd. Capitalism brings increasing misery, exploitation, and unemployment to the masses. The overwhelming majority of the population have been forced into the proletariat. They have no stake in the existing system and nothing to lose by revolution.

After the revolution, the first stage will be socialism. The industrial working class will come to power and destroy the inhuman market economy of capitalism. Only in the higher stage of socialism will workers be free of the industrial system. In this higher stage, communism, there will be an abundance of material goods and free development of the individual. There will be no classes and no conflict. The division of labor will be wiped out. The state will disappear. "From each according to his ability, to each according to his needs" will become the reigning principle of distribution.

Another important element of Marxism that was to affect Russian politics profoundly was the belief that class loyalties would and should override loyalties based on nationality and ethnic background. Nationalism might be a weapon against feudal society, but it then continued to serve the interests of the bourgeoisie, who used it to divide the workers of different countries in an effort to prevent them from coming to the realization of their common interest in opposing capitalism. The workers' movement should be international in scope.

Although Plekhanov was the Father of Russian Marxism, Lenin turned Marxism into an instrument of revolution. In his 1902 pamphlet *What Is to Be Done?* Lenin wrote that revolution requires a disciplined elite of professional revolutionaries. The working class, by itself, will develop only trade union consciousness. Revolutionary consciousness must be brought to the worker from without. This requires an organization of professionals. Leadership must be centralized. It is impossible to have democracy in a conspiratorial organization, especially when there is a constant danger from the regime's police. Democracy requires openness, whereas conspiracy requires secrecy.

At the Second Congress of the Russian Social Democratic Labor Party in 1903, a battle over party rules was waged. Lenin and Julius Martov, who had been allied to that point, presented rival drafts. The ostensible issue was party membership; the real issue was the nature of the party. Lenin wanted a narrow, closed party of dedicated revolutionaries, operating in strict subordination to the center and serving as a vanguard of leadership for the workers who would surround the party but not belong to it. Martov wanted a broad party open to anyone who believed in the program and was willing to work under its direction. At the congress, Martov's version won. When, at a later stage in the proceedings, after some participants had left, Lenin and his followers won a temporary majority, he promptly labeled his faction Bolsheviks, or the majority. Martov's group was called Mensheviks, or the minority. The formal split into two parties did not take place until 1912.

After the Congress, Trotsky warned that Lenin's view of the party would encourage the growth of dictatorship. Similarly, Fainsod argued that Lenin's organization of the Party planted the seed of the monolithic and totalitarian party.[6] The question, given Lenin's determination to use the party as an instrument of revolution, is whether there was any real alternative to Lenin's method of organization under Russian conditions.

Another issue dividing the RSDLP concerned the timing of the revolution. Marx had argued that the chances of success for the revolution were greatest in highly industrialized countries with large working classes. Two revolutions were needed. First, the bourgeoisie must overthrow feudalism and proceed to create a capitalist society. Only after capitalism has created the necessary industrial base can there be a successful social revolution in which the workers overthrow the capitalists. The time must be ripe for action. The problem was that Russia was economically backward with a weak and undeveloped proletariat.

The Mensheviks saw socialism as the end of a long process of capitalist development. The bourgeois revolution, carried out with the aid of the proletariat, would need to come first. The Mensheviks were therefore willing to conclude alliances with middle-class liberals against the autocracy. They hoped to establish a bourgeois republic with civil liberties and universal suffrage. In such a republic, the Social Democrats could function as a legal party, which might arrive at power through parliamentary means after industrial development and the growth of the working class had laid the basis for socialism.

Trotsky advanced a view at the opposite extreme. He argued that Russian industrial backwardness was an advantage. The Russian bourgeoisie was so weak that the bourgeois revolution could be made only by the proletariat. But once they had made the revolution, the proletariat should not hand it over to the bourgeoisie. Rather, it should hold onto power through the establishment of minority dictatorship and keep the revolution going until socialism was established. This Russian revolution would ignite a series of revolutions in the West. So, in Trotsky's view, the two Russian revolutions could be telescoped into one.

Lenin and the Bolsheviks, like the Mensheviks, argued that Russia was ripe only for a bourgeois-democratic revolution and that a two-stage revolution was necessary. Like Trotsky, Lenin recognized that the bourgeoisie in Russia were weak and unreliable. The proletariat, therefore, must take the lead in completing the bourgeois revolution. He looked to an alliance with the peasantry to provide the mass base to complete the democratic revolution. Then an alliance of the proletariat and poor peasantry could initiate the socialist revolution.

Lenin attacked Trotsky's view, warning that any attempt to arrive at socialism without passing through bourgeois political democracy would inevitably lead to reaction. In 1917, though, Lenin adopted Trotsky's position in practice. A 1988 editorial in *Izvestia* commented: "We were too clever. We thought we could skip over capitalist problems. Now we have to go back—we couldn't do it."

## THE COLLAPSE OF THE TSARIST REGIME

World War I had a tremendous impact on the regime. Once again a foreign war exposed the corruption of the system. Although there was an outpouring of popular patriotic support at first, this dissipated quickly with disasters on the fronts. The army was unprepared for war against Germany. The regime was unable to adequately supply the army with rifles and ammunition. In 1915 Russia lost 2 million killed and wounded while 1.3 million were taken prisoner. These immense losses were so harmful to Russian morale that industrialists, Duma representatives, *zemstvo* members, and other leading figures became alarmed and urged reforms. They were the backbone of conservative patriotic society, but they were largely ignored. The Tsar, who had no military training, took command of the armed forces in August 1915, leaving the government in the hands of his wife, the German-born Empress Alexandra. She was under the influence of the notorious monk, Valentin Rasputin. The military situation did not improve. In 1916 Russia lost over 2 million killed and wounded and another 350,000 taken prisoner. The morale of the Russian army was ruined.

On the domestic front, there was skyrocketing inflation. Wages could not keep up with prices. There were food and fuel shortages and transportation difficulties. Food riots and strikes broke out. Government ministers were appointed and dismissed in rapid succession. Rumors spread that the empress and Rasputin were betraying Russia to the Germans. On November 1, 1916, the conservative, nationalist Duma met. Miliukov, a prominent deputy, demanded, "Is this stupidity or is this treason?" Other speeches condemned Rasputin. Finally, three ultraconservative nobles assassinated Rasputin in an effort to save the regime, but it was too late.

By 1917, Russia had lost 12 million killed, wounded, or captured. Inflation had advanced further and there was an increasing number of strikes. Food shortages had become increasingly severe. The country was in a prerevolutionary situation.

On International Women's Day, March 8, women workers from a textile factory in Petrograd protested against living conditions and food shortages. The protest grew into a wider movement of workers and students. When the government ordered soldiers to fire on the crowds, they went over to the side of the demonstrators. The refusal of the soldiers was the key to the success of this unplanned revolution. By the night of March 12, the revolution was in control in Petrograd, and it was spreading throughout the country.

The Duma was in session in the Taurida Palace in Petrograd on March 12 when the Tsar dissolved it, leaving it without any legal standing. The deputies, faced with a political vacuum, organized a temporary committee to establish order. On the same day the Soviet of Workers' and Soldiers' Deputies, dominated by the Mensheviks and the Socialist Revolutionaries, assembled across the hall in the same building and became involved in practical and immediate problems, organizing food supplies and establishing a militia to maintain order. Most members of the Duma wanted to preserve the monarchy and, in pursuit of that end, asked the Tsar to abdicate in favor of his brother, Grand Duke Michael. The Tsar abdicated March 16, and Michael refused the throne. The Tsarist system, which had appeared immutable, slipped into the pages of history.

Duma leaders were forced to form a Provisional Government, headed by Prince Georgi Lvov. The leaders of the Soviet, without whose backing the government could never have survived, granted conditional support as long as the government was faithful to the revolution. The Soviet leaders did not want to form a government themselves. Not only did they lack experience in government, but they believed that this was a bourgeois revolution and therefore power should go to the leaders of the bourgeoisie. The Soviet banned participation in the government by socialists, insisting that socialists should serve as the opposition. Alexander Kerensky, a Socialist Revolutionary, was the only person in both the Soviet and the Provisional Government. As minister of justice, he linked the two bodies. In practice, what had been created was a dual government, in which real power was split between the Provisional Government and the Soviet. The middle class moderate or conservative leaders of the Provisional Government were aware that withdrawal of support by the Soviet would lead to its downfall. The Soviet, dominated by moderate socialists, commanded the loyalty of the workers and soldiers.

The Provisional Government instituted broad civil liberties and legal equality. It promised immediate preparations for a constituent assembly to be elected by universal, direct, equal, secret suffrage to write and adopt a constitution. The government, however, continued to prosecute the war and took no action to carry out land reform or solve the desperate food shortage.

On April 16, Lenin arrived at Finland Station in Petrograd. The next day he presented his April Theses, which called for the overthrow of capitalism, no support to the Provisional Government, power to the Soviets, and the breakup of large estates. He thus scuttled the idea of two revolutions, essentially adopting Trotsky's view, which he had earlier condemned. Lenin's platform was initially opposed by the Bolsheviks, but Lenin continued to push for it, and, in May, it was finally accepted by the Bolsheviks.

In the July Days, workers and soldiers, impatient with the failure of the government to withdraw from the war, carry out land reform, or alleviate the food shortage, took to the streets, demanding "All Power to the Soviets." The Bolsheviks, believing that the time was not yet ripe, tried to restrain them. But when that proved impossible, they decided it was necessary to lead them or risk losing their support. The Soviet refused to accept power from the demonstrators. The government still had enough power to restore order. It retaliated by raiding offices of *Pravda*, the Bolshevik paper, and Bolshevik headquarters. It published documents charging Lenin and other Bolshevik leaders with treason and issued warrants for the arrest of Bolshevik leaders. Lenin fled to Finland. Trotsky and others were arrested but were soon released. Although the government could have used the situation to eliminate the Bolsheviks, it could not muster the resolve to do so.

The Provisional Government had a new opportunity when Kerensky replaced Lvov as premier and socialists took twelve of the sixteen cabinet positions. Kerensky, who had almost dictatorial powers, moved into Alexander III's suite at the Winter Palace. But the new government, too, failed to satisfy the demand for peace and land. Believing it had no legitimate authority to make fundamental decisions, the government wanted to wait for the Constituent Assembly before carrying out land reform. It continued to pursue the war. Because of the chaotic situation in the country, it kept postponing elections for the Constituent Assembly. It did nothing to win over the masses.

Russian opinion polarized. Conservatives and liberals were frightened by the socialist composition of the government and felt that strong leadership was needed to stem the spreading anarchy. They had no faith in Kerensky's ability to govern. The urban masses were increasingly attracted to the Bolsheviks, who called for peace, land, and bread. The conservatives looked to General Kornilov, the commander-in-chief of the armed forces, to save the country. On September 9 General Kornilov marched on Petrograd, assuming he would gain the backing of all patriotic forces. To stop Kornilov, Kerensky freed the Bolsheviks who had been jailed following the July Days and distributed arms to factory workers and Red Guards. Trotsky, who had just left jail, took over the Petrograd Soviet and organized the forces opposed to Kornilov. Soldiers of the Petrograd garrison sabotaged railroads and telegraph communications of the army. Kornilov's troops deserted him. The failed coup revealed the emptiness of the power of the Right and the officer corps. It threw moderate socialists and Bolsheviks into each other's arms, and it led to a rise in mass militancy. The Bolsheviks and their supporters were now armed. Kerensky was left with no counterweight to the Left.

The radicalized masses were increasingly dissatisfied with the moderate socialists. Soldiers began to fraternize openly with the enemy and leave the front. Lenin said they "voted with their feet." By mid-September there were

Bolshevik majorities in the Soviets of Petrograd, Moscow, and some provincial cities. Trotsky headed the Petrograd Soviet. Kerensky tried to counter the rising strength of the Bolsheviks by moving to the Left. He proclaimed a republic. It was, however, too late to stem the radicalization of the masses. Soldiers became even more disaffected as the war dragged on, worker strikes increased, and peasant impatience rose. Since other socialist parties participated in the government, disillusion with the government led to disillusion with moderate socialism.

At the end of October, Lenin was able to persuade the majority of the Central Committee of the Bolshevik Party to support armed insurrection. The seizure of power was almost bloodless. It was backed by considerable mass support, but the support was for an all-socialist Soviet government, not an exclusively Bolshevik government. Trotsky disguised the seizure of power by the Bolsheviks as a transfer of power to the Soviets, composed of Bolsheviks and non-Bolsheviks. The Military Revolutionary Committee, established by the Petrograd Soviet on October 29 to prepare for the armed rising, was controlled by the Bolsheviks and chaired by Trotsky. On November 5, Trotsky persuaded the Petrograd garrison to join the insurrection. The government was unable to defend itself. The coup began at midnight of November 6–7. On the morning of November 7, Lenin announced the overthrow of the Provisional Government. Mensheviks and Socialist Revolutionaries resigned from the Congress of Soviets in protest, leaving the Bolsheviks in control of the centers of power.

## LOSS OF CONTROL OVER THE PERIPHERY

Although we have concentrated on the dissolution of power at the center, it is important to be aware that power was disintegrating on the periphery as well. Upon coming to power, the Provisional Government took some immediate steps to placate minorities, abolishing all restrictive legislation and promising full equality regardless of race, religion, or nationality. The actual administration was left largely to local leaders. But, as with so many other pressing concerns, the government refused to make any fundamental changes until the Constituent Assembly. Just as the refusal to take action caused increasing chaos at the center, it resulted in loss of control throughout the borderlands.

The military disasters and the failure to deal with fundamental problems radicalized the populations, but in the borderlands that radicalization led not only to socialism but to a growth in nationalism. We have noted that as the Provisional Government continued the war, peasant soldiers deserted the front. Non-Russian soldiers organized national units, left the front, returned home as units, and then backed local political organizations. When the government failed to institute land reform, much of the resentment was directed against Russian colonizers. National minorities had organized in preparation for the Constituent Assembly. There was no intent to challenge the authority of the Provisional Government, but as the Provisional Government weakened, local centers took on a greater and greater role. When the Bolsheviks seized power, local organizations declared sovereignty and took over control of the government in their territories.[7]

The Tsarist system was not really overthrown; rather, it dissolved, leaving a vacuum that was filled reluctantly by the Provisional Government. When the Provisional Government found itself unable to establish order out of chaos, the Bolsheviks took over, almost bloodlessly. Unlike the members of the Provisional Government, they would not hesitate to use the force necessary to reestablish control over the center.

As the government lost power at the center, control over the borderlands began to slip from their hands as well. Not just Tsardom, but the Russian Empire had disappeared. But just as the Bolsheviks would reestablish control over the center, so, too, would they reestablish control over the periphery.

It is interesting to compare Gorbachev with Kerensky. In order to forestall too radical reform, Kerensky tried to balance the forces of the Left with the Right. When Kornilov actually tried to carry out a coup, Kerensky resisted. The failed coup led to growth in the power of the Left, undermining Kerensky's power. One might add that both cases led to the loss of empire.

## NOTES

1. Merle Fainsod, *How Russia Is Ruled*, rev. ed. (Cambridge: Harvard University Press, 1963), 20–24.

2. Ibid., 24.

3. Barrington Moore, Jr., *Social Origins of Dictatorship and Democracy: Lord and Peasant in the Making of the Modern World* (Boston: Beacon Press, 1966), 418.

4. Gerald A. Heeger, *The Politics of Underdevelopment* (New York: St. Martin's Press, 1974), 137.

5. Richard Pipes, *The Formation of the Soviet Union* (Cambridge: Harvard University Press, 1954), 3.

6. Fainsod, *How Russia Is Ruled*, 148.

7. Pipes, *The Formation of the Soviet Union*, 50–53.

*Chapter 3*

# ESTABLISHING CONTROL: THE LENIN YEARS

After the revolution the Bolsheviks found themselves in control of Petrograd, Moscow, and about ten other cities. The country was in chaos. The formidable tasks facing Lenin and his party included restoring order in the center, winning a civil war against domestic opponents, eliminating foreign control, and then reestablishing control over the periphery. In accomplishing these tasks, the Bolsheviks felt that they must somehow justify their actions in terms of an ideology that they were applying to a situation for which it had not been intended. The final and in many ways most difficult task facing the Bolsheviks was creating the industrial base that Marx had stated was the historic task of the capitalists. By skipping over capitalism, the party itself had to perform this task, which necessitated exploiting the workers and peasants. But this task fell to Stalin.

## ESTABLISHING CONTROL OVER THE CENTER

The first and most immediate question facing the Bolsheviks was whether to govern alone, thereby establishing a minority dictatorship, or to share power with other socialists and establish a government that could claim the loyalties of a majority of the population. The problem, of course, was that the other socialist parties had been in a majority in the Provisional Government that the Bolsheviks had just overthrown. How could the party carry out a revolution and then invite its opponents to join it in a new regime? Furthermore, bringing the moderate socialists into the government would introduce the same indecisiveness that had characterized the Provisional Government, and that was something Lenin would not tolerate. Minority dictatorship, on the other hand, risked the danger that Lenin had pointed out when it was originally advocated by Trotsky—the danger of creating a reactionary system adverse to the interests of the people. There was considerable controversy among the Bolshevik leaders, but it was finally decided to work only with the left wing of the Socialist Revolutionary Party. The Bolsheviks held all important posts in the new government: Lenin became chairman of the people's commissars; Trotsky, commissar of foreign affairs; Stalin, commissar of nationalities. Lenin recognized that if the problems facing Russia were to be dealt with, what was needed was a sharp instrument able to act quickly and decisively, not a debating society. The need for action took precedence over democracy.

The problem facing Lenin and the Bolsheviks was similar to that facing modernizing elites when they take power in underdeveloped countries. Gerald Heeger in *The Politics of Underdevelopment* points out that if the elite seeks alliances with other elites and social groups, the result is immobilism. Intra-elite conflict prevents any one elite from attacking the problems of social change. If a coalition is formed, elites are inhibited from implementing policies that might challenge the position of their partners. This usually perpetuates the status quo and makes underdevelopment a chronic problem. The alternative to coalition, governing alone, requires coercion, since patronage is limited.[1] The decision on the part of the Bolsheviks to govern alone freed them to take the action necessary to alter the social and economic structure and deal with the problem of development, but it also made the terror inevitable.

Lenin indeed acted quickly. He established the Cheka under Feliks Dzerzhinsky, a Polish noble who was totally incorruptible and totally dedicated to the Bolshevik cause. It was the Cheka's task to root out and eliminate opponents. Lenin also issued decrees that nationalized all banks, annulled all debts of the Russian government including foreign debts, nationalized industry, redistributed land, abolished capital punishment, introduced separation of church and state, nationalized church property but permitted churches to use it, and proclaimed the equality of women. All of this, of course, was on paper only, since the Bolsheviks did not have the ability to enforce their decrees.

Before its overthrow, the Provisional Government had finally set a date, November 25, for elections to the Constituent Assembly. The Bolsheviks had repeatedly called for the elections. Lenin now felt that the Constituent Assembly was part of bourgeois democracy, and they had moved on beyond that stage. It was decided to allow the elections, let the Constituent Assembly meet, and dissolve it if it proved troublesome. The Bolsheviks won less than 25 percent of the seats. When the assembly met January 18–19, it was surrounded by armed troops. Lenin demanded that it vote all power to the Soviets, which the Bolsheviks controlled. The assembly refused. The Bolsheviks and Left Socialist Revolutionaries withdrew and the meeting adjourned. It was declared dissolved and not allowed to reconvene.

Lenin was aware that the war had been instrumental in bringing about the fall of Tsardom and the Provisional Government. German troops were on the soil of the Russian Empire. The Bolsheviks were divided over what to do. Some wanted to continue the fight against the Germans. Trotsky proposed a policy of "no war, no peace," according to which the Bolsheviks, while refusing to fight, would hold the lines at the front and refuse to cede lands to the Germans. Lenin insisted that the country needed peace. Soldiers were deserting the front—the country was simply unable to continue to wage war. The war, in any case, was a fight among capitalist states and of no concern to socialists. When the international revolution came, it would not matter whether they had ceded land or not. Protracted negotiations with the Germans began almost immediately after the revolution.

The Treaty of Brest-Litovsk was finally signed in March. Russia surrendered all land occupied by the Germans: Finland; the Baltic states of Estonia, Latvia, and Lithuania; Poland; Ukraine; and much of Byelorussia. This meant the loss of almost all the European territory acquired by the Tsarist Empire, more than 1.3 million square miles with more than 60 million people. Russia lost three-quarters of its iron and coal mines, one-third of its factories, and the breadbasket of the empire. The Left Socialist Revolutionaries protested and left the government. For Lenin, the losses were secondary. The most important task was to establish control over the center. To try to fight the war or hold on to the borderlands at this point would only jeopardize this essential task.

In discussing the Treaty of Brest-Litovsk, Adam Ulam holds the experience of Brest-Litovsk responsible for changing the nature of the Bolsheviks:

They emerged from the experience of Brest-Litovsk as politicians. Many of them still felt in the vanguard of revolution, but all of them now realized that they were primarily masters of Russia. Rapidly there now developed those state institutions which even the most cynical among them had believed they were casting aside forever when they seized power: a standing army with an officer corps, a bureaucracy, a *permanent* political police.[2]

He also stresses the importance of the shift of the Soviet government to Moscow on March 10. St. Petersburg had represented the opening of Russia to Western ideas. Now, however, "the new rulers, like the Tsars before Peter the Great, resided in the Kremlin, sought their inspiration in Russian history, made Russian nationalism the mainstay of their power."[3]

Lenin and the Bolsheviks were still faced with civil war. The Whites, led by former Tsarist officers associated with the old order, wanted to restore landlords' estates. This antagonized the peasantry. They spoke of Russia as one and indivisible and opposed any concessions to minority nationalities, thus alienating non-Russians. The Allies, Britain, France, the United States, and Japan intervened in support of the Whites. This Allied intervention turned the civil war into a patriotic war to save Russia from foreign enemies. Mensheviks and Socialist Revolutionaries opposed the Bolsheviks but hesitated to fight them because they opposed a reactionary restoration.

Trotsky built the Red Army, hiring Tsarist noncommissioned officers to serve as officers. By the middle of 1920, Russia was rid of most of the White armies and the Allied intervention forces, and the Bolsheviks began to reclaim some of the ceded territory. As the civil war came to an end, the Russo-Polish War broke out over the issue of the border between the two. As a result of this war, interwar Poland included what is now western Ukraine. The Poles also took Vilnius, the capital of present-day Lithuania.

War communism was the attempt to build communism and serve practical needs during the civil war and was prompted by ideological idealism and cold necessity. It consisted of five key points:

1. Forcible requisitions of agricultural surpluses to feed the army and workers in the cities;
2. Nationalization of all branches of the economy, at least on paper;
3. Prohibition of private trade;
4. Strict egalitarianism; and
5. Elimination of money as a means of exchange.

The Bolsheviks, faced with the task of feeding the army and workers, had no choice but to institute the "forcible requisitions," which amounted to sending raiding parties into the countryside to seize food. With money worthless and no consumer goods to purchase, there was no incentive for peasants to sell their produce—they produced only enough to feed themselves and their families. Although the raiding parties were supposed to take only surplus food production, this was usually not adhered to. War communism, however, was not just a policy of necessity. There were also a strong ideological element and a determined effort to destroy the market economy. This was a period of social experimentation in education, postcard divorce, abortion on demand, and equality of the sexes. New forms of art and literature flourished. War communism abolished inequality but did so by leveling down and making poverty universal.

The country's industry, transportation system, and agriculture were in ruins after six years of war. Millions of people had been killed or had died of hunger, while others had joined bands, killing and looting. Once the civil war and Polish war were over, the Bolsheviks had to face severe domestic problems. The half-starved workers and peasants turned against the Bolsheviks. A peasant revolt broke out, and there were strikes in Petrograd (St. Petersburg) itself and a naval mutiny in Kronstadt. The sailors of the Kronstadt naval base, who had been among Trotsky's strongest supporters, demanded freedom for workers and peasants and free elections to soviets. They called for the overthrow of the Bolsheviks and the establishment of socialist democracy. The Kronstadt Rebellion was put down by force. In this sobering atmosphere the Tenth Party Congress of 1921–22 was held.

The Bolsheviks, as Isaac Deutscher points out, now claimed that they were pursuing a policy with which the working class, in its interest, ought to agree, and with which it would eventually agree, even though it did not yet agree.[4] The first issue concerned the role of trade unions. Could the Bolsheviks permit trade unions to push forward the interests of their members when such might conflict with the overall good as viewed by the Bolshevik Party, which represented the interest of the entire working class? After considerable debate, it was decided that, temporarily, the party must control the trade unions because of the economic crisis. If necessary, the party would dismiss their leaders and prevent free speech and criticism of government policies. Lenin argued that there was no obligation to allow freedom of speech to critics when the government knew that what it was doing was right and in the true interest of the working class. After the crisis, Lenin insisted, there would be a return to proletarian democracy.

Lenin introduced the New Economic Policy (NEP), intended as a temporary retreat from building communism and necessitated by the disastrous economic circumstances in which the country found itself. Lenin stated that it was necessary to take "one step backward to take two steps forward." The main points involved:

1. abandoning the policy of forced requisitions from the peasantry and encouraging private farming;
2. allowing small private or cooperative industries to produce consumer goods;
3. permitting private trade; and
4. encouraging a free labor market.

The major industries or "commanding heights" would remain under the state but would use commercial principles.

Lenin, like Stolypin before him, would bank on the peasant to solve the economic crisis. Stolypin had hoped to see the emergence of well-to-do peasants who would form a conservative petit bourgeoisie and stem the tide of socialism. This was exactly what Lenin feared. Although the economic reality necessitated reliance on peasants, traders, and small-business men, Lenin had no intention of permitting them to block the advance of socialism. He envisaged only a temporary retreat in the economic realm, but a retreat that might last one to two decades.

At the same time that the party loosened control over the economy, it tightened political controls. Lenin feared the growing popularity of the Mensheviks and Social Revolutionaries and feared even more the possibility that they might become vehicles for the expression of the interests of the new classes being created by NEP. The decision was made to outlaw all other political parties. Soviet Russia officially became a one-party state.

Leonard Schapiro argues that a single party might have been justified under war communism and civil war but that Marxist logic demanded more than one party under NEP.[5] Under NEP, there would be a growth of different economic interests. Therefore, according to Marxism, there would be a growth of disparate political interests. Unchecked, this should have led to multiple parties expressing their disparate interests and to separate centers of power. Lenin essentially shared Schapiro's reasoning as to what would occur if the different interests were not checked. He had no intention, however, of submitting passively to Marxist economic forces.

A single party, though, could operate as an umbrella party, permitting a variety of different factions to operate under its aegis. Under such circumstances, the factions might end up representing different class interests. Not only would they undermine the class basis of the party, but the party itself would be transformed from a powerful instrument of change into a debating society. Given Russia's dire condition, action, not discussion, was required. By a large majority, the Congress therefore made the crucial and fateful decision to outlaw factions within the party. A secret clause empowered the Central Committee to expel any offenders, even party leaders. Publicly, the Central Committee would have to stand as a bloc regardless of previous disagreement. This, too, was intended as a temporary measure until the crisis was over. An article in *Pravda* in the fall of 1990 lamented, "It was Lenin's party which made Stalin possible." However, while it is true that the tight-knit party of Lenin with its prohibition against factions facilitated the rise of Stalin and Stalinism, it did not make this outcome inevitable.

## ESTABLISHING CONTROL OVER THE PERIPHERY

Lenin had recognized the value of nationalist movements as a tool to weaken Tsarist authority. Prior to World War I, he developed a national program proclaiming the right of all nations to self-determination, by which he meant the right to secede from an oppressor nation. He opposed federalism and did not favor secession. He was convinced that if nationalities had the right to secede, they would no longer choose independence. What Lenin wanted was free unification.

Immediately after the revolution, on November 15, the Bolsheviks issued the Declaration of the Rights of the Peoples of Russia, calling for the equality of all the peoples of Russia; the right to self-determination, including secession and the formation of independent states; the abolition of all national privileges; and the free development of all national minorities and ethnic groups. Lenin hoped that the minority nationalities would choose to join Russia now that Tsardom and the bourgeoisie had been defeated. Despite his hopes, the empire rapidly fell apart.

The best study of the disintegration of the Russian Empire and its reconstitution as the Union of Soviet Socialist Republics in 1922 is found in Richard Pipes's *The Formation of the Soviet Union*. This discussion is heavily indebted to that work.

The reaction of the Bolsheviks, particularly when faced with the prospect of Ukrainian independence, was to reinterpret the concept of self-determination. It was decided that the right to secession could be exercised only by the working class as represented by the Bolshevik Party. The governments of the breakaway lands were labeled counterrevolutionary. National self-determination could not be permitted to serve as a cloak for the bourgeoisie. The Bolsheviks now adopted federalism in an effort to hold the empire together. Nevertheless, it was not until the end of the civil war that the borderlands were brought back under central control.

The Ukraine was of particular concern: Lenin said, "If we lose the Ukraine, we lose our heads." Immediately following the Bolshevik revolution, power in the Ukraine was divided between the Ukrainian Central Rada in Kiev, dominated by moderate socialists, and city soviets in Kharkov and elsewhere, dominated by Bolsheviks. Armed struggle broke out. By February 1918 Bolshevik forces occupied most of the Ukraine, and a Ukrainian People's Republic in Kharkov declared the Ukraine to be in a federal relationship with Soviet Russia. However, the Treaty of Brest-Litovsk ceded control of the western borderlands. The Rada entered an agreement with the Central Powers providing for their occupation of the Ukraine. Once they were in control, the Germans dissolved the Rada and set up a puppet government. The entire Ukraine was soon the scene of anarchic peasant rebellion.

The surrender of the Central Powers in November 1918 led to their withdrawal from the Ukraine. At this juncture the Ukraine was in total chaos. Roving bands of peasants attacked estates, killed Jews, and launched raids on cities. The heads of the old Rada established the Directory, which depended on the politically disorganized peasantry for support. A Soviet government of the Ukraine had a base of support in cities and towns with a pro-Russian flavor. Soviet troops moved in, and by the beginning of February they were in control of almost the entire Ukraine. Agents of the Russian Communist Party arrived in force. Although the Soviets withdrew in the face of General Anton Denikin's White forces at the end of August, Soviet forces reentered in December 1919 when they established what was supposedly a sovereign Soviet republic. This was intended to undercut the drive for independence, but in practice the Ukraine was run by the Russian Communist Party.

Armenia, Azerbaijan, and Georgia proclaimed the Transcaucasian Federative Republic in April 1918, but when the three nationalities proved unable to reconcile their differences, the federation fell apart. The Azeris were under Turkish occupation until the end of the war, when British troops landed. The British backed General Denikin and his White army, thereby alienating Azeri nationalists, who had no desire to see a reversal of land reform or a restoration of Tsarist domination. The Armenians were in a desperate situation, flooded with refugees and facing famine. After the Germans and Turks evacuated, Armenia collaborated with Denikin and soon became involved in hostilities with Georgia and Azerbaijan.

Georgia was in a far better situation than Armenia or Azerbaijan, since it had an educated intelligentsia experienced in government service and party organization. It was under German occupation for five months and then under British occupation, but both countries limited their interference in Georgian affairs. Although the Georgian Social Democratic government tried to model itself on West European democracies and introduced socialist and democratic reforms, it opposed the strivings of national minorities on its territory. Georgian nationalism then, just as today, has refused to accommodate the concerns of Ossetians and Abkhazians.

After the defeat of Denikin, the Great Powers recognized the de facto independence of all three Transcaucasian republics. However, Russia regarded their separation as temporary. Russia was heavily dependent on the area for fuel and mineral resources, so that its retention was considered vital to future development.

Since Azerbaijan was most crucial because of its valuable oil reserves, the Bolsheviks moved against it first. At the end of April 1920, the Red Army crossed the Azerbaijan border and marched on Baku. The government surrendered following an ultimatum from the Azerbaijan Communist Party. The Soviets captured Baku without bloodshed. The Red Army then crossed the Armenian and Georgian borders. The Georgians counterattacked, and when the war with Poland broke out, Lenin withdrew from Armenia and Georgia. The Soviets entered a treaty with Georgia granting unconditional recognition and renouncing all interference in its affairs. In exchange, Georgia agreed to allow the Communist Party freedom of action.

After defeat by the Turks in a full-scale war in September 1920, Armenia's situation became more hopeless than ever. Stalin, as commissar of nationality affairs, issued an ultimatum to the Armenian government and the Red Army crossed the border. Because of the danger of Turkish occupation, the Soviet invasion was not unwelcome to the Armenians. By the end of 1920, Azerbaijan and Armenia were both back in the fold.

The conquest of Georgia took longer, led to strong differences of opinion among Soviet communist leaders, and was apparently carried out without Lenin's knowledge. Although Lenin had approved the invasions of Armenia and Azerbaijan, with the end of the civil war and the need for reconstruction, Lenin was trying to curry favor with the West. Military operations began on February 16–17. On March 18, the Georgians surrendered.

The Muslim borderlands raised a difficult situation for the Bolsheviks. Lenin supported independence for the Muslim areas of the British Empire, believing that the colonial peoples of the East would play a major role in the international revolution against imperialism. How then could the Bolsheviks reassert Russian control over these lands, which, after all, were colonial dependencies? In December 1917, in an effort to win over the Muslims, Lenin promised to respect their beliefs, customs, and cultural institutions.

Fighting broke out between local Russian urban inhabitants and peasants, on one hand, and local Muslims, on the other. The local Russians allied with the communists to preserve their privileges. Local Muslim intellectuals wanted to create a Turkic Communist Party and a Turkic Republic to include all Muslims in Central Asia and elsewhere. They wanted an independent army and the withdrawal of all non-Muslim units. Further, they insisted that all anti-imperial activity in the East must rely exclusively on Muslim revolutionary forces. Stalin, as commissar of nationality affairs, was adamantly opposed to a unified Muslim movement and sought to prevent any pan-Islamic or pan-Turk movement. Lenin, too, found the demands of the Muslim leaders unacceptable. However, Lenin realized that an effort to continue colonial rule would antagonize the Muslims. He recognized that local Soviet power had been in the hands of a small group of Russian workers with a colonial mentality. When the Soviets conquered the borderlands in 1919 and 1920, Lenin proposed that land be taken from Russian settlers and redistributed to Muslim peasants, Russian *kulaks* (well-to-do peasants) disarmed, and communists infected with Great Russian nationalism transferred. When this proved unacceptable to the Muslim Communist Party, Lenin seized control, purging those Muslims who had challenged Soviet control. Lenin made economic and cultural concessions and strove to work with Muslim nationalists for common goals, but he was not prepared to cede control to local Muslims.

Lenin argued for the necessity of disassociating the Communist regime from Great Russian nationalism. He proposed the creation of a Union of Soviet Republics, a federal government standing over all the republics: Russia, Ukraine, Byelorussia, and Transcaucasia. Under the Soviet Union, the republics would possess equal rights, including the right to secession. A commission under Stalin's chairmanship prepared a draft agreement. On December 30, 1922, the First Congress of the Union of Soviet Socialist Republics ratified the agreement establishing the Soviet Union.

Lenin was too ill during the fall and winter of 1922–23 to take an active role in this process. However, he became increasingly concerned about Great Russian dominance. He warned:

It is quite natural that in such circumstances the "freedom to secede from the union" by which we justify ourselves will be a mere scrap of paper, unable to defend the non-Russians from the onslaught of that really Russian man, the Great-Russian chauvinist, in substance a rascal and a tyrant, such as the typical Russian bureaucrat is.[6]

Lenin supported the union but wanted concessions for the minorities. Stalin argued that "the political basis of the proletariat is primarily and chiefly the central, industrial regions, and not the border regions, which are peasant countries." Therefore "the right of self-determination cannot and must not serve as an obstacle to the working class."[7]

The Constitution of the Union of Soviet Socialist Republics (USSR) was ratified on January 31, 1924, seven days after Lenin's death. It created a single union state with a federal structure and granted, on paper, the right to free secession. The Tsarist Empire was in effect reconstructed with the exception of Finland, Poland, the Baltics, the Western Ukraine and Western Byelorussia, and Bessarabia.

## NOTES

1. Gerald A. Heeger, *The Politics of Underdevelopment* (New York: St. Martin's Press, 1974), 9.

2. Adam Ulam, *Stalin: The Man and His Era* (New York: Viking, 1973), 162–63.

3. Ibid., 168.

4. Isaac Deutscher, "Defeat in Victory," in *The Soviet Crucible*, ed. Samuel Hendel, 5th ed. (North Scituate, Mass.: Duxbury Press, 1980), 93.

5. Leonard Schapiro, "The Origin of the Communist Autocracy," in *The Soviet Crucible*, ed. Hendel, 104–7.

6. Quoted in Bohdan Nahaylo and Victor Swoboda, *Soviet Disunion: A History of the Nationalities Problem in the USSR* (New York: Free Press, 1990), 54.

7. Ibid., 56–57.

## Chapter 4

# CONSOLIDATION OF POWER
# AND RECONSTRUCTION

Although the Lenin years were crucial for the development of the Communist Party, the major formative and institution-building years took place under Joseph Stalin. This chapter deals with the first stage of the process by which power was consolidated and society transformed to create what became known as the Stalinist model. What was perhaps the greatest social and economic revolution in history was carried out from above against the opposition not only of the masses but of much of the elite. To achieve this required the amassing of an enormous amount of power in the hands of one man and the unleashing of unprecedented terror. The economy was industrialized rapidly while every effort was expended to prevent the development of a civil society in which associations would act independently of the state. The Stalinist years set the course for the future of the Soviet Union.

## AGGREGATING POWER TO RULE

Elitist mobilization movements such as the Bolshevik Party are held together by party discipline, ideology, and quasi-charismatic leadership. The weakening of any one of these is likely to turn the movement into a collection of rivals representing competing interests. This, in turn, weakens the ability of the movement to carry out an economic transformation that will modernize the country. The country becomes condemned to backwardness.

In his discussion of the politics of underdevelopment, Gerald Heeger points out, "The problem of political consolidation, of aggregating sufficient power to rule, has been an age-old concern in the study of politics."[1] In many states, no single leadership group has been able to consolidate control. The complexity of the center combined with the increase in the scope of government activities means that power becomes increasingly fragmented. He states:

The question must ultimately be asked as to how "uncruel" this kind of a political system really is. True, its capacity to coerce is minimal. Yet, so too is its capacity to satisfy the aspirations of its citizens. . . . The power to accomplish national goals remains a scarce resource. In its absence, a government not only cannot deal with bettering the human condition of its people, it cannot even save itself.[2]

Stalin, certainly, did not hesitate to aggregate the power to rule—he did so by eliminating any real or potential rivals for power. In reviewing Stalin's actions, we need to assess the appropriateness of the means to the end desired. If the end may be considered to justify the means, it does not justify *any* means, but, as Machiavelli pointed out, only those means necessary to achieve the end.

The consolidation of Stalin's power proceeded by slow steps, beginning during the period of Lenin's last illness. The incapacity of Lenin, the quasi-charismatic leader, permitted the growth of increased ideological friction within the party and threatened the unity of the party. Stalin, Lev Kamenev, and Grigory Zinoviev formed a triumverate within the Politburo to prevent Leon Trotsky from succeeding to the leadership. Trotsky was a powerful orator and the hero who had created the Red Army, but he was considered arrogant and even dangerous because of his radical views. Stalin originally seemed unthreatening and conciliatory, a gray presence willing to take on the boring, routine assignments that needed to be done but brought no personal glory. In 1922 he was appointed to the newly created position of General Secretary of the party—a position that put him in charge of the machinery of the party. Stalin used the powers of the Secretariat to put his supporters in other positions of power.

On December 25, 1922, after suffering a severe stroke, Lenin dictated a memo he intended the party to see after his death. In this "testament," Lenin warned, "Comrade Stalin, having become General Secretary, has concentrated an enormous power in his hands; and I am not sure that he always knows how to use that power with sufficient caution." He then turned to Trotsky, saying, "Comrade Trotsky . . . is distinguished not only by his exceptional abilities . . . but also by his too-far reaching self-confidence." Lenin also raised questions about other potential successors. On January 24, 1923, Lenin added a postscript to the testament, saying, "Stalin is too rude" and calling for his removal as General Secretary. Although the memos were not made known until January 1924, Lenin openly criticized Stalin as an administrator and attacked his nationality policies.

When Trotsky sought to take advantage of Lenin's attack on Stalin by calling for a revival of criticism in the party, Zinoviev demanded Trotsky's arrest. Stalin called for caution, saying that chopping off heads was dangerous. He did accuse Trotsky and his supporters of factionalism, adding that factional freedom would lead to the destruction of the party and play into the hands of its enemies. The party called for a systematic battle against Trotskyism, which was labeled a "petty-bourgeois deviation." The Secretariat then removed or transferred Trotsky's supporters from strategic party and government posts, replacing them with loyal followers of Stalin.

After Lenin's death on January 21, 1924, the party Central Committee voted to suppress Lenin's testament. When the party Congress met on May 24, Zinoviev led the attack on Trotsky, demanding that he confess his errors. Stalin did not go as far as Zinoviev, asking only for a halt to oppositionist activities. He was conciliatory and called for unity. However, for Stalin unity required that Trotsky and his followers subordinate themselves to the Politburo majority, and this the Opposition refused to do. Stalin used the very logic that Trotsky had accepted in 1921 when he supported the resolution against factionalism at the Tenth Party Congress. In January 1925, Trotsky was dismissed from his position as head of the War Commissariat and chairman of the Revolutionary War Council.

Stalin now abandoned Zinoviev and Kamenev, whom he labeled the Left Opposition. He allied with Nikolai Bukharin, the strongest defender of NEP and the advocate of building "socialism in one country" (the view that the Soviet Union should concentrate on building a powerful self-sufficient state rather than concentrating on world revolution), Alexei Rykov, chairman of the people's commissars; and Mikhail Tomsky, the trade union leader. At the Fourteenth Party Congress in December 1925, Zinoviev and Kamenev were in much the same position Trotsky had been previously. Then Zinoviev and Kamenev had led the call for party unity and the elimination of factions. Now they seemed to be challenging those very principles. Kamenev attacked Stalin and the idea of vesting supreme power in a single leader, but he was shouted down. The Congress was a triumph for Stalin.

Stalin moved to destroy his opponents politically. First, the Leningrad party organization, which had been Zinoviev's base of support, was purged. Zinoviev was removed from the Politburo. In late October 1926, Trotsky was dropped from the Politburo, Kamenev lost his position as an alternative member of the Politburo, and Zinoviev was removed as head of the Comintern. Although the Left Opposition renounced factional activities, it continued to hold clandestine meetings, run an illegal press, and stage public demonstrations. In October 1927, Trotsky and Zinoviev were expelled from the Central Committee, accused of participating in a military conspiracy against the regime in league with White Guardists. In November, Trotsky and Zinoviev were expelled from the party. On January 17, Trotsky was exiled. He continued to attack Stalin, accusing him of betraying the revolution.

The Fifteenth Party Congress in December 1927 was the scene of the complete defeat of the Left Opposition. Zinoviev and Kamenev surrendered. Although later readmitted to the party, they were a spent force. The Trotskyites who refused to recant were exiled or imprisoned.

Stalin next moved against Bukharin, Rykov, and Tomsky. He began by insisting that differences among Politburo members could be expressed only behind closed doors. All would be bound in public by a majority vote. Since Stalin controlled a majority of the Politburo, this ensured that only his position could be voiced. This was in accord with the decision of the Tenth Party Congress they had all supported. In early January 1929, Stalin announced that he had discovered a right-wing faction led by Bukharin, Rykov, and Tomsky. In April, the Central Committee denounced the views of the Right Opposition and warned that they would be expelled from the Politburo if they persisted in defying the ban on factionalism. By the end of 1930, despite stating publicly that their views were mistaken, all three had been removed from their leadership positions and dropped from the Politburo.

The question we need to consider at this point is whether it was necessary for Stalin to eliminate other senior leaders and, if so, whether the means used were appropriate to the goal. Not only Trotsky, Zinoviev, and Kamenev but Bukharin, Rykov, and Tomsky as well shared "a fervent hope of achieving an industrialized and socialist Russia and of seeing Communism prevail in the world."[3] They agreed on the goal but, as is discussed later, disagreed on the appropriate means. They also agreed on the importance of a centralized party without organized factions. But the Left at least was unwilling to submit to party discipline. As Adam Ulam states, "No one could really believe that the three dissident leaders would cease criticizing and plotting, no matter how many times they pledged good behavior."[4] If the intra-elite conflict had continued, it would have prevented any one elite from attacking the problems of social change. This is not to argue that Stalin's approach to social change was the appropriate one, but rather that for any approach to be implemented, unity of leadership would have to be forged. To ensure that once defeated, they stayed defeated, Stalin not only needed to defeat his opponents politically but discredit their views. What better way than to require them to recant and themselves admit publicly that their views were erroneous? If one accepts the goal of transforming Russia, then the means to this point were appropriate.

By the end of 1929, Stalin was the only member of Lenin's Politburo still in power. The men who replaced the Old Guard were personal followers of Stalin, utterly dependent upon him for their positions. They would exercise power and indeed become instruments for the transformation of the system, but they would operate only in accord with the dictates of Stalin. Sergei Kirov, the only one to build an independent base of power and gain a measure of popularity, would soon become a victim. The others, the Molotovs and Mikoyans, would outlast the dictator. But Stalin and his policies would not be publicly opposed until after his death. Stalin had aggregated power and forged the monolithic instrument necessary for rapid industrialization and modernization.

## TRANSFORMATION OF THE ECONOMY

The introduction of NEP following the disastrous harvest of 1921 improved agricultural production as peasants responded to incentives. By substituting a tax in kind for forced requisitions and enabling peasants to dispose of their surplus as they chose, peasants had reason to produce a surplus. The regime relied on persuasion and education, stressing gradualism. But as the peasants increased their output, the price of food fell while that of industrial goods rose. Peasants began to hold back their surpluses, endangering the supply to the cities and export markets. Nevertheless, there was an overall improvement in economic conditions. By 1927, the prewar level of the economy had been reached.

While NEP permitted economic recovery, it also led to the reemergence of the problem of a dual society. Robert C. Tucker states:

NEP Russia . . . could be described as a society with two uneasily coexisting cultures. There was an officially dominant Soviet culture comprising the Revolution's myriad innovations in ideology, government structure, political procedures, economic organization. . . . Side by side with it was a scarcely sovietized Russian culture that lived on from the pre-1917 past as well as in the small-scale rural and urban private enterprise that flourished under the NEP. It was a Russia of churches, the village *mir*, the patriarchal peasant family, old values, old pastimes, old outlooks along with widespread illiteracy, muddy roads.[5]

Tucker adds, "It was the declared objective of the new one to transform the old one."[6]

The central question was how to achieve this transformation. As Stephen Cohen stresses, Bukharin was committed to the NEP economic framework, in which large-scale industry, transportation, and banking were in the state sector while private farms, small manufacturing, trade, and service enterprises constituted a private sector.[7] Bukharin believed in offering price concessions to the peasants to get increased production for the market. The government would obtain produce from the *kulaks* through increased taxation. More and cheaper consumer goods would also be needed to tempt the peasants to produce more than their households required and to bring that surplus to market.

Trotsky insisted that greater attention had to be paid to heavy industry and planning. He feared the consequences of allowing the economic future of the country to remain in the hands of the *kulaks*, who could withhold the grain supply if their demands were not met. But, Cohen argues, neither Trotsky nor the Bolshevik Left "ever advocated imposed collectivization, much less wholesale collectivization as a system of requisitioning or a solution to industrial backwardness."[8]

In December 1927, the Fifteenth Party Congress adopted the first Five-Year Plan for economic development. As originally approved, it called for ambitious expansion of heavy industry and partial voluntary collectivization. Collectivization was intended not only as a means to transform the countryside but as a means to carry out an industrial revolution from above. Since long-term foreign loans were not available, the only alternative was to extract a surplus from the agricultural sector. This would necessitate lowering prices for agricultural goods, increasing the tax on peasants, taxing *kulaks* more heavily, and persuading poor peasants to join collectives.

In 1929 Stalin jettisoned this approach and instituted a relentless struggle for rapid industrialization and total collectivization carried out with unbridled coercion. Peasants were forced to give up their land, their tools, and their livestock as they were herded into collective farms (*kolkhozy*) or state farms (*sovkhozy*). Collective and state farms would put the rural population under control, thereby simplifying the task of extracting grain. Stalin called for emergency measures against the *kulaks*, who, supposedly, were hoarding surpluses, but the fury of collectivization fell on the mass of the peasants, not just the *kulaks*. Stalin sent thousands of party members to the countryside to confiscate surpluses, liquidate *kulaks* as a class, and force the peasants into the collectives. Peasants resisted in the only way they could, by destroying their crops and slaughtering their livestock. The chaos and confusion led to a temporary retreat; but after a successful harvest in 1930, Stalin pushed ahead. The harvests of 1931 and 1932 were poor, but Stalin was relentless. Millions of peasants were exiled to Siberia. The Great Famine of 1932–33, in which 5–10 million lives were lost, was caused in large measure by the chaos of collectivization. Although agricultural production declined in the 1930s, the export of grain increased. Robert Tucker calls forced collectivization a "state-initiated, state-directed, and state-enforced revolution from above."[9]

The original cautious approach was abandoned in the industrial sector just as it was in the agricultural. Totally unrealistic goals were imposed. All industries were again nationalized. Government-directed planning under Gosplan replaced the market in all respects.[10] Heavy industry and war industry were given absolute priority. The emphasis was on machine building, steel mills, and hydroelectric dams. There was little investment in consumer goods or agriculture. "Shock methods," intensive campaigns, were used to increase productivity in key sectors; but what was produced had little relation to any plan. A.F.K. Organski states that the average rate of increase in large-scale industrial output from 1928 to 1937 was about 15 to 16 percent per year. The gross national product rose 6.5 to 7 percent each year. In 1926, more than 80 percent of Russia's workers were in the agricultural sector. During the next thirteen years, 25 million moved to cities, doubling the urban population.[11] This vast stream of peasants strained the already inadequate housing supply.

The rapid development of a modern industrial society requires more than financial investment—an illiterate peasant population has to be molded into a modern work force. The need for managerial, engineering, and technical personnel was so great that the country used remnants of the old intelligentsia and foreign specialists. It then embarked on a vast training program to create a Soviet technical intelligentsia. The enormous demand for trained technical personnel led the regime to emphasize technical ability for important positions, not just party membership or class origins. Peasants who had never seen a watch had to be transformed into a disciplined urban work force. A work ethic had to be developed. The educational system had to be expanded and remodeled in order to inculcate students with the virtues of efficiency and discipline. They had to be taught the importance of getting to work on time, sticking to the job, not leaving early. Sanctions were introduced to keep workers on the job and prevent labor-flitting, absenteeism, and tardiness. Egalitarianism was scuttled. Large-scale factories necessitated that authority and responsibility be located in the hands of factory managers.[12]

## IMPACT ON THE PERIPHERY

During the period of NEP, beginning in 1923, the Party followed a policy of *indigenization*, which entailed encouraging the involvement of members of the local nationalities in the work of the party and local governments, encouraging literacy in the native languages, providing education in native languages, and fostering cultural development. In Muslim republics, Latin-based alphabets were created for each ethnic group. Within each republic, minority rights, including the right to education in the native language, were protected. National literatures and arts flourished.[13]

The onset of collectivization was bound to have a particularly cruel effect on the population of the borderlands. As Stalin had noted, the urban population was largely clustered in the center, while the periphery was populated by peasants and herdsmen. Collectivization and the Five-Year Plan were intended to put the burden of industrialization on the peasantry, and this meant that there would be a disparate impact on the nationalities of the periphery. Bohdan Nahaylo and Victor Swoboda describe how the terror was initially directed against the national intelligentsia and then against the population as a whole. Collectivization in Kazakhstan was unspeakably brutal, involving the forced settlement of herdsmen and nomads. Kazakhstan lost 73 percent of its cattle and 88 percent of its horses. Over 1.5 million Kazakhs, about one-third of the population, perished. "Relative to the size of their population, the Kazakh holocaust exceeded that of any other nation in the Soviet Union at that time."[14] Denomadization and collectivization, directed primarily by Russians, were also implemented in the rest of Soviet Central Asia despite opposition and even open rebellion.[15]

Nahaylo and Swoboda contend that the Ukraine was a deliberate and intended target because the loyalty of all Ukrainians was suspect. They maintain that the famine, in which at least 5 million Ukrainians died, was deliberately engineered by Stalin. They cite the fact that the Russian-

Ukrainian border was closed to prevent starving peasants from going to the Russian side to get bread.[16]

Whether or not there was genocidal intent in the attack on the Ukrainian peasants, there is no question but that the Ukrainian peasantry suffered disproportionately. The Ukraine was the richest agricultural region with a large number of relatively well-to-do peasants—the hated *kulaks*. If the peasants were to be made to bear the brunt of the burden of industrialization, and if the *kulaks* were to be eliminated, there is no way that the Ukraine could have escaped disproportionate suffering.

If Stalin's consolidation of power can be justified in terms of the requirements of modernization, what about Stalin's mass collectivization and rapid industrialization? How do the achievements balance off against the costs? Isaac Deutscher argues:

In a titanic struggle with the inefficiency, the sluggishness, and the anarchy of Mother Russia, Stalinism has carried its industrial revolution almost to every corner of its Eurasian realm. The core of Stalin's genuine historic achievement lies in the fact that he found Russia working with the wooden plow and left her equipped with atomic piles.[17]

In view of Chernobyl, this assessment is unintentionally ironic. But it did not take Chernobyl to raise doubts about Deutscher's assessment. Tucker has argued that "the terroristic collectivization" was not necessary for the results achieved in industrialization.[18] Stalinist socialism, he says, "was a socialism of mass poverty rather than plenty; of sharp social stratification rather than relative equality; of universal, constant fear . . . ; of national chauvinism . . . ; and of a monstrously hypertrophied state power."[19] Similarly, Ulam states, "Quite apart from its immediate catastrophic effects, collectivization has been an economic disaster in the long run."[20]

The Soviet Union, through forced collectivization and the relentless struggle for industrialization, created a powerful industrial state. If Deutscher overstresses the constructive aspects of Stalin's economic strategy and his "historic achievement," Ulam and Tucker ignore the fact that the Soviet Union, despite its weaknesses, was able to direct enough resources into heavy industry and the military to challenge the United States and to be considered one of the world's two superpowers. A major question is whether this goal could have been achieved by less horrific means. We need to consider whether a slower pace, retaining the NEP framework, might have achieved the same result. In 1928 there were 25 million inefficient, primitive small farms tying up labor needed for industrialization. How could these be transformed into modernized, efficient, surplus-producing farms? One alternative might have been to continue to rely on the *kulaks*. As they prospered, they would enlarge their farms and modernize. While the *kulaks* might have prospered, the poor peasants would have been driven out of the countryside in search of urban employment. Many would have lived in dreadful circumstances. The state would have needed to use its tax powers to siphon off at least a part of the *kulaks'* productivity to use for investment in heavy industry. The process of industrialization might have been painfully slow. But once the country modernized, it would have had a strong base of support in an independent class of farmers who would identify their well-being with that of the country. The state could have retained its control of the heights of industry and even instituted planning. This approach, because of the need to placate the *kulaks*, would not have been able to throw all its resources into heavy industry. A consumer goods sector would have been necessary.

In fact, though, what Stalin created was a distorted economy that formed the basis for the current economic catastrophe. Economic Stalinism left the Soviet Union with an inefficient and distorted system of production. Heavy industry, especially defense, had absolute priority. The planning process itself distorted production, as industries strove to meet production targets rather than producing what the economy needed. Consumer goods were sacrificed. What was produced was of shoddy quality. There was a housing shortage as more workers poured into the cities. The chaos of collectivization, peasant resistance, the lack of incentives for the individual peasant, and the low investment in agriculture have continued to plague the Soviet economy. What the Soviet people have discovered is that their enormous sacrifices produced an economy that no longer works.

## NOTES

1. Gerald A. Heeger, *The Politics of Underdevelopment* (New York: St. Martin's Press, 1974), 133.

2. Ibid., 137–38.

3. Adam Ulam, *Stalin: The Man and His Era* (New York: Viking, 1973), 258.

4. Ibid., 267.

5. Robert C. Tucker, "Stalinism as Revolution from Above," in *Stalinism: Essays in Historical Interpretation*, ed. Robert C. Tucker (New York: W. W. Norton, 1977), 80.

6. Ibid.

7. Stephen F. Cohen, "Bolshevism and Stalinism," in *Stalinism*, ed. Tucker, 22.

8. Ibid., 23.

9. Tucker, "Stalinism as Revolution," 83. See also Robert C. Tucker, *Political Culture and Leadership in Soviet Russia* (New York: W. W. Norton, 1987), 72–107.

10. Tucker, "Stalinism as Revolution," 83.

11. A.F.K. Organski, *The Stages of Political Development* (New York: Alfred A. Knopf, 1965), 103–5.

12. Merle Fainsod, *How Russia Is Ruled*, rev. ed. (Cambridge: Harvard University Press, 1963), 103–8.

13. Bohdan Nahaylo and Victor Swoboda, *Soviet Disunion: A History of the Nationalities Problem in the USSR* (New York: The Free Press, 1990), 60–65.

14. Ibid., 67–68.

15. Ibid., 70.

16. Ibid. For elaboration of this argument, see Robert Conquest, *The Harvest of Sorrow* (New York: Oxford University Press, 1986).

17. Isaac Deutscher, *Russia: What Next?* (New York: Oxford University Press, 1953), 65.

18. Tucker, "Stalinism as Revolution," 87–88.

19. Ibid., 95.

20. Ulam, *Stalin*, 356.

*Chapter 5*

# CENTRALIZATION OF CONTROL

By 1934, Stalin had completed the first stage of the total transformation of society. The peasants had been subdued and the economy was on the upturn. At the Seventeenth Party Congress in January 1934, Stalin was in total control. It might seem that this would be the time to build up positive support for the regime, especially in view of the growing menace of Hitler's Germany. Instead, Stalin chose to unleash the terror. Bolsheviks under Lenin had never shrunk from the use of terror. Terror was used by both sides during the civil war, and Lenin did not hesitate to order the Cheka to shoot or arrest class enemies or opponents of the regime, including Mensheviks and Socialist Revolutionaries. During collectivization, terror was used against *kulaks* and other peasants, Nepmen (those who engaged in buying and selling during NEP), and anyone else who stood in the way of the vast social transformation being imposed on the country. Now Stalin was to unleash the terror against ever larger proportions of the population, including the Communist Party itself. This was accompanied and followed by the fastening of controls on all aspects of society. Peasants were once again enserfed, tied to collective or state farms. Workers were tied to factories. The party, the military, the intelligentsia, and the technical elite were under tight, centralized control. The state swallowed up society as all voluntary associations were transformed into instruments of the regime.

## THE GREAT PURGE

On December 1, 1934, Sergei Kirov, the head of the Leningrad Party organization, member of the Politburo, and heir apparent to Stalin, was assassinated.[1] Although it is likely that Stalin himself ordered the assassination, Stalin blamed a terroristic "Leningrad Center" that allegedly also planned to kill Stalin. All members of this alleged counterrevolutionary organization were executed. Hundreds of Leningraders were arrested. This inaugurated a massive campaign of repression. In January 1935, Zinoviev, Kamenev, and seventeen of their allies were tried and sentenced to terms of five to ten years. In the spring, thousands of Leningraders were deported to Siberia. These early stages of the Great Purge were conducted under NKVD chief Genrikh Yagoda, who also prepared the first of the Moscow show trials.

In August 1936 Zinoviev and Kamenev, in a staged open trial in Moscow, confessed to planning and instigating the murder of Kirov and to acting as agents of foreign powers. They and fourteen other defendants were found guilty and shot. During the trial, they implicated former Right Opposition-ists. Tomsky committed suicide.

In September 1936, Yagoda was replaced by Nikola Yezhov. The ensuing period, until he was replaced by Lavrentii Beria in December 1938, is known as the Yezhovshchina, the Yezhov Time. Terror became pervasive. No one was beyond its reach. Everyone suffered, and the more influential suffered the worst. The party, the army, and security forces were all targets as violence spiraled. A second show trial, in January 1937, was aimed at alleged economic "wreckers" and saboteurs who, supposedly on orders of the German and Japanese intelligence services as transmitted by Trotsky, had deliberately mismanaged and wrecked the economy. They were blamed for shortages and economic failures of collectivization and the first Five-Year Plan.

The purge of the Red Army took place next, after fake evidence impli-cated the top commanders in treason. In fact, "from all available evidence it is certain that there was no military plot against Stalin."[2] On June 11, 1937, it was announced that Marshal Tukhachevsky and seven other generals were being tried for espionage and treason. This one-day trial was held in secret session and all defendants were executed. After the trial, their families and aides were rounded up. Any officer who had ever received a favorable recommendation from any of them was liquidated. This was followed by a mass purge of the armed forces. About 40,000 Red Army officers, three-fourths of the officer corps, were "unmasked" as traitors.

The third and most famous of the Moscow show trials, the Trial of the Twenty-One or the Anti-Soviet Bloc of Rightists and Trotskyites, was held in March 1938. The defendants were former Politburo members, govern-ment ministers, diplomats, and doctors. Primary among them were Buk-harin, Rykov, and Yagoda. It was charged that not just the Left Oppositionists, but also the Right Oppositionists, had been involved in the murder of Kirov. Defendants were accused of serving the Germans, the Japanese, the Poles, and the British. They were accused of participating in nationalist plots to detach parts of the Soviet Union, instigating economic wrecking activities, inciting rebellion, and having plotted to kill Lenin. Eighteen of the condemned were shot, and three received long prison sentences.

In July 1938, Beria, the party boss of Transcaucasia, was brought to Moscow as Yezhov's deputy, and on December 8 Yezhov was replaced by Beria. Now began what Merle Fainsod has called "the purging of the purgers."[3] Beria purged the NKVD, staffing top positions with men loyal to him. Yezhov and his men were blamed for "excesses." Some thousands of lesser victims were released from forced labor camps and the pressure of the purge relaxed, at least as it affected ordinary citizens. A wave of arrests targeted the NKVD. The Great Purge slowly came to a halt, but terror was now institutionalized in the system.

The Communist Party was almost destroyed. Of the 1,966 delegates to the Seventeenth Party Congress in 1934, 1,108 were arrested. Of the 139 Central Committee members and alternates elected at that Congress, 98 were shot. Of 15 full and candidate members of the Politburo, only 7 survived until 1939. By 1939, 850,000 party members had been purged. The Old Bolsheviks were eliminated, and the party began to put increasing emphasis on recruiting a new, technically oriented managerial elite that could supervise the economy.

Political leaders of the non-Russian republics were accused of "bourgeois nationalism" and purged, to be replaced by Stalin's henchmen. The entire pre-1938 government and party leaderships of the Ukraine were branded as foreign spies. The cultural intelligentsia of Ukraine, Georgia, and Armenia suffered heavily. Deportations began in the North Caucasus in 1937. Control by the center was strengthened.

Anyone with foreign contacts was automatically suspect during these years. This included diplomats, foreign communists, and veterans of the Spanish civil war. The terror moved in ever-widening circles until everyone was a potential victim independent of the actions or beliefs of the individual. The total number of victims, including arrests and deaths, may have reached 12–15 million. The vast majority of the population spent these years in fear. But many also believed that while they and their family and friends were innocent and while there may have been excesses, nevertheless most of the victims were guilty. Ulam points out that hundreds of thousands of Russians cheered resolutions demanding that enemies of the people be shot.[4]

The purges eliminated all real or potential opposition to Stalin's further consolidation of autocratic power. They directly benefited a new generation who could step into positions of power opened up by the purges.

Robert Tucker argues that the Stalinist revolution recapitulated the Tsarist pattern of rule wherein all classes of the population from the lowest serf to the highest noble were bound in compulsory service to the state.[5] He cites the anti-*boyar* terror of Ivan IV and the *oprichnina*, stating that Stalin consciously took it as a model during the Great Purge, casting the Old Bolsheviks in the role of the *boyars*. Tucker's argument highlights the element of continuity in Russian politics. It is useful especially in throwing light on one aspect of the purges, the elimination of all real and potential rivals for power. As long as the Old Bolsheviks existed, even out of power or in jail, they were a potential alternative to Stalin's power. The Great Purge, by eliminating and thoroughly discrediting them as traitors, assured that neither they nor their positions could be used to challenge Stalin in the future. In the process, Stalin implicated the hundreds of thousands who cheered and the tens of thousands who benefited by moving into positions of power.

Stalin's Great Purge then can be seen in part as an attempt to ensure that the transformation of the social and economic structure of the country could be institutionalized without opposition, even when problems arose, as surely they must. It can also be seen as a necessary measure, in view of the impending war with Nazi Germany, to ensure the total unity of the country when it would face its greatest peril. These rationales, however, are inadequate in face of the ever-spiraling terror and its millions of victims. Stalinism was clearly not a purely utilitarian ideology.

The regime established tighter and tighter controls over society. A vast network of labor camps at times held 10 to 15 million prisoners, who were forced to build canals and railroads and labor on other projects under inhuman conditions. In industry, the power of the managers was strengthened, but they were punished drastically for failure to meet performance goals. Labor discipline was tightened and the power of trade unions was curbed. Internal passports were revived—since peasants were denied them, they were restricted to their villages and lost any freedom of movement. Numbers of them were drafted to work in industry. In 1938, to tighten control over workers and prevent "flitting," labor books with a record of work history were issued to each worker. No one could be hired without handing the book over to management, which retained it, thus tying the worker to his place of employment. Violators of labor discipline could be punished by dismissal, which entailed the loss of social benefits, including housing. In practice, because there was a severe labor shortage, managers often overlooked infractions. In 1940, as the danger of war increased, labor rules were tightened even further. Employees who were late to work could be sentenced to compulsory labor at their workplace with wage deduction up to 25 percent. Petty theft and hooliganism at work could lead to a one-year prison sentence. All workers were frozen at their jobs. A worker in a defense industry who quit without authorization was subject to court-martial and a sentence of five to ten years of forced labor.

Controls were supplemented by a system of incentives. In 1931, wage differentials, piece rates, and rewards for exceeding production norms were introduced. Egalitarianism was labeled a petty bourgeois deviation. Shock workers who exceeded production records were rewarded with special privileges, including better food, housing, and consumer goods. A miner, Aleksei Stakhanov, had supposedly exceeded work norms by fourteen times. The Stakhanovite movement urged others to emulate his achievement. Workers who exceeded the norms were showered with honors and special rewards. But the mass of workers were poorly paid, poorly housed, poorly fed, and tightly controlled.

## PATRIOTISM AND THE WARTIME EXPERIENCE

A patriotic revival began in the 1930s with a return to traditional Russian values, as Russian nationalism was merged with Marxist-Leninism. Peter the Great and Ivan the Terrible became heroes. Traditional family values, with emphasis on childbearing, were restored, as was the traditional educational system, with school uniforms and emphasis on discipline.

In an effort to delay or prevent war with Germany, the Nazi-Soviet Pact was signed on August 23, 1939. This agreement and its consequences were to play a significant role in the ultimate dissolution of the Soviet Union. Although this was a nonaggression agreement, not an alliance, it served Hitler's purposes by allowing him to attack Poland on September 1 without fear of a two-front war. The infamous secret protocols established spheres of influence in Eastern Europe. The eastern portion of interwar Poland, an area that was ethnically primarily Ukrainian and Byelorussian, went to the Soviet Union, as did Finland, Estonia, and Latvia. Lithuania was later added. The Soviets were also granted an interest in Bessarabia, then under Romania. The Soviet Union invaded Poland on September 17. Single-slate elections were held in western Ukraine and western Byelorussia, which then unanimously voted to join the Soviet Union. Their requests were granted November 1 and 2, 1939. In June 1940, the Soviets invaded Bessarabia and the ethnically Ukrainian area of northern Bukovina. The latter, along with part of Bessarabia, went to the Ukraine. The Romanian part of Bessarabia was joined with the Slavic Trans-Dniester region to become the Moldavian Soviet Socialist Republic. Banks, industry, and trade were nationalized, and large estates were distributed to poor peasants. The Soviets then unleashed terror, deporting more than 1 million people from Ukraine and Byelorussia, primarily Poles and Jews.

The Soviets demanded that Finland and the Baltic states enter mutual assistance pacts with the USSR. Finland refused, precipitating the Winter War, in which the Soviet Union annexed some territory that served to improve the defense of Leningrad. Latvia, Lithuania, and Estonia bowed to the ultimatum. In June 1940, Soviet troops entered all three. Rigged elections were held, and the new parliaments voted to join the Soviet Union. They were admitted in August 1940. The Baltic states were later to declare this procedure illegal. The acquisition of the Baltics could, perhaps, be defended as necessary to defense. The Baltics had, after all, been part of the Tsarist Empire, and they provided the Soviets with ice-free ports. Their takeover did, of course, violate solemn treaties entered into by Lenin. Here, too, the Soviets nationalized banks, industry, and trade and unleashed terror. In the single night of June 13–14, just eight to nine days before the German invasion, approximately 10,000 Estonians, 15,000 Latvians, and

25,000 Lithuanians were rounded up for deportation. In total, during the single year of occupation, over 125,000 were deported from the three Baltic states. Their memories of the horrors of the deportation affected their behavior during the war, leading them to view the Germans as liberators. It continued to influence their attitudes after the war and was a strong factor in their determination to reestablish their independence.

The Great Patriotic War gave powerful impetus to Great Russian nationalism. To rally the peasants and workers who had suffered so much from World War I, the civil war, collectivization, and the Great Terror, Stalin appealed to Great Russian patriotism. Russian military heroes of the past were glorified and an informal concordat was reached with the Russian Orthodox Church. Marxist slogans were downplayed. A new national anthem replaced the "Internationale." The costs of the war were appalling. The Soviets suffered 20 million dead, including 7 million military casualties. Cities, villages, farms, and factories were destroyed. The war served to strengthen Russian patriotism, and the memory of their heroic struggle became sacred to the Russians. The Soviet regime had become identified with Russia.

What was less noticed was that this identification of the war with Great Russians had implications for other nationalities whose loyalty was suspect. About 800,000 ethnic Germans whose ancestors had arrived in the eighteenth and nineteenth centuries were deported from the Ukraine, the Crimea, and the Volga German Autonomous Republic. Other nationality groups whose loyalty was suspect were also deported. Among these, the Crimean Tatar catastrophe was later to become a rallying cry for dissenters. About 250,000 Tatars, the entire population, were accused of collaboration with the Germans and deported in May 1944. Almost half died. Altogether, about 2 million Muslims were expelled from their homelands. At the end of the war, about 500,000 Ukrainians and 600,000 from the Baltics were deported for collaboration. They were rounded up to fill quotas, and the question of individual guilt or innocence was often ignored. There were mass deportations from Moldavia as well. With the cooperation of the Russian Orthodox church, the Ukrainian Catholic church was abolished.

## THE POSTWAR PERIOD

At the end of the war, the Soviet people hoped for a breathing space, a respite from the horrors of Sovietization and war. But this was not to be. Returning Soviet soldiers, prisoners of war, and others considered to have been exposed to alien ideas were sent to labor camps. Ideology was reimposed as victory approached. Andrei Zhdanov, the ideological chief, emphasized an amalgam of Great Russian nationalism and Marxist-Leninism. The dominance of Russians was stressed. Campaigns were instituted against bourgeois nationalism in the republics. In 1946, Zhdanov proclaimed his two-camp theory: the world was divided into two hostile camps, one headed by the Soviet Union and the other by the United States and Britain. Stalin warned of the dangers of capitalist encirclement and future war. Controls were restored over intellectual life. The fourth Five-Year Plan emphasized rebuilding heavy industry. Beginning in 1948 an official campaign against "cosmopolitanism" was directed against Jews. In Leningrad, 3,000 senior party officials were arrested, and most were shot.

In 1952, at the Nineteenth Party Congress, Stalin increased the size of the Politburo from ten to twenty-five members and renamed it the Presidium. He also doubled the size of the Central Committee. It looked to many as if he were preparing a purge of the top party leaders. This was confirmed by the announcement in January 1953 of the Doctors' Plot, an alleged conspiracy by nine Kremlin doctors, seven of them Jews, against the leadership of the country. A government-sponsored anti-Semitic campaign with arrests and shootings followed. Questions were asked as to who knew of the conspiracy and who should have known. There were strong indications that a new Great Purge was in the making when Stalin died on March 5, 1953.

Although Stalin ruled until his death in 1953, the fundamental economic and social transformation of the country had been achieved by the close of the 1930s. What came to be called the totalitarian model had taken shape. Its most familiar incarnation was that developed by Carl Friedrich and Zbigniew Brzezinski in their 1956 publication, *Totalitarian Dictatorship and Autocracy*.[6] Almost from its inception, this approach was highly controversial. However, the model is useful as a framework for the discussion of high Stalinism.

Friedrich and Brzezinski point out that autocracy has been the prevailing form of government over long stretches of history. They argue that totalitarianism is a form of autocracy, but a new species. Totalitarian regimes use modern technical devices to achieve total control in the service of an ideologically motivated movement dedicated to the total destruction and total reconstruction of a mass society.

The authors present a syndrome or pattern of six interrelated traits common to totalitarian dictatorships:

1. An elaborate ideology: an official doctrine covering all aspects of man's existence that everyone is supposed to adhere to, at least passively. The ideology is focused toward a perfect final state and entails a radical rejection of existing society.
2. A single mass party typically led by one man: a single party consisting of a small percentage of the population, including a hard core of dedicated members. It is hierarchically organized and superior to, or intertwined with, the government bureaucracy.
3. A system of terror: the terror, carried out through the party or secret police, supports and supervises the party for its rulers. The terror is directed not only against demonstrable enemies but against arbitrarily selected classes of the population.

4. A technologically conditioned, near-complete monopoly of all means of effective mass communications.

5. A technologically conditioned, near-complete monopoly of effective use of all weapons of armed conflict.

6. Central control and direction of the entire economy.

Friedrich and Brzezinski argue that for a state to be considered totalitarian, it must have all six of the characteristics. All modern states, unless engaged in civil war, have near-complete weapons monopolies. Constitutional systems may have a centrally directed economy. Unlike Tucker, who sees Stalinism as a reversion to the Russian past,[7] Friedrich insists that totalitarian regimes could arise only in the context of mass democracy and modern technology. Although both Tsarism and Stalinism are forms of autocracy, Friedrich considers there to be a qualitative difference.

## THE STALINIST IDEOLOGY AND CONTROL OF MASS COMMUNICATIONS

The Stalinist ideology was an official doctrine used to mobilize the population in support of regime goals. From Marxist-Leninism, Stalinism borrowed a vocabulary and an analytic framework that permitted the reinterpretation of Marxist thought largely through selective references and Stalin's own "creative" contributions.[8] The Marxist concept that progress meant moving toward increased economic equality was pushed into the distant future, despite the fact that Stalin proclaimed in 1936 that the Soviet Union had eliminated the last vestiges of capitalism and entered the period of socialism. According to Stalin, differential economic rewards and inequality of status were justified under socialism.

Russian nationalism became a core system value. The outside world was viewed as menacing. In 1924, Stalin argued that it was necessary to build socialism in one country, rather than waiting for a world revolution. This evoked a patriotic response and in time the survival of communism became identified with the well-being of the Soviet Union. Seweryn Bialer says that the essence of internationalism became a willingness to defend the Soviet Union.[9] Russian nationalism thus merged with Marxist-Leninism. During the war, nationalism and patriotism were invoked, and Stalin came to be seen as a great nationalist leader. The national anthem that replaced the "Internationale" in 1944 included lines praising Stalin.

This is connected to the development of a personality cult. Stalin first built a cult of Lenin, embalming his body and placing it in a mausoleum in Red Square. Statues of Lenin were erected in the central square of every city and town, his portrait hung everywhere, his sayings quoted everywhere. The name of Petrograd was changed to Leningrad. In some ways, the cult of Leninism replaced Russian orthodoxy. In time, the cult of Stalin began to rival that of Lenin. Stalin came to be referred to as the Vozhd', or Leader, the modern counterpart of Peter the Great. He was also referred to as the Great Teacher, the Helmsman, and the Father of the People. Books, poems, and plays were written about, and dedicated to, him. The victory in World War II was attributed to his magical powers.[10]

The Stalinist ideology was pervasive—it blared from loudspeakers and radios, and its slogans appeared on posters. Agitprop centers in neighborhoods, villages, factories, and apartment houses repeated the message. Literature, theater, and films were required to conform. Not only were alternative views not tolerated, but writers were attacked for taking an individualistic nonparty approach to literature. Zhdanov attacked followers of Albert Einstein for their absurd ideas. Modern music and art came under attack. The media were required to carry the party line and only the party line. Since the party knew what was right, to permit other views would be tantamount to propagating lies. All books, articles, and radio broadcasts had to be submitted to official censors before publication. In the Stalin era most radios were closed-circuit instruments that had to be wired into government-controlled broadcasts, so alternatives were simply not available to listeners. The media were expected to play an active role in building communism, in inculcating citizens with proper values. Ellen Mickiewicz comments that the primary mission of media was to "change the ethical and moral outlook of the population."[11]

The existing Stalinist society was expected to lead to the perfect final state of mankind, but that state was put off into the distant future. Meanwhile, the official message was the only one that had access to publication or broadcasting.

## THE PARTY AND THE LEADER

We have already seen the process by which single-party rule was established at the Tenth Party Congress through the outlawing of other parties and factions within the party itself. Nevertheless, under Stalin it would be incorrect to speak of one-party rule. Fainsod stresses that with the consolidation of Stalin's power, "the operative theory of the role of Party leadership underwent profound changes." Stalin mastered the party, and "the figure of the infallible dictator emerged as the operative theory of Bolshevik leadership."[12] Similarly, Bialer states, "the Communist party became extinct as a political movement."[13]

This is not to say that the party disappeared. To the contrary, its membership grew rapidly from about 2.5 million in 1939 to 6.9 million in 1952. While all politically important individuals belonged to the party, most of the members of the party were not politically powerful. There was a vast party bureaucracy of some 200,000 full-time paid employees, or *apparatchiki*, who were deeply involved in administration of the state. Fainsod calls the party apparatus the "institutionalized projection" of Stalin's will.[14]

In any case, the party apparatus was only one of the bureaucracies administering the Stalinist state. There were "vastly overlapping lines of control, rights, and responsibilities among the diverse bureaucratic hierarchies" and "shifting lines of responsibility and control."[15] There was no point of resolution short of the dictator himself.

The Party Congresses became rallies of the faithful. No word of opposition or dissent disturbed their unanimity. The Central Committee rarely met. While the highest organs, the Politburo, Secretariat, and Orgburo met regularly, they lost any decision-making capacity and were purely advisory to Stalin. Stalin's mode of operation was to meet with one or more members of the Politburo rather than with the Politburo as a body. The Politburo and Secretariat were divided into subcommittees that reported to Stalin separately. He was the only one able to coordinate the information. All discussion ended once Stalin expressed a definite opinion. He "kept the elite off balance and made the formation of an alliance within its ranks, a challenge against him, hard to conceive."[16]

## THE SYSTEM OF TERROR

No group or individual was exempt from the terror—the higher one's position, the more vulnerable one became, but no one was exempt. As Fainsod wrote, "The insecurity of the masses must be supplemented by the insecurity of the governing elite who surround the dictator."[17] Because the terror was arbitrary in the sense that it was not based on any actual behavior or opinions, no one could be sure he or she would not be a victim. Not only was everyone involved in the terror as a potential victim, but hundreds of thousands were involved as informers.

The political police penetrated all parts of the political system, including the Communist Party. Secret police dossiers were maintained on high officials. The police network paralleled the structure of the entire society and reached into every administrative unit of party and government, every enterprise, factory, and rural machine tractor station. It controlled ministries in charge of lumber, heavy construction, and nonferrous metals. "Enemies of the people" were tried by Special Boards, controlled by the political police, that set punishments for the accused in the absence of the accused or counsel and with no right of appeal. The police ran enormous forced labor camps with millions of prisoners working on huge construction projects. They made the political police one of the country's largest economic enterprises, using prisoners to perform work where otherwise it would have been impossible to get a labor force. Scientific research prison establishments ensured that the talents of eminent scientists would not be lost to the regime. The police gained economic and political benefits from their contribution to the Soviet economy. The need for additional labor may have encouraged mass arrests. The political police commanded internal security units and border troops, putting them in control of major military force. They controlled armed forces counterintelligence and directed external intelligence.[18]

Thirty years after Stalin's death a dissident criticized the view that terror was an outgrowth of Stalin's personality, saying that this view was too simple and overlooked underlying factors:

Stalin could not have done what he did without many people supporting, or at least acquiescing, in his murderous ways. You cannot kill millions without tens of thousands, or perhaps I should say hundreds of thousands, collaborating. Who were the informers? Who were the people who came in the night and took husbands and brothers and sons away? Who were the guards who watched over the camps as vast populations died? These people were all loyal Soviet citizens, and they were accomplices.[19]

## WEAPONS OF ARMED COMBAT

A primary goal of the Stalinist regime was to ensure that the armed forces would serve the purposes of the political leadership.[20] There was deep concern with the potential power of the military—the possibility of Bonapartism haunted the leaders. Originally, Lenin and Trotsky favored replacement of the regular army with a citizens' militia. However, the civil war forced Trotsky to create the Red Army, using about 50,000 officers and 200,000 noncommissioned officers from the Tsarist army. Political commissars in each military unit ensured their loyalty. They were even empowered to countermand orders of military commanders if they were considered suspect. Officer privileges were reduced, insignia and epaulets disappeared, and rank was de-emphasized. Once the civil war was over, the size of the military was cut back to 600,000 troops. The emphasis was on training new commanders. By 1934, over 68 percent of the Red Army officers were communists. Despite the strength of the communist element, political commissars were retained and operated independently of the army chain of command. They served as a check on the growth of a professional esprit de corps. Political workers indoctrinated annual contingents of peasant recruits as army barracks were transformed into schools of communism. The regime made remarkable progress in transforming the army into a dependable political instrument.

With the growing threat of Hitler, a decision was taken in 1934 to greatly expand the size of the standing army. There had been both a regular army and a territorial army based on the militia system. Now the territorial structure was abolished, all national military units were dissolved, and their troops were scattered and merged in the regular army. This served to increase centralized control over the military and was intended to ensure that units would not put the interest of their republic over that of the union. Universal military service was introduced in 1939, and, in view of the imminent danger, tests of class origin were eliminated.

If, as seemed likely, war occurred, the stature of military leaders was likely to increase, endangering Stalin's control. The officer corps, as noted earlier, was a prime target in the purges. The trial and execution of Marshal Tukhachevsky and seven other high-ranking generals in 1937 were followed by an extensive purge of the officer corps. Measures were taken to strengthen political leadership control over the armed forces. The authority of the political commissars was strengthened and they were made equal with the commanding officers in military and political affairs. All orders had to be signed jointly. The reconstructed officer corps received higher rates of pay and better living conditions in an effort to mollify them, but every effort was made to prevent them from developing into an independent base of power. Although the officers were party members, the fear was that they would develop a greater loyalty to the armed forces than to the party. The presence of political commissars could make this less likely. The problem was, however, that they could detract from the ability of the commanders to form an efficient fighting force. In 1940, political commissars were replaced by *zampolity*, or assistant commanders for political affairs, who were restricted to political training and education. After the disastrous defeats following the Nazi invasion, political commissars were reestablished, but when the tide of battle turned, unity of command and *zampolity* were restored.

Although the army's heroic feats were celebrated, Stalin took no chances that the military might become a rival force. Once victory seemed assured, Stalin downgraded the military, increased party control, and strengthened political police surveillance. Marshal Zhukov, the most celebrated military leader, was moved to an inconspicuous command. Stalin's wartime leadership was stressed, and the military was thoroughly subordinated to political control.

## CONTROL OVER THE ECONOMY

We have already seen the process by which Stalin transformed the economy of a largely peasant state into one geared to rapid industrial growth regardless of the costs involved. Once collectivization was completed and the first Five-Year Plan declared a success, the process was institutionalized. The economic goal, set by the center, was to achieve a highly unbalanced economy with emphasis on heavy industry, in particular, industry geared to the military. Economic criteria were of secondary concern. Consumer goods production was to be held to the minimum. The achievement of this goal could not be left to free market forces that would dictate a different outcome.

The decision to counter market forces necessitated tight centralized control. So did the decision to set almost unattainable goals and then command that they be achieved in the shortest possible amount of time. Since workers could not be rewarded with material goods, they were subjected to coercion and exhortation. The emphasis was on quantity and speed. Lacking any market mechanisms, the economic system of planning and management stressed detailed output targets and instructions on "what should be done, when, how, and according to what sequence."[21] Centralized controls pervaded the entire system. An enormous economic-political bureaucracy was required to set the goals, provide the plans, issue the detailed instructions, supervise implementation, and coordinate the several parts of the system. The intent was to ensure that the economic system served the political goals of the leadership.

Stalinism overcame the problem of underdevelopment, but it created the problem of economic misdevelopment. Stalin left a country that had managed to industrialize at heavy cost in human terms. Until the 1960s, the Soviet economy grew rapidly, but it continued to require ever-greater infusions of manpower, capital, and natural resources. The economic bureaucracy proved unable to coordinate the millions upon millions of details the system required. The system proved inappropriate as the economy matured. Coercion and exhortation in time proved insufficient to develop a more sophisticated, technologically oriented economy. The system was geared to the production of steel and basic machine tools, when modern technology, food, and consumer goods were needed. The imbalances and distortions of the Stalinist economic system created the problems that his successors struggled with and that, in time, played a central role in the dissolution of the Soviet Union.

## NOTES

1. For thorough discussions of the Great Purge, see Adam Ulam, *Stalin: The Man and His Era* (New York: Viking, 1973), 370–99, 407–34, 438–66, 474–90; Robert Conquest, *Stalin and the Kirov Murder* (New York: Oxford University Press, 1989); Robert Conquest, *The Great Terror: Stalin's Purge of the Thirties* (New York: Macmillan, 1968); Alexander Solzhenitsyn, *The Gulag Archipelago*, trans. Thomas P. Whitney (New York: Harper and Row, 1973).

2. Ulam, *Stalin*, 448.

3. Merle Fainsod, *How Russia Is Ruled*, rev. ed. (Cambridge: Harvard University Press, 1963), 442.

4. Ulam, *Stalin*, 486.

5. Robert C. Tucker, "Stalinism as Revolution from Above," in *Stalinism: Essays in Historical Interpretation*, ed. Robert C. Tucker (New York: W. W. Norton, 1977), 98–101; Robert C. Tucker, *Political Culture and Leadership in Soviet Russia* (New York: W. W. Norton, 1987), 72–107, 108–16.

6. Carl J. Friedrich and Zbigniew K. Brzezinski, *Totalitarian Dictatorship and Autocracy* (Cambridge: Harvard University Press, 1956).

7. Tucker, *Political Culture*, 116.

8. Seweryn Bialer, *Stalin's Successors* (Cambridge: Cambridge University Press, 1980), 23.

9. Ibid.

10. Ibid., 29–30.

11. Ellen Mickiewicz, "Political Communication and the Soviet Media System," in *Soviet Politics: Russia After Brezhnev*, ed. Joseph L. Nogee (New York: Praeger, 1985), 35–36.

12. Fainsod, *How Russia Is Ruled*, 159–61.

13. Bialer, *Stalin's Successors*, 14. Much of the following is dependent on Bialer, 14–35.

14. Fainsod, *How Russia Is Ruled*, 161.

15. Bialer, *Stalin's Successors*, 16.

16. Ibid., 34.

17. Fainsod, *How Russia Is Ruled*, 441.

18. Bialer, *Stalin's Successors*, 12–13.

19. *New York Times*, March 6, 1983.

20. This section relies heavily on Fainsod, *How Russia Is Ruled*, 473–81; Raymond L. Garthoff, *Soviet Military Policy* (London: Faber and Faber, 1966), 6–36.

21. Bialer, *Stalin's Successors*, 21.

## Chapter 6

# EXPERIMENTATION, DE-STALINIZATION, AND DISSENT

The death of Stalin on March 5, 1953, opened a decade of experimentation. The aim was to reform the system, to return to Leninism, to preserve Stalinism without the excesses of Stalin, and to move ahead to build communism. Belief in the ideology was jarred, the Leader was exposed as a tyrant, and terror was no longer the primary instrument of rule. For a time there was an atmosphere of cautious relief, as people put out antennae to test whether they could once again live and breathe without constant fear. For some there was a heady atmosphere of newfound, though limited, freedom. For many there was a faith that things would get better and better and that Nikita Khrushchev's call to catch up and overtake the United States was not a foolhardy dream or a vainglorious boast. The loosening of controls permitted the slow growth of institutional pluralism and the emergence of social groups, the initial steps toward the re-creation of civil society. By the end of Khrushchev's rule, society was increasingly characterized by cynicism and apathy. Only Khrushchev, with his attempts to stir up the country by the use of old-fashioned oratory, seemed out of place. In the future, the legitimacy of the system and its ability to govern would depend upon the viability of the Communist Party and whether it could improve the economic well-being of the people.

## SUCCESSION

Immediately upon Stalin's death, his lieutenants formed a collective leadership for self-preservation and called on the population to avoid "panic and disarray." They reduced the party Presidium[1] to ten members. Measures were taken to win popular support, censorship and ideological controls were loosened, and there was a thaw in literature. Behind the facade of the collective leadership, various contenders were using different bases of power in a struggle for succession.

Beria was the lieutenant most seriously endangered by the fabricated Doctors' Plot. Stalin had already taken steps to weaken his control over the secret police and to purge his followers in Transcaucasia. Now Beria regained control over the police and repudiated the Doctors' Plot, stating that those who dreamed it up would be punished. He reinstalled his followers in Transcaucasia and appealed to the nationalities with promises of greater autonomy. His control of the secret police was seen as a threat by the other leaders, who feared that he would use his base in the police to strike out for leadership. He was arrested in June 1953 and probably executed immediately, although his execution was not announced until December. He and his six associates were the last Soviet leaders to be executed. The police organization was purged of his followers. The secret police, Stalin's chief instrument of rule, were now stripped of considerable authority and put under party control.

Georgi Malenkov was at first the most powerful of Stalin's lieutenants. Upon Stalin's death, he took over the chairmanship of the Council of Ministers (the premiership) and was also the senior member of the party Secretariat. After one week, he resigned from the Secretariat, leaving Khrushchev as its most senior member. Malenkov lost control of the party apparatus, and his position became dependent on control of the state administration. In August 1953 he called for a New Course that would ease up on development of heavy industry in favor of consumer goods and housing construction. Stating that nuclear war would lead to worldwide destruction, he called for mutual coexistence with the West and a relaxation of cold war tensions.

Khrushchev built his base in the party. On September 13, 1953, he was elected first secretary of the Central Committee of the party.[2] Using the powers of the Secretariat, he began putting his supporters in key positions. In contrast to Malenkov, he favored continued primacy for heavy industry and defense, and he insisted that nuclear war would mean the end of capitalism, not the world. By early February 1955, Khrushchev was able to force Malenkov to resign as chairman of the Council of Ministers in favor of Nikolai Bulganin, but Malenkov remained in the Presidium. Khrushchev's use of the party against the state apparatus demonstrated that the Communist Party had been restored as the primary political institution. Khrushchev continued to use his powers as first secretary to extend his influence in the top party organs. He was clearly the most powerful member of the Presidium. Khrushchev now renounced the inevitability of war between capitalism and socialism and called for peaceful coexistence with the West.

The most significant and dramatic event of his leadership was the Twentieth Party Congress of February 14–25, 1956, at which he gave his Secret Speech in closed session on the last day. He attacked Stalin's Great Terror, illegal mass repression, and the cult of personality. The costs of Stalinism were detailed. This was the initial salvo in the de-Stalinization process. Earlier, the Congress had strengthened Khrushchev's position by establishing regional economic councils, or *sovnarkhozy*, which siphoned power from the state apparatus in Moscow and distributed it to local party leaders. Not only did he weaken the state apparatus, but he took firmer control over the party through the Central Committee elections. Of 125 Central Committee members elected at the Nineteenth Party Congress, only 79 were reelected. In addition to the vacated positions, the Central Committee was expanded so that 54 new members were elected, enabling Khrushchev to consolidate his position.

Events in Poland and the Hungarian revolution in October and early November opened Khrushchev to vehement criticism from conservatives who argued that Khrushchev's liberal policies were responsible. They argued that such events would not have been possible "under the old man." They demanded an end to de-Stalinization. At a meeting of the party Presidium in June 1957, Khrushchev found himself in a minority. His opponents called for his resignation as first secretary, but Khrushchev insisted that he had been elected by, and was responsible to, the Central Committee, which was the only organ that could dismiss him. Marshal Zhukov, the defense minister and Khrushchev ally, flew in loyal Khrushchev supporters. When the Central Committee met, not only did Khrushchev prevail, but his opponents were labeled the antiparty group. By the end of 1958, all of his opponents had been removed from the Presidium and assigned to obscure positions outside Moscow.

Marshal Zhukov was first rewarded by being elected a full member of the Presidium of the party, where he spoke on behalf of the armed forces in pledging support to the party leadership under Khrushchev.[3] Khrushchev was wary of Zhukov, realizing that if he could use his power and prestige to support Khrushchev, he could also use it against him. Furthermore, Zhukov began to insist that the professional competence of career military officers should not be judged by the party political officers or in party meetings. The danger was that the military would "become a self-contained professional body," and this was something Khrushchev refused to accept. On November 2, 1957, it was announced that Zhukov had been removed from the Presidium and the Central Committee. He was accused of attempting to abolish the leadership and control of the party over the armed forces.[4] It was clear that the military was no challenge to the party.

By January 1959, Merle Fainsod and others considered Khrushchev's position beyond challenge. Khrushchev's victory symbolized the ascendancy of the party. Unlike Stalin, Khrushchev did not base his power on overlapping and competing hierarchies. The party was his instrument of rule.[5]

## DE-STALINIZATION

Khrushchev's Secret Speech at the Twentieth Party Congress in 1956, although not made public in the Soviet Union, severely shocked party members. We have noted earlier that hundreds of thousands were in some way implicated in the crimes of the Stalin years, and millions of others had found ways to excuse the "excesses" while worshiping the Vozhd' and his achievements including, above all, the miraculous victory in the Great Patriotic War. Now the cult of personality and the purges were attacked. Khrushchev charged that far from being a heroic war leader, Stalin had suffered a breakdown at the beginning of the war and was responsible for early defeats.

Khrushchev denounced Stalinist terror but in no way renounced the Leninist use of terror against enemies.[6] But mass terror came to an end. Nearly 8 million victims of Stalinist terror were amnestied, and many were legally and politically rehabilitated, often posthumously. Victims, including large numbers of Ukrainians and Baltic peoples, poured out of the camps. Accompanying the renunciation of Stalinist terror was a stress on "socialist legality," codification of laws, and the establishment of procedural norms in the judicial process.

De-Stalinization was renewed at the Twenty-Second Party Congress in October 1961, when, for the first time, individuals were publicly accused as accomplices of Stalin. Khrushchev used de-Stalinization as a weapon to purge his rivals and consolidate his own power. Following the Congress, Stalin's embalmed body was removed from the mausoleum in Red Square and reburied. Places and institutions named after Stalin were renamed. Symbols of the Stalin cult were removed, except in Georgia, where, as a native son, he remained a hero.

The attacks on Stalinism and loosening of censorship encouraged writers to speak out. Ilya Ehrenburg's *The Thaw* gave its name to the period. The authorities permitted the publication of Vladimir Dudintsev's *Not by Bread Alone* and poems about the purges soon appeared. The journal *Novy Mir* encouraged writers who were testing the limits of the permissible. Although there were fluctuations in what Khrushchev was willing to tolerate, writers found the courage to push for greater freedom. In October 1962, Yevgenii Yevtushenko's *The Heirs of Stalin*, which had become well known through poetry readings, appeared in *Pravda*. It attacked not just Stalin, but Stalinists.[7]

This was followed by Solzhenitsyn's *One Day in the Life of Ivan Denisovich*, a searing description of life in a forced labor camp that was published at Khrushchev's urging. Patricia Blake reports that 1962 looked to be a year of unprecedented triumph for liberal writers, who even achieved important positions in the cultural apparatus. However, there was an abrupt shift after Khrushchev visited an exhibition of nonrepresentational art at the Manege Gallery in Moscow on December 1, 1962. He was genuinely appalled and expressed his feelings in a crude outburst. Liberal artists and intellectuals came under attack for seven months, but they fought back. "At issue was nothing less than the responsibility of the Stalinist generation of officials and bureaucrats for the crimes of Stalin."[8]

Blake uses the events on the literary scene to throw light on the nature of the post-Stalin Soviet system. Pointing out that "the outstanding characteristic of the Stalin era, mass terror directed against both the bureaucracy and the people, has been abolished," she goes on to say, "When terror is absent, all other instruments of control are less effective, and, often, altogether useless."[9] Intellectuals and artists were able to challenge authority and speak out. They were no longer instruments of the party or dictator.

## THE ECONOMY

At the time of Stalin's death, the rural sector was in many ways more backward than it had been in 1928 because of the unbalanced growth path of the Five-Year Plans. Agriculture was showing signs of exhaustion. Khrushchev attempted to tinker with the system to make the Stalinist model work. He understood the crucial importance of the agriculture sector not only for improving the well-being of the peasantry but for improving the standard of living of the urban households.[10] As early as February 1954, Khrushchev proposed the Virgin Lands program to cultivate semiarid tracts of land east of the Urals. Hundreds of thousands of volunteers, huge amounts of capital, and vast irrigation networks transformed 90 million acres, an area equivalent to the entire cultivated area of Canada, into vast state farms operated on the model of state industrial enterprises. In 1957, Khrushchev replaced centralized industrial ministries with *sovnarkhozy*—one hundred economic regions to develop and administer economic programs without undue central controls. Since local party bosses soon gave priority to local interests at the expense of the overall national priorities, some recentralization was introduced in 1959.

In 1958, Khrushchev took more radical measures to restructure agriculture. In-kind transactions, including taxes, were replaced by monetary ones, bringing peasants into the modern economy. Khrushchev eliminated the machine tractor stations (MTS) established by Stalin as an urban outpost in rural areas. They were centers of party and police control at a time when peasants were highly suspect and collective farms had few or no Communist Party members. Since few peasants knew how to operate machinery, they concentrated heavy agricultural equipment and rented it to the *kolkhozy*. Khrushchev's plan was to sell the equipment to the *kolkhozy*, but many went into debt to raise enough capital to purchase the equipment. They had difficulty keeping it in repair and many lacked the skill to operate the machinery. Khrushchev consolidated the farms into larger units, assuming that this would create economies of scale, and also reduced the size of the peasants' private garden plots. The result was lowered agricultural productivity. He then moved to improve the standard of living of the peasants, lowering their taxes, raising prices for collective farm products, and writing off a large proportion of the *kolkhoz* debt.

In 1959, the sixth Five-Year Plan for 1956–60, which gave priority to producer goods, was replaced by a Seven-Year Plan for 1959–65. This was an ambitious plan for transformation and economic growth suffused with optimistic belief in the possibility of catching up to, and eventually overtaking, the United States. There was increased emphasis on consumer goods, the expansion of urban housing, and an increase in meat and milk production. Overall, the plan envisaged a 70 percent increase in agricultural production. Although Khrushchev increased investment in agriculture, he relied primarily on pressure and exhortation to produce results.[11] Total agricultural production for the plan rose only about 10 percent and there were sharp year-to-year fluctuations. The need to spend scarce foreign currency on imports of food held back the growth of the industrial sector.[12]

A more fundamental problem was that the entire planning system, successful in promoting rapid industrialization, was no longer able to handle the tasks of an increasingly complex economy. Industrialization now required keeping track of a larger number of products and more varieties of them. The emphasis on gross output targets created serious problems. Managers found that the easiest way to fulfill their quotas was to lobby for a low target—many spent as much time in bargaining as in production. Further, since exceeding targets would lead planning authorities to increase them in the next cycle, managers were likely to hold back on production. In order to avoid the possibility that targets might not be met because suppliers failed to deliver inputs, managers tried to make their factories self-sufficient. The practice of *storming* was common—little work was done at the beginning of the month, while about 60 percent was completed in the last ten days. Little attention was paid to quality control; the emphasis was on quantity. Since new techniques, however promising in the long run, disrupt the production line, managers were reluctant to innovate.[13] Since purchase costs were included in gross output, managers were actually encouraged by the system to use the most costly inputs.

Soviet economists recognized the need to rethink the entire system. Some pushed for the use of advanced computer technology. Others, especially Evsei Liberman, called for new incentives and the substitution of "profitability" for gross output as the principal measure of performance. The intent was not to abandon, but to strengthen, effective economic control.[14] Despite his recognition of many of the problems of the Soviet economy, Khrushchev was unwilling to risk this significant a reform of the system. He had a genuine commitment to innovative change, but in the end he left most of the Stalinist economic model intact.

## CONTROL OVER THE PERIPHERY

Khrushchev's early policy reached out toward minority nationalities stressing Leninist norms. He put strong emphasis on the special relationship between Russia and the Ukraine, the two Great Peoples of the Soviet

Union. In 1954, he gave the Crimea to the Ukraine to mark 300 years of indissoluble ties. This gift, of little significance at the time, was to become a major point of contention between Russia and Ukraine.

The Virgin Lands project inadvertently had a devastating impact on the herdsmen of Kazakhstan. As a consequence of the vast influx of volunteers, the Kazakhs were reduced to only one-third of the population by 1959. Kazakhstan became a major grain producer, rivaling the Ukraine.

At the Twentieth Party Congress, Khrushchev stressed Leninist norms and the equality of peoples. He pledged to make better use of national cadres and enlarge the power of republics. Despite pro-Stalinist demonstrations in Georgia, economic decentralization continued. Russification eased. The Chechen-Ingush and some other deported peoples were rehabilitated and allowed to return to their territories. There were revivals of national cultures and national assertiveness.[15]

After 1958, Khrushchev adopted a more militant policy against "vestiges of capitalism" and called for the drawing together of nations. He moved against party leaderships considered too nationalistic and campaigned against local nationalism. There were political arrests and trials in the Ukraine, where clandestine groups were uncovered and accused of treason. There were political arrests elsewhere and an official anti-Zionist campaign. Khrushchev launched an antireligious campaign that pulled down or closed hundreds of churches, mosques, and synagogues. The Khrushchev leadership stressed the importance of exchanging cadres among republics and encouraged migration, settlement, and the intermixing of peoples.[16] The goal was to move toward the creation of a single Soviet people in preparation for the victory of communism. Khrushchev was not a liberal—he was a Leninist. For him, nationalism was something to be tolerated temporarily but not encouraged. In time, it would need to be overcome.

## THE GROWTH OF PLURALISM

Khrushchev's period of ascendancy was characterized by a growing heterogeneity of the elite accompanied by increasing differentiation within society.[17] The institutional rivalry meant that the governing apparatus was shot through with competition. Soviet society experienced the formation of various groupings with their own interests and values, eager to influence but not actually rule. These groups were in some cases able to influence policy. The lawyers with their close professional ties and common interest in preserving legality were able to influence law reforms. Educators had some influence on the implementation of Khrushchev's reforms in their field. Discussions by economists and planners clearly influenced government policy. Trade unions increased their role to the point that managers complained they were unable to discharge anyone. The intellectuals began to exert influence on government policies and to stand up to Khrushchev himself.

Much attention focused on the army as a highly organized group with a strong esprit de corps. The army was even seen as a potential rival to the party, and some observers hypothesized that if the Soviet Union were to experience serious difficulties or fail to achieve significant successes, the army might stage a coup. There is no question but that the influence of the army increased enormously in the last year or two of Khrushchev's rule and that it was able to influence military policy. However, the military was not a solid phalanx; rather, it was characterized by differentiation of views on military doctrine and shot through with interservice rivalry. It was a powerful group whose leaders had to be listened to, but it was more interested in influencing government policy than in actually attempting to seize power. Its influence in the military field did reverberate throughout Soviet society, since it was deeply concerned with economic priorities. Its interest in heavy industry and military hardware created conflicts with the economists and managerial groups with other priorities.

The technical intelligentsia played an increasing role and began to act in terms of professional criteria rather than slavishly following the party line. Other less well integrated groupings in Soviet society—minority nationalities, youth, peasants, workers, consumers—were also developing interests of their own and becoming more articulate in expressing their common interests and aspirations.

In order to have group politics it is necessary not only to have groups, but for the groups to have access to the means of influencing government policy. Such means were not totally lacking in the Khrushchev era. Groups attempted to influence policy through articulation of their views at professional meetings. Newspapers and journals expressed the vital concerns of various organized groups and even reflected differences of opinion within groups. It became possible to speak of liberal and conservative journals, liberal and conservative editors. Interest groups even came to have some influence on policy at the very summit of power. Under Khrushchev, Presidium members were given assignments in specific areas and often became spokesmen for the areas they supervised. This provided a channel for interest groups and an arena for bargaining and compromise.

## THE COMMUNIST PARTY AND THE FALL OF KHRUSHCHEV

We have previously emphasized that Khrushchev did not base his power on competing hierarchies as Stalin had done but instead used the party as the instrument by which to gain and maintain ascendancy. After 1959, his position seemed beyond challenge. Perhaps because he felt himself a prisoner of the party that he had done so much to strengthen, beginning in 1961 Khrushchev began to weaken party control. New party rules providing for rotation in office that were promulgated at the Twenty-Second Party Congress in October 1961 carried a threat to members of the Presidium and other leading party organs.[18]

The reorganization of the party in November 1962 into agricultural and industrial branches below the republic level threatened administrative chaos. *Oblast* (regional) party secretaries were key figures in the party, with considerable independence and power. Although very few lost their positions, their power was divided and diluted. They had a common group interest in eliminating the changes introduced by Khrushchev. This endangered Khrushchev's support base since most of them sat on the party Central Committee.[19]

In October 1964 while Khrushchev was on vacation, the Presidium met and decided to oust him. Khrushchev was brought back to Moscow, and, on the following day, the Presidium informed him of the decision, which was then ratified by the Central Committee. Khrushchev was replaced by his own appointees: Leonid Brezhnev became first secretary; Aleksei Kosygin, chairman of the Council of Ministers; and Nikolai Podgorny, the chairman of the Presidium of the Supreme Soviet. Richard Lowenthal argues that the crucial factor was the institutional question, the relative power of the leader and the highest organs of the party. Khrushchev had depended on the party machine, but, after 1958, he tried to free himself from its constraints. He appealed to "the people" against "the bureaucrats." The Presidium became the focus of oligarchic resistance to Khrushchev's efforts at personal rule. The men of the Presidium acted to protect the power of the Presidium, which, they believed, was threatened by Khrushchev.[20] His successors accused Khrushchev of creating a cult of personality and violating the principles of collective leadership. They stressed the responsibility of the leader to the Presidium and the necessity of holding the leader accountable.

## NOTES

1. The Politburo had been renamed the Presidium at the Nineteenth Party Congress in 1952. It was called the Presidium throughout the Khrushchev years.

2. This title was used by Khrushchev in place of the title General Secretary.

3. For a discussion of the role of the military in the Khrushchev era, see Raymond L. Garthoff, "Khrushchev and the Military," in *Politics in the Soviet Union*, ed. Alexander Dallin and Alan Westin (New York: Harcourt, Brace and World, 1966), 243–74.

4. Garthoff, "Khrushchev and the Military," 253–54.

5. Merle Fainsod, *How Russia Is Ruled*, rev. ed. (Cambridge: Harvard University Press, 1963), 173–75.

6. Robert Conquest, "De-Stalinization and the Heritage of Terror," in *Politics in the Soviet Union*, ed. Dallin and Westin, 51.

7. Patricia Blake, "Freedom and Control in Literature, 1962–63," in *Politics in the Soviet Union*, ed. Dallin and Westin, 165–66.

8. Ibid., 180–81.

9. Ibid., 202.

10. James Millar, "Post-Stalin Agriculture and Its Future," in *The Soviet Union Since Stalin*, ed. Stephen F. Cohen, Alexander Rabinovitch, and Robert Sharlet (Bloomington: Indiana University Press, 1980), 138–39.

11. George W. Breslauer, "Khrushchev Reconsidered," in *The Soviet Union Since Stalin*, ed. Cohen, Rabinovitch, and Sharlet, 58.

12. Arthur Wright, "The Soviet Economy," *Current History* 51 (October 1966): 220.

13. Marshall I. Goldman, *The Soviet Economy* (Englewood Cliffs, N.J.: Prentice-Hall, 1968), 90–95.

14. Wright, *The Soviet Economy*, 222–24.

15. Bohdan Nahaylo and Victor Swoboda, *Soviet Disunion: A History of the Nationalities Problem in the USSR* (New York: Free Press, 1990), 109–28.

16. Ibid., 129–46.

17. For a discussion of interest groups in the Soviet Union at this time, see H. Gordon Skilling, "Interest Groups and Communist Politics," *World Politics* 18 (April 1966): 435–51.

18. Barbara B. Green, "Soviet Politics and Interest Groups," *Current History* 51 (October 1966): 214–15.

19. Ibid., 214.

20. Richard Lowenthal, "The Revolution Withers Away," in *The Soviet Political System*, ed. Richard Cornell (Englewood Cliffs, N.J.: Prentice-Hall, 1970), 185–94.

## Chapter 7

# THE SEARCH FOR POLITICAL STABILITY AND ORDER

Khrushchev's successors stressed the importance of holding the leader responsible to the Presidium and condemned "subjectivism" and "harebrained schemes." They wanted to reverse some of Khrushchev's experimental policies, increase harmony, and avoid confrontation among top leaders. Their greatest fear was of destabilizing the system through regime-initiated change or by arousing unrealistic hopes for economic improvement or intellectual freedom. The Presidium inner group of Brezhnev, Kosygin, Mikhail Suslov, and Podgorny emphasized collective rule, although Brezhnev soon emerged as first among equals. Robert Tucker speaks of "consensual leadership for order and stability."[1] The Party *apparatchiki* were the main beneficiaries of the coup. The first major decision of the new leadership was to rescind the 1962 division of the party and to reinstate the old regional party secretaries. The slogan "trust in cadres," promising security of tenure, won the loyalty of an elite that had suffered from the unpredictability of Stalin and Khrushchev. The removal of Khrushchev appeared to herald a new era of stable, impersonal, bureaucratic dictatorship.

Although most of the regime's efforts were concentrated on assuring the party *apparatchiki* of its ability to provide stable leadership, overtures were made to the intellectuals. The regime hoped that if artistic experimentation and free expression were permitted, economists, scientists, and writers would be reconciled to the system and would make a positive contribution. There was a growing sense of optimism among liberal and moderate members of the intelligentsia.[2]

The optimism was short-lived. By early September 1965, there were growing pressures to reassess the Stalinist era, accompanied by calls to strengthen ideology and increase social discipline. Then, in the second week of September, Andrei Sinyavsky and Yuli Daniel were arrested for publishing slanderous anti-Soviet literature abroad. Their fate became the central issue for Soviet intellectuals. The trial in February took place in the face of petitions and letters from every important liberal Moscow intellectual.[3] When Sinyavsky and Daniel were condemned to seven and five years, respectively, at forced labor, conservatives felt vindicated while liberal intellectuals protested in letters to the party leadership. Timothy McClure speaks of "the remarkable strength and unity demonstrated by various segments of the moderate and liberal intelligentsia."[4] The regime, encouraged by military leaders who deplored the lack of discipline in the armed forces, imposed increasingly repressive policies on deviant intellectuals.

## THE TWENTY-THIRD PARTY CONGRESS: SETTING THE STAGE

This atmosphere set the stage for the Twenty-Third Party Congress in March 1966.[5] Prior to the opening of the Party Congress, there was a spate of rumors that a reassessment of Stalin was pending. The rumors aroused protests among writers, artists, scientists, and others who feared a return to Stalinist practice. These protests culminated in public demonstrations and collective letters to party leaders. They had some effect. There was no clear reassessment of Stalin, but rather a compromise. The personality cult was denounced, but it was emphasized that this should not lead to denigrating the Soviet Union's heroic history. Khrushchev's successors wanted respect for collective leadership, elimination of concentration camp excesses, and party control over the security police. They did not want public criticism, accusations against individual Stalinists, or spectacular rehabilitations. The *apparatchiki* wanted a halt to attacks on the *period* of the cult of personality, since most of them were heirs of Stalin. They felt such attacks discredited the party as a whole. Therefore they favored limited re-Stalinization, a balanced image of Stalin, noting his favorable aspects. They wanted to speak as little as possible of the purge victims, without disavowing the rehabilitations that had already taken place. They denounced the anticult literature of the Khrushchev years.

The Party Congress that opened March 29 was the largest in history, with almost 5,000 delegates. There seemed to be a fear of innovation and risk accompanied by a desire to draw the line between the permissible and the forbidden. The leaders seemed to be saying, "So far and no further." Brezhnev noted that the division of the party into agricultural and industrial hierarchies had been revoked, and he condemned the disruption caused by constant shifts in personnel. The slogan "trust in cadres" originated at this Congress. The provisions on rotation in office introduced at the Twenty-Second Party Congress were abolished. The leadership was intent on stability, not change. A change in name from Presidium back to Politburo and the resuscitation of the title general secretary were of symbolic importance, signifying continuity with the past.

In the economic field, Brezhnev spoke of miscalculations in the Seven-Year Plan completed in 1965, asserting that its goals were not always "actual possibilities." He then stated, "There must be no unrealistic provisions in our plans for the future." The new Five-Year Plan, while more modest in its goals, still provided for a rapid rate of growth. More resources were to go into the consumer field than in the past, but heavy industry still received priority. In accord with the Kosygin-sponsored economic reforms introduced in 1965, an increase in centralized planning was to be combined with greater initiative for individual enterprises. Again, caution was the watchword.

The tremendous concentration on writers and literary matters at the Congress revealed deep-seated concern on the part of the leadership. Mikhail Sholokov, with the prestige of a recent Nobel Prize, was brought in to chastise Soviet writers in vociferous language. Brezhnev insisted that the party opposed administration by fiat or arbitrary decisions, but would fight all manifestations of alien ideology. He attacked those who denigrated the system.

The basic theme of the Twenty-Third Congress was stability and caution. The leaders were determined to prevent change from going too far too fast. They wanted to get on with the job of internal development without taking the risks inherent in radical innovations. They were bureaucrats who wanted to administer. The first secretary of the Moscow party committee stated:

The most characteristic feature of the style of leadership of the CPSU [Communist Party of the Soviet Union] Central Committee and its Presidium and of the Central Committee Secretariat today is a thoughtful, realistic approach to the solution of important and complex economic and political problems.[6]

This Congress set the tone for the ensuing years. It is important to note that the first decade of Brezhnev's ascendancy was marked by major achievements. The last six years of his rule were marked by domestic stagnation, resistance to change, growing corruption, and foreign adventures.

## STABILIZATION AND RECONCILIATION

The primary goal was to preserve social and political stability without resorting to mass terror. Symbols of order and stability—patriotism, duty, family, army—received emphasis. The leadership opposed top-down efforts to revolutionize society through Stalinist terror or Khrushchevian experimentation.

Experts were increasingly brought into the policy-making process. The leaders stressed scientific management, careful planning, clear procedures, and close consultation not only with leaders in the government, party, and military but also with technically trained specialists.[7] Economists and legal scholars were called upon for advice. Soviet publications carried policy debates on issues and advisers were even urged to conduct public opinion surveys as part of their research. The leadership, of course, could still draw the line to prevent debate on sensitive issues and control the way views were expressed, but the range of topics discussed and argued was impressive.[8]

Elites from all major institutions were brought into the Politburo, where conflicts were settled through bargaining and compromise. There was a growth of institutional pluralism, with economic ministries, regional organs, and prestigious scientific bodies influencing the allocation of resources.[9] The military were a prime beneficiary of the regime's conservatism and search for order. Military spending grew at a steady 4 to 5 percent a year until 1977. In addition to a buildup of strategic and conventional forces, civil defense, basic military training in secondary schools, and pervasive military-patriotic education were supported. The minister of defense gained a seat on the Politburo in 1973.[10]

By 1970, the Soviet economy, second only to the United States in gross national product (GNP), accounted for 15.5 percent of the world's GNP, while the United States accounted for 27.7 percent. Soviet growth was more rapid than the American.[11] Moreover, the Soviets were first in the world in steel, pig iron, and cement production and second in aluminum and gold. Their aerospace industry challenged the American, and they exported arms, were self-sufficient in oil production, and exported oil and gas.[12] An economic management proposal to provide price and profit incentives was announced in 1965 and introduced gradually on a piecemeal basis. A mood of sober optimism prevailed.

Consumer policy played a major role in the Brezhnev strategy. The intent was to provide "assurances to the masses . . . that political conformity ensures physical security and that hard work means the opportunity for advancement and a higher standard of living."[13] The promise of increasing consumer goods and a welfare state became the dominant belief, justifying and legitimating the system in the eyes of the masses. The regime made a continuing effort to improve the standard of living by expanding production and improving the quality of food, consumer goods, and services.[14] It recognized that the availability of quality consumer goods was a crucial incentive for increased labor productivity. With nothing worth buying, higher wages alone were not an incentive. The two plans covering 1966–75 allotted a greater proportion of state investment to the consumer goods sector than ever before.[15] In the second half of the 1960s, per capita consumption increased by over 5 percent a year. In increasing numbers people acquired refrigerators, television sets, and washing machines.[16] However, complaints arose because of the shoddy quality of many of the factory products and the unavailability of spare parts. Because of difficulties in obtaining quality goods and services, the private entrepreneurial "second economy" grew. This included theft and black market purchases of spare parts and goods not regularly available, private work done during regular work hours, and bribes to obtain goods and services. This "second economy," while illegal, was generally tolerated.[17] Social welfare policies provided employment security, low inflation, free education, health care, pensions, subsidized housing, food, and transportation.

Agriculture rose to near the top of nondefense priorities.[18] To offset fluctuations in productivity from year to year, the regime devoted an enormous amount of foreign exchange to the importation of grain. Emphasis was put on research and development, mechanization, and the use of mineral fertilizers and pesticides. In response to consumer demand, livestock production was pushed even though this increased the need for large importation of grain and fodder from the West. Peasants on collective farms now received increased earnings, a minimum guaranteed annual wage, pensions, and internal passports. By the Brezhnev era, the Soviet Union was no longer primarily an agrarian economy. Less than 40 percent of the population was rural, and the rural sector was literate and had access to health care.[19] So, despite problems with quality and availability of consumer goods, not only did the regime provide comprehensive social benefits, but it seemed to be making good on the promise that the material conditions of life would continue to improve.

## INTELLECTUAL REPRESSION

The social and political stability of the early Brezhnev years was dependent on political repression. Imprisonment, camps, police intimidation, psychiatric confinement, and exile were used to silence dissidents. Following the trial of Sinyavsky and Daniel, the government took a series of measures to strengthen party control of literature and intellectual life. It condemned "unpatriotic" writings and stopped their publication. A campaign for "military-patriotic" education of youth was launched while military power was glorified. Persecution not only revived the tradition of the social responsibility of intellectuals to speak truth to power but led to increasing ties among critical writers, scientists, and even some independent-minded party members. The regime responded with a series of criminal prosecutions.

In January 1967, two young poets, Aleksandr Ginzburg and Yuri Galanskov were arrested and charged with compiling a *White Book* on violations of Soviet law in the Sinyavsky-Daniel trial and with publishing the dissident journal *Phoenix*. When, in violation of Soviet law, they were not brought to trial for a year, another writer, Vladimir Bukovsky, organized a protest. Bukovsky and two associates were arrested and sentenced to prison. Other Soviet intellectuals became interested in the Ginzburg-Galanskov case, protesting violations of legality. Andrei Sakharov wrote to the party Central Committee in protest. The trial of Ginzburg and Galanskov attracted a large group of protesters. Many prominent intellectuals protested violations of Soviet legality. There were arrests and trials in Moscow, Leningrad, and the Ukraine.

Soviet intellectuals were inspired by the liberalization in Czechoslovakia during the Prague Spring, but the invasion of Czechoslovakia in August 1968 crushed any hope for evolutionary change. It was followed by increased domestic repression. Intellectuals in 1968 founded the *Chronicle of Current Events*, an important underground publication that coordinated various civil rights groups. In 1969 they established the Initiative Group to Defend Human Rights, and in 1970 the Moscow Human Rights Committee was founded.

Although the regime repressed the liberal intelligentsia, it tolerated and even encouraged neo-Slavophilism.[20] Village prose writers, including Valentin Rasputin, perhaps the most popular writer in Russia, began to search for pure traditional Russian culture uncontaminated by Western ideas, urbanization, and industrialization. They yearned for the innocence of a mythical past. Russian nationalists wrote of the purity of "simple" Russian villagers. The intelligentsia were accused of having a narrow, money-grubbing attitude, suffering from Americanization of spirit. Although the nationalists praised the purity of the prerevolutionary way of life, many saw Communism, particularly Stalinism, as a means toward attaining the greatness of the Russian state and society. Much of this Russian movement was characterized by its belief in the messianic role of Russia, anti-Semitism, and scorn for non-Russians. In 1968, *Molodaya gvardiya* (Young Guard), the Komsomol monthly, was taken over by nationalists who pursued an ethnocentric, anti-Western line. *Nash sovremennik* (Our Contemporary), an extreme Russian monthly publication, first appeared in 1970, and in 1971 the extremist *samizdat* (self-published or underground press) journal *Veche* made its appearance.[21]

In December 1971, the regime initiated a new repression of the liberal intelligentsia. It used threats, intimidation, arrests, imprisonment, confinement to psychiatric hospitals, and loss of jobs. The *Chronicle* came under heavy attack but managed to survive. When Alexander Yakovlev, then the party's acting chief of agitation and propaganda, attacked reactionary Russian nationalism in November 1972, *Veche* denounced him as a traitor to Russia's interests. Yakovlev was appointed ambassador to Canada. A massive propaganda campaign was unleashed against Sakharov and Solzhenitsyn.[22] Although liberals were repressed, Vladimir Osipov, an extremist, was the only well-known Russian nationalist imprisoned in the 1970s. Russian nationalism, National Bolshevism, and neo-Slavophilism continued.[23]

## THE PERIPHERY

Along with the growth of Russian nationalism, nationalist sentiment was growing in the borderlands. As Ralph S. Clem notes, "The invocation of ethnicity by one group as a means of attaining a more favorable position is likely . . . to provoke a similar reaction in defense from groups that are threatened."[24] The lessened faith in an overarching supranational ideology encouraged increasing identification with nationality groups. As the fear of mass Stalinist repression and deportations lessened, nationalities were increasingly likely to express their national aspirations. Although it was not apparent at the time, the movements that resulted in the dissolution of the Soviet Union had their origin in this period.

As early as April 1965, Armenians demonstrated to mark the fiftieth anniversary of the Turkish genocide and to demand the return of Nagorno-Karabakh and Nakhichivan, which had been placed under Azerbaijan control.[25] They opposed improving Turkish-Russian relations. Crimean Tatars and their supporters became active, demanding their right to return to their homeland in the Crimea, from which they had been expelled by Stalin. In 1967, Crimean Tatars were politically rehabilitated but still not permitted to return to the Crimea. When they tried to settle there, they were forcibly expelled. Their demands received support from leaders of the human rights movement. The Tatar movement became a symbol of the nationalities problem.

In the Ukraine, arrests and trials of nationalist intellectuals led to protests. Ukrainian national assertiveness was supported by the Ukrainian Party first secretary, Pyotr Shelest, and his faction of the party. He defended the Ukrainian language, encouraged revival of historical studies, and opposed diversion of funds from the Ukraine for development of Siberia. Economic interests fused with cultural nationalism.

The Soviet leadership was becoming increasingly aware of two major issues. The first was the growing national feeling in the borderlands. The emphasis was on cultural nationalism, on traditions and languages. Although there were calls for increased autonomy, political independence was not yet on the agenda. The effort was primarily to prevent Russification. The second issue involved demographic factors. The Russian share of the population fell from 55.65 percent in 1959 to 53.37 percent in 1970. Not only Russians, but Ukrainians and the Baltic peoples had low birthrates, with a reproductive index below 1. In contrast, the Muslim population was increasing at about three and a half times the rate of the Russians. The non-European share of the population increased from 11.5 percent in 1959 to approximately 17 percent in 1977.[26] The 9.2 million Uzbeks had become the third largest nationality. Although Khrushchev had pushed Russian as the language of the Soviet people, other nationalities continued to view it as the language of the Russian people. Jeremy Azrael states that what was troubling was not the shift in ethnic composition, but the economic implications of the fact that the "Central Asian nationalities have remained outside the mainstream of the country's economic development and contain a heavy preponderance of undereducated peasants with a weak-tononexistent knowledge of Russian and a tenacious aversion to interregional or even intraregional migration."[27]

Beginning in 1971, Brezhnev tried to clarify nationalities policy. The fusion of nationalities would be delayed since the attainment of communism would take longer than Khrushchev had anticipated. The drawing together of the nations was an objective process that would occur naturally as the country progressed further toward communism. While those attempting to hold the movement back would be opposed and measures, such as improving the teaching of Russian in non-Russian republics, could be taken to speed up the process, Brezhnev indicated his opposition to forcing matters. Instead, he promoted the concept of the Soviet people, an effort to recognize the multinational nature of the Soviet state while attempting to create a higher unity that could transcend national distinctions. The regime seems to have decided to concentrate on creating a Russian-speaking Slavic core. If fusion of the hundred or so different nationalities was not immediately feasible, surely, it seemed, fusion of the Slavic peoples was possible. If their numbers were added to the Russians, the total would account for about 70 percent of the population. Manifestations of Ukrainian nationalism were therefore particularly disturbing. In 1972–73 Shelest was purged, and many Ukrainian national schools were closed in an effort to stifle Ukrainian nationalism.

In the spring of 1972, the regime decided to crack down on the pervasive corruption, nepotism, and economic crimes in Georgia. There were tales of millionaire palaces, Mafia-like activity, and capitalistic tendencies. Eduard Shevardnadze, the head of the Georgian MVD, was appointed first secretary of the Georgian Communist Party with a mandate to carry out an anticorruption campaign. His efforts were met by bombings and arson, including destruction of the opera house in Tbilisi. About 25,000 were arrested before order was restored.

In Lithuania, the *samizdat* publication *The Chronicle of the Catholic Church in Lithuania* first appeared in 1972. In May of that year, a student set himself on fire in the city square of Kaunas to protest Soviet oppression. His funeral led to rioting. Troops had to be called in to restore order, and the organizers of the demonstrations were imprisoned. National dissent increased in all three Baltic republics, and cooperation among them began at this time.

Some liberal Russian dissidents recognized the salience of the nationality issue and began to sympathize. Bukovsky, while still a political prisoner in 1975, echoed Karl Marx's indictment of Tsarist Russia by stating, "It pains me that [today] Russia is a prison of nations on a greater scale than was the case 60 years ago." He affirmed the existence of national discrimination and forcible Russification.[28]

Nevertheless, despite national problems, the issue seemed to be one that could be handled within the existing framework. There was national dissent in the Baltics, corruption in Georgia, Crimean Tatar agitation, and problems with spreading the Russian language to Central Asia, but none of these seemed urgent.

John Bushnell speaks of a surge of confidence and optimism that pervaded the country in the late 1950s.[29] Soviet citizens were proud of their country's accomplishments, confident that the Soviet Union was the rising world power, convinced that rapid economic advances would improve their well-being and provide unlimited opportunities, especially for the young. He states that middle-class optimism peaked by the early 1960s and then remained at a constant high level into the second half of the 1960s. By the late 1960s, intellectuals had become pessimistic, largely as a result of re-Stalinization, but the bulk of the middle class remained reasonably optimistic until the beginning of the 1970s. They saw no threat to those who observed the rules of society, and they had no fear of political repression.

What Brezhnev tried to do was to draw a wedge between the intellectuals and the mass of the population. By improving living conditions, equalizing incomes, satisfying the most pressing demands of workers and peasants, and encouraging Russian nationalism, the leadership hoped to isolate the intellectuals, who would come to seem more and more irrelevant to the concerns of the nation. This strategy was reasonably successful as long as the regime could deliver on its economic promises of more and better consumer goods and a welfare state, while meeting the demands of national security.

## NOTES

1. Robert C. Tucker, *Political Culture and Leadership in Soviet Russia* (New York: W. W. Norton, 1987), 127.

2. Timothy McClure, "The Politics of Soviet Culture, 1964–1967," in *The Soviet Political System*, ed. Richard Cornell (Englewood Cliffs, N.J.: Prentice-Hall, 1970), 229–34.

3. Anatole Shub, *The New Russian Tragedy* (New York: W. W. Norton, 1969), 52.

4. McClure, "The Politics of Soviet Culture," 240.

5. Barbara B. Green, "Soviet Politics and Interest Groups," *Current History* 51 (October 1966): 216–17, 246.

6. *Pravda*, March 31, 1966, 2.

7. Timothy J. Colton, *The Dilemma of Reform in the Soviet Union* (New York: Council on Foreign Relations, 1984), 4.

8. Ibid., 7.

9. Jerry Hough, *The Soviet Union and Social Science Theory* (Cambridge: Harvard University Press, 1977), Chapter 1.

10. Colton, *The Dilemma of Reform*, 4–5.

11. Zbigniew Brzezinski, *The Grand Failure* (New York: Collier, 1990), 35.

12. Tucker, *Political Culture*, 130.

13. George W. Breslauer, "Khrushchev Reconsidered," in *The Soviet Union Since Stalin*, ed. Stephen F. Cohen, Alexander Rabinowitch, and Robert Sharlet (Bloomington: Indiana University Press, 1980), 62.

14. Jane P. Shapiro, "Soviet Consumer Policy in the 1970s: Plan and Performance," in *Soviet Politics in the Brezhnev Era*, ed. Donald R. Kelley (New York: Praeger, 1980), 104–28.

15. Ibid., 104–9.

16. Colton, *The Dilemma of Reform*, 8.

17. Shapiro, "Soviet Consumer Policy," 120.

18. This section is heavily dependent on James R. Millar, "Post-Stalin Agriculture and Its Future," in *The Soviet Union Since Stalin*, ed. Cohen, Rabinowitch, and Sharlet, 135–54.

19. Ibid., 140–41.

20. On Russian nationalism, see Stephen K. Carter, *Russian Nationalism: Yesterday, Today, Tomorrow* (New York: St. Martin's, 1990).

21. Bohdan Nahaylo and Victor Swoboda, *Soviet Disunion: A History of the Nationalities Problem in the USSR* (New York: The Free Press, 1990), 159–60, 171–72.

22. In 1973, Solzhenitsyn published his *Letter to Soviet Leaders*, calling on Soviet leaders to abandon any claims to lead a world communist movement and instead to concentrate on specifically Russian national concerns. He urged the leadership not to hold onto the non-Slavic nationalities in the borderlands or to Eastern Europe. He said that Russia was not ready for a democratic multiparty system, which would produce only anarchy. Freedom of thought or discussion is not an end in itself, but a means to discover truth, and truth lies in Russian orthodoxy. Solzhenitsyn criticized Marxist-Leninism, which he attacked as an alien ideology. What he wanted was a resurrection of orthodox Tsarist Russia. Solzhenitsyn was expelled from the Soviet Union in 1974, but his profoundly conservative outlook was shared by many Russians.

23. Nahaylo and Swoboda, *Soviet Disunion*, 182–83, 195.

24. Ralph S. Clem, "The Ethnic Dimension, Part II," in *Contemporary Soviet Society: Sociological Perspectives*, ed. Jerry G. Pankhurst and Michael Paul Sacks (New York: Praeger, 1980), 38.

25. This section is heavily dependent on Nahaylo and Swoboda, *Soviet Disunion*, 146–98.

26. Jeremy Azrael, "Emergent Nationality Problems," in *The Soviet Polity in the Modern Era*, ed. Erik P. Hoffmann and Robbin F. Laird (New York: Aldine, 1984), 608.

27. Ibid., 610.

28. Nahaylo and Swoboda, *Soviet Disunion*, 195.

29. John Bushnell, "The 'New Soviet Man' Turns Pessimist," in *The Soviet Union Since Stalin*, ed. Cohen, Rabinowitch, and Sharlet, 179–99. By *middle class*, Bushnell means white-collar professionals.

## Chapter 8

# STAGNATION

In 1976, Brezhnev boasted, "Never before over the length of its entire history has our country enjoyed such authority and influence in the world."[1] The Soviet Union had obtained nuclear parity with the West, achieved detente, maintained control over Eastern Europe, and challenged the West in the Third World. Domestically, it had reduced conflicts among elites by bringing all major institutional actors into the Politburo, where differences could be resolved through bargaining and compromise. Policy was an outgrowth of competing bureaucratic interest representing the military, heavy industry, agriculture, and regional party secretaries. This institutional pluralism would become a major source of stagnation since any action needed at least the passive consent of these bureaucratic institutions.

Despite Brezhnev's boast, by 1976 serious problems were evident in the regime's ability to deliver on its promises. The stability of cadres was leading to stagnation, with little or no turnover in the aging leadership since 1965. Writing in 1979, John Dornberg said, "The most significant thing that seems to have happened in the past 15 years is that Brezhnev and his team have simply gotten older."[2] There were a loss of momentum and a lack of direction. The country suffered an agricultural disaster of unprecedented proportions in 1975, inducing the leadership to increase investments in agriculture and cut back plans for increased consumer goods. Although this was assumed to be temporary, agriculture and, in fact, the entire economy were entering a period of decline. In 1976, Brezhnev suffered a stroke, clearly impairing his abilities and putting the country's leadership in doubt. Despite his increasing incapacity, Brezhnev took the title of president of the USSR in 1977, forcing Podgorny into retirement. Party and state bodies became increasingly reluctant to undertake long-term planning or policy commitments, waiting for a new leadership to establish direction. If Brezhnev and his aging team had been replaced by more dynamic leadership at this time, it is conceivable that incremental economic changes might have put the system back on course. But Brezhnev remained in office until November 1982. By the later Brezhnev years, a "growing awareness of decay, of ideological rot, of cultural sterility was setting in."[3] The problems were so severe that incremental, within-system efforts at reform would no longer suffice.

## THE ECONOMY

Agriculture was plagued by chronic inefficiency. Leon Baradat sets forth a catalog of problems and their consequences: workers were careless in harvesting and handling crops; there were not enough boxes and bags; storage facilities were often primitive; there were shortages of canning equipment, grain elevators, food bins, drying facilities, and refrigerated storage. Most roads were dirt and became impassable in rain—trucks became bogged down, and produce rotted, or they crossed fields, ruining crops. The roadside was strewn with grain that had blown off uncovered transport. The shortage of refrigerated trucks and railroad cars added to the problem of spoilage. Although the Soviet Union produced more tractors than the United States, the best were exported, leaving collective farmers with poor-quality tractors often unsuited to their needs. Spare parts were scarce, leading to cannibalization of other machines or to machinery sitting idle. Since there was a lack of barn space to house machinery, it was left outside, cutting its useful life. Baradat states that at least one-fourth of Soviet food crops failed to reach the table because of waste and spoilage.[4]

The rate of growth of agricultural output slowed down to just short of 1 percent in the 1970s, with most of the growth attributable to increased inputs. The Soviets invested about $78 billion a year in agriculture, with another $50 billion going for subsidies. By 1980, close to one-third of total investments went to agriculture or to the industrial sectors that served it.[5] Not only did enormous investment not lead to a significant increase in productivity, but it also did not lead to a significant release of labor from agricultural employment. James R. Millar stresses the "inordinate absorption of current resources of labor, land, and capital . . . to produce a still inadequate and thus very costly output."[6] The record of the 1970s was worsened by four straight years of poor weather beginning in 1979. Output for 1979–82 was so far below planned levels that the Soviets withheld production statistics.[7] The country was forced to spend about $8 billion per year in hard currency for import of grain, dairy products, and meat while the drop in oil and gold prices after 1980 cost the Soviets billions in foreign exchange.[8]

Industry was not in much better shape. The reforms introduced by Kosygin were defeated by bureaucratic resistance since they would have reduced the bureaucracy's control over the economy. There was a return to earlier performance criteria. The prerogatives granted economic units were eroded and by 1977 all investments were again planned centrally. The bureaucracy expanded to over one hundred ministries. Decision-making facilities were overloaded. Resources went not where they were needed, but where influence was the strongest. The growth rate of the early 1980s was the lowest since World War II. The Soviets' extensive approach to growth was dependent upon an abundance of labor, capital, land, energy, and raw materials, but assets were becoming scarce. There were no longer backlogs of modern technology from which to borrow, nor were there plentiful reserves of skilled or trainable labor. What was needed was improvement of the efficiency with which resources were used. Timothy J. Colton, however, pointed out that redirection of the bureaucracy would be a difficult task.[9]

Although in retrospect it seems evident that there were fundamental systemic problems with the Soviet economic system, at the time this was not evident. The United States Central Intelligence Agency reported in December 1982 that unsatisfactory results "do not mean that the Soviet economy is losing its viability as well as its dynamism . . . we do not consider an economic 'collapse' . . . even a remote possibility."[10] Similarly, Alec Nove stated, "There is no catastrophe imminent, the system is not in chaos, the quality of its planning and of its production are not in decline."[11]

The effort to provide increased consumer goods and raise the standard of living was further jeopardized by the reluctance to cut back on military expenditures. With the growth of institutional pluralism, the military-industrial complex became increasingly influential in asserting the priority of heavy and defense industries. Defense spending was absorbing about 20 percent of the GNP, but real costs were higher because the highest quality of material and most skilled personnel were used for defense industries. The regime, committed to parity with the United States, poured increasing resources into the military. Although the Soviets signed the Helsinki Accords in 1975 and two Strategic Arms Limitation Treaties (SALT) were agreed to by Brezhnev and U.S. presidents, deteriorating relations led to reductions in Soviet-American trade, American grain embargoes, boycotts, technology transfer bans, and the 1979 refusal of the U.S. Senate to ratify SALT II. When the Soviets entered Afghanistan in December 1979, they embarked on a costly, futile war that not only drained their resources but destroyed what remained of detente with the West.

Although the Brezhnev regime had made some headway in closing the gap between Soviet and Western living standards in the first decade, by the mid-1970s the gap was opening up again. Even when the system was able to produce needed goods, shortages resulted from the chaotic distribution system. There were periodic shortages of goods such as soap, toothpaste, toilet paper, and socks. Rumors of shortages led consumers to react by hoarding goods, thus creating artificial shortages. The system was unable to meet the demand for meat, fruit, and vegetables.[12] Most fruit and vegetables were grown on peasants' private plots rather than on state or collective farms. The private plots constituted about 4 percent of the arable land but produced about 60 percent of the potatoes, more than 40 percent of fruits, berries, and eggs, and about 30 percent of the meat, milk, and vegetables.[13] These were sold in private farmers' markets, often at exorbitant prices. There were long lines outside food stores even in major cities. In provincial towns there were reports of no cheese, milk, butter, and even on occasion, bread. Some cities introduced rationing in 1981. The central distribution system stocked cities better than provincial areas or farms, and the more prestigious the city, the better it was stocked. Peasants took trains into Moscow to join the lines for food and clothing.[14] Peasant resentment of the privileged citizens of Moscow grew, while Muscovites were angered by seeing outsiders buy up the goods in their stores. Increasingly, goods were being distributed to workers at their workplaces, bypassing the retail network.[15]

Consumers became increasingly frustrated at the lack of goods and the poor quality of those available. Soviet citizens were aware that conditions abroad, even in Eastern Europe, were better. The problem was due not to a reduction in supply but to the fact that incomes had been rising, the government was reluctant to increase retail prices, and there was little to spend their income on. Meat prices had remained frozen for eighteen years, while average salaries increased by almost 70 percent.[16] From 1975 to 1979, savings deposits in Soviet savings banks increased faster than retail sales. Cash income simply exceeded the availability of goods. This created the "ruble overhang," basically, pent-up inflation with too much money chasing too few goods. If prices were freed, this "ruble overhang" could create runaway inflation, but that would be a problem for Mikhail Gorbachev and Boris Yeltsin, not Brezhnev. Meanwhile, with nothing to buy, there was little incentive to work harder and increase one's salary; therefore, shortages persisted. The excess cash income helped to fuel the black market or second economy. Frustrated consumers bought goods *nalevo*,[17] from store clerks, waiters, and others with access to scarce goods, often stolen or misappropriated from state channels. Hedrick Smith speaks of "entire underground industries . . . illegal factories within legal ones, operating with the same workers and the same raw materials . . . . There were underground millionaires managing wholesale production and marketing enterprises with links all over the country."[18] Marshall I. Goldman estimates that the second economy accounted for 10 to 20 percent of the GNP.[19]

In the cities there was an enormous demand for automobiles, which might have soaked up surplus rubles, but they were difficult to obtain. Production rose from 344,000 a year to 1,327,000 in 1980, but of these, 328,000 were for export and 50 to 75 percent of the rest were for government use. There was only one car for every forty-six citizens. The unfilled demand meant that there was a three- to four-year wait to purchase a car.[20] Often it was more expensive to buy a used car than a new car if the used car could be bought without a waiting period. Spare parts for cars were almost impossible to find.

Housing continued as a major problem. Investment in housing dropped from 23.2 percent of all capital investment in 1956–60 to just 13.3 percent in the eleventh Five-Year Plan for 1981–85.[21] Drab neighborhoods of huge, monotonous blocks of apartment houses on the city outskirts were often constructed well before telephone cables, stores, or recreation facilities. In 1981, 20 percent of Moscow's population still lived in crowded communal apartments, each family in its own room, sharing a kitchen and toilet with another family in the same apartment. Most housing was run by the municipality or by factories for their employees. Apartments were small and overcrowded, but rent was nominal, rarely exceeding 10 percent of family income. The drawback of the low rent was that authorities could not collect enough money to maintain the buildings. Dusty courtyards; broken front stoops; cracked pavement; broken mailboxes; dingy, half-lit staircases; and tiny, malfunctioning elevators came to typify Soviet housing. The housing shortage was so bad that people schemed and bribed to get a tiny apartment in one of these blocks. Cooperative apartments, while better built and better maintained, were very expensive and not readily available.[22]

Although housing in Moscow was crowded, the right to live there was a coveted privilege. Moscow, Leningrad, Kiev, and other provincial capitals were closed cities, open only to those with special permits. The peasants lived in villages with wooden huts, outhouses, and unpaved roads. But even the most primitive huts had television, which brought in pictures of Moscow, nurtured envy, and raised expectations.[23]

The agricultural crisis of 1975 was a devastating blow to middle-class confidence in the regime's ability to improve economic performance.[24] Although the problem was largely one of rising expectations, people believed that things were getting worse and would continue to get worse. They no longer believed that hard work would pay off. The discontent of engineers, teachers, doctors, and other professionals was exacerbated by the fact that they were poorly paid, often receiving lower wages than skilled workers. Most earned less than bus drivers.[25] Cynicism and apathy became pervasive. The middle class became "indifferent to rampant petty corruption and pilferage, and increasingly, these phenomena meet with approval."[26] John Bushnell attributes the growing cynicism not just to the regime's failure to deliver on economic promises but to the decline in ideological fervor and the growth of materialism.[27] Western material levels were out of reach and hence irrelevant, but Soviet citizens were increasingly aware that consumer standards in Eastern Europe were far ahead of those of the Soviet Union, and this contributed to their pessimism. Bushnell states that there was still a belief that the Soviet socialist system was superior to Western capitalism. The assumption was that there were problems with the leadership and that new leaders could remedy the problems. But:

Because the legitimacy of the Soviet regime, in the eyes of the middle class, rests so heavily on the promise and expectation of material betterment, the perception that the economic system is being mismanaged must inevitably erode the regime's political legitimacy.[28]

While the Soviet middle class was becoming disenchanted, the working class was increasingly alienated, denied even the rewards and privileges available to the middle class. They resented the relative privilege accorded the middle class in what was supposedly a workers' state.[29] Although the regime took measures to increase equality by reducing wage differentials, raising the minimum wage, increasing old age pensions, and freezing the salaries of managerial and technical staffs, intellectual and cultural occupations were more highly valued. Intellectual occupations "promote a way of life culturally distinct from those occupied in routine, manual jobs."[30] While the workers resented the middle class, the intelligentsia had only contempt for the workers. David K. Shipler says, "The man who works with his hands is silently despised by the man who does not."[31] Nove speaks of the "wide gulf of mutual incomprehension" between workers and the middle class and notes that the regime has often manipulated the anti-intellectualism of the masses.[32]

## THE CRISIS IN HEALTH CARE

Meanwhile, the health care system was experiencing unprecedented difficulties.[33] From Stalin through Khrushchev, the health care sector had received a large share of the funds for social service. The results showed that Soviet citizens were receiving inexpensive, quality health care. Through 1970, there was a considerable decline in the incidence of infectious diseases. In 1897, life expectancy had been about 30 years; in the late 1950s, it reached 68.7, higher than that of the United States; by 1971, it was 70 years. Infant mortality (deaths in the first year) rates showed a similar pattern: in 1913, the rate was 269 per 1,000; in 1950, 60 per 1,000; and in 1971, 22.9 per 1,000. Attainment of these figures would have been impossible without a massive transformation of living conditions, especially in the Asian areas of the Soviet Union. In 1960, Soviet Central Asians lived 15 years longer than Iranians, 20 years longer than Pakistanis, and twice as long as Afghans. The Soviet Union had more hospital beds than all European hospitals combined.

Under Brezhnev, from the mid-1960s on, health care deteriorated. The expenditure on health care fell from 6.5 percent of the state budget in 1965 to 5.2 percent in 1975 and to 5.0 percent in 1980. According to Soviet statistics, infant mortality increased by more than one-third between 1970 and 1975. After 1975, the government stopped reporting infant mortality rates, but estimates reached 39 or 40 per 1,000 by 1980. Murray Feshbach points out that the Soviet Union was the first industrialized nation to experience a long-term rise in infant mortality.[34] With the exception of teenagers, nearly every age group had higher death rates in 1975 than 1960. Death rates for people in their fifties increased 20 percent; for those in their forties, the increase was 30 percent. Life expectancy for men fell from 67.0 in 1964 to 61.9 in 1980 while life expectancy for women in the same period fell from 75.6 to 73.5. Life expectancy was below that of every country in Europe, East or West.

The reasons for these appalling figures were multiple. The leading cause of death was heart disease, followed by cancer and alcohol-related illnesses. Soviet alcohol consumption was among the highest in the world. In the early 1970s, the per capita intake of hard liquor was double that of the United States and Sweden. Doctors rated alcoholism the third most frequent cause of illness for women and blamed it for the increasing incidence of birth defects, miscarriages, and premature births. In 1978, 51,000 deaths were due to alcohol poisoning. Smoking, diet, and lack of exercise affected health statistics. Given the poor quality or unavailability of alternatives, abortion was the primary means of birth control. The high rate of repeated abortions created a health risk for women, and uterine damage was a factor in increased infant mortality. There was a rising incidence of respiratory diseases linked to air and water pollution and birth abnormalities linked to pollution and radiation exposure. Industrial accidents caused by heavy machinery and electrical equipment produced on shoddy assembly lines by drunken workers accounted for 20 percent of the rise in male death rates. With only 10 percent of the number of motor vehicles as in the United States, the Soviets had the same number of traffic fatalities. Influenza killed thousands of babies annually. Hospitals lacked necessary medical supplies and pharmaceuticals. Effective drugs, thermometers, surgical gloves, insulin, and disposable bedding and needles were often unavailable.

Although there was an extensive network of hospitals, polyclinics, and neighborhood doctors, access to the better hospitals and doctors depended on connections, influence, and bribery. Even in the best hospitals, septic measures were careless.[35] Not surprisingly, there was a very high rate of hospital-induced infection. In March 1987, the Ministry of Health revealed that a large percentage of hospitals had no hot water and inadequate sewage and lacked basic sanitation.

Russians believe that medicine you do not pay for is worthless and accept the need to "oil the system." Gift giving is common. The *nomenklatura* (political elite), top military officers, prominent scientists, athletes, dancers, and other members of the elite had access to exclusive, well-equipped hospitals, including the Kremlin Clinic.[36]

## PRIVILEGE AND CORRUPTION

Ruling party officials, top military officers, and the managerial elite had access to special closed shops, good hospitals, and special vacation centers.

These privileges of the *nomenklatura* class evoked deep resentment in a state allegedly ruled by the workers. Under Brezhnev, once someone "made it" into the privileged caste, he was in it for life, as were his children. The country that had once prided itself on having careers open to talent now had a relatively closed class system with sharply limited opportunities for advancement and mobility. Fewer than 5 percent of the population had access to the closed stores, which were the only place to buy imported clothing, electronic equipment, and items in short supply, such as meat, fruit, and vegetables. Instead of rationing by money, the Soviets rationed by privilege. The *nomenklatura* were entitled to go to the head of the long list of those waiting to buy cars; were entitled to larger, better-constructed apartments; and were entitled to travel abroad. Tickets for the ballet, opera, theater, and music were allocated on a ranked system to members of the *nomenklatura*. The very top of the elite had extraordinary privileges, with luxurious apartments and dachas. They received part of their pay in "gold rubles" or "certificate rubles," which could be exchanged for hard currency and used in special stores where they could buy foreign or Soviet goods at reduced prices. The ruling elite bought its food at the "Kremlin canteen," open only to people with special passes, where they were able to purchase high-quality food never seen in ordinary stores, American cigarettes, and Scotch whiskey.[37]

In Moscow and other large cities, the center strip in the main avenue was reserved for members of the party Central Committee and top government ministers. Powerful leaders had government cars and drivers, and most had their own luxury cars. Brezhnev had a fleet of foreign cars including Mercedes, Rolls Royce, Lincoln Continental, and others.[38] Gordon Smith speaks of "the ostentatiousness, the flaunting of wealth and position by the elite."[39]

Corruption became increasingly widespread, reaching from the very apex of the privileged down throughout the fabric of society. Brezhnev's daughter had an affair with a gypsy circus performer who was arrested for accepting bribes. Her husband, the deputy minister of internal affairs, was convicted of bribery. Konstantin Simis states that "the atmosphere of corruption . . . bred the conviction in the minds of the people that everything can be attained by bribery: a good job, a university diploma, or an undeserved judicial verdict. . . . It has led to the climate of tolerance toward corruption that holds sway in Soviet society."[40]

## INTELLECTUALS, DISSENT, AND RUSSIAN NATIONALISM

The Soviets signed the Helsinki Accords in 1975, including the broad humanitarian declarations constituting the so-called Third Basket. Dissenters used the Helsinki Accords as a lever to push for liberalization. A Helsinki Watch Group was established in Moscow in 1976. Soon others, favoring human rights and national self-determination, were established in the Ukraine, Lithuania, Georgia, and Armenia. The monitoring groups brought together different kinds of dissidents who met in each other's apartments, sent messages, traveled to each other's cities.

With the collapse of detente the KGB began to arrest the founders of Helsinki Watch Groups and Jewish refusniks (individuals refused the right to emigrate for political reasons). Controls over printing and duplicating equipment were tightened, and new provisions were introduced for deprivation of citizenship. The dissidents fought back by calling press conferences, circulating banned books and manuscripts, and sending protests to Washington, Paris, and the Vatican. Andrei Sakharov, the unofficial leader of the human rights movement, regularly received foreign newsmen, but he and his family were subjected to continual harassment. The persecution was inconsistent and unpredictable. Some were arrested, some were sent to mental institutions, some were harassed in their homes or on the streets, and some were exiled. Dissidents were tried under laws forbidding the dissemination of anti-Soviet propaganda or for the crime of hooliganism. Exchange programs that had brought Soviet scientists to the West broke down, and jamming of foreign broadcasts in Russian was resumed in August 1980. There was a drastic reduction in the emigration of Jews and Germans. Sakharov was sent into internal exile in the city of Gorky in 1980, three weeks after the invasion of Afghanistan. The Moscow Helsinki Watch Committee disbanded itself, and the dissident movement ended as a viable force. Many of the country's best known intellectuals left or were forced into exile. Robert Kaiser calls this "an incredible exodus of talent, a devastating loss to the country."[41]

The message of Russian nationalists vied with that of liberal dissidents.[42] The village prose writers, as noted earlier, tended to equate true Russian values with the Orthodox church or even pre-Christian Russian naturalism. Rasputin expressed nationalistic and anti-Semitic views, attacking mixed marriages between Russians and other races. Igor Shafarevich, the noted mathematician and friend of Solzhenitsyn, denounced Marx, Engels, and Trotsky for hatred of Russia. Gennady Shimanov, a leading right-wing dissident, endorsed a powerful Soviet state based on Russian orthodoxy and the attachment of man to the soil. He opposed Western technology and the craving for foreign goods, attacking Lenin and his Politburo as non-Russians. Ilya Glazunov's enormously popular paintings glorifying the tsars, the saints, and the old Russia were shown in a long-running one-man exhibition at the Manezh Gallery in 1978. Liberal dissidents denounced him as anti-Semitic and suspected him of being a KGB agent. He was an influential leader in the movement to preserve historical monuments, which became increasingly associated with right-wing Russianism.[43]

These views found fertile soil among Russians who believed that other nationalities were treated better than Russians and lived better. They feared that as a result of demographic trends, Russians would soon be a minority in the Soviet Union. Russians called Central Asians by the racial epithet Chuchmek, blaming them for rising crime rates. Although the only blacks were foreign students and diplomats, racist attitudes toward blacks were pervasive. Anti-Semitism was never much below the surface and often blatant. *Samizdat* pamphlets spoke of a Jewish-Masonic conspiracy, and mimeographed pamphlets charged that control of the Politburo had been seized by Zionists. Some extremists supported Anatoly Shcharansky and the emigration movement, arguing that all Jews should leave Russia.[44] On April 20, 1982, a group of young fascists in black shirts and swastikas attempted to celebrate Hitler's birthday in Moscow's Pushkin Square.

## PROBLEMS AT THE PERIPHERY

Manifestation of dissident nationalism continued. In Tbilisi, Georgia, in 1978, hundreds of demonstrators took to the streets to protest attempts to alter the constitutional provision making Georgian the official state language of the republic. The authorities were forced to retreat, and similar attempts to alter the constitutions of Armenia and Azerbaijan were abandoned. An extremist Armenian organization was responsible for a bomb explosion in the Moscow metro that killed seven and injured thirty-seven. Ethnic minorities within these republics expressed their frustrations as well. Abkhazians protesting violations of their rights by the Georgians campaigned to be allowed to secede from Georgia and join the Russian Federation, where they thought they would receive more protection. Although their goal was rejected, they were granted cultural and economic concessions. Armenians in Nagorno-Karabakh claimed that the Azerbaijanis were deliberately keeping the region backward and pressuring Armenians to leave.[45]

Nationalist dissidents were active elsewhere as well. In the Baltics, activists called for independence. The example of Lech Walesa and the election of a Polish pope were particularly encouraging in Catholic Lithuania and the Western Ukraine. The Crimean Tatar demonstrations continued. Members of the "diaspora" nationalities, most prominently the Jews and Volga Germans, campaigned for the right to emigrate. In his 1978 evaluation of nationalism, Jeremy Azrael argued that although the situation at that time was not explosive, problems were likely to increase. However, he concluded, "There is little likelihood that national protest will rise to unmanageable levels."[46]

Demographic trends were of increasing concern to the regime, as they produced problems for the work force and the army.[47] For 1981–85, all of the population increment came from non-Russian republics, primarily Central Asia, Kazakhstan, and Azerbaijan. Essentially, Gertrude Schroeder points out, the government had three options for dealing with the problem: (1) it could encourage or compel migration from labor-surplus regions to labor-deficit regions, primarily the Russian Federal Republic (RSFSR); (2) it could reallocate investment and locate new industries in labor-surplus areas; or (3) it could follow a combination of the two. The government, in fact, did none of these, choosing rather to evade the issue.[48] The problem for the military was even more severe.[49] In 1979 more than 35 percent of non-Russians, almost 45 million people, spoke no Russian, the language of the military and the only language spoken by senior officers. The ethnic mix in the military was "changing in favor of the nationalities that are technically least developed and culturally and politically most alienated."[50] Antagonisms between Muslims and Europeans and between Russians and non-Russians were endemic, with ethnic-based mutual protection groups engaging in ethnic infighting.[51]

## ANDROPOV AND CHERNENKO

When Brezhnev died in November 1982, he was replaced as General Secretary by the sixty-eight-year-old Yuri Andropov. Although Andropov had been appointed chief of the KGB in 1967 and was the first Soviet leader to come from the police, he had a long career in party administration, serving as a member of the Secretariat prior to joining the KGB. Along with his KGB appointment in 1967, he was made a candidate member of the Politburo. In 1973, he became a full member. After Mikhail Suslov died in January 1982, Andropov gave up his post as chairman of the KGB and moved to the Central Committee Secretariat, where he took responsibility for ideology and foreign policy. In June 1983, he took the ceremonial position of chairman of the Presidium of the Supreme Soviet, the Soviet presidency. Andropov moved swiftly to rejuvenate the party apparatus and install his supporters in key positions. In his fifteen months in office, half the voting members of the Politburo, one-fifth of all regional party secretaries, and one-third of the department heads of the Secretariat were replaced. The turnover on the Central Committee was at the annual rate of 20 percent. In recruitment and promotion, emphasis was put on professional competence.

For Andropov, the first step was to enforce order, move against bribery, and clean up corruption and incompetence. His experience in the KGB had heightened his awareness of the pervasiveness of corruption in Soviet life, and he was determined to end it. He shed the luxurious trappings of office, visited factories, limited the privileges of the elite, and stressed the importance of discipline. He opened attacks on the elite for misuse of state and public property and use of their official positions for personal gain. Thousands of officials were arrested for corruption and thousands of others in the upper ranks of government were demoted or transferred. Forty of the 150 regional party secretaries were fired. Three well-known figures were shot by firing squads for corruption. Although attacks on elitist privilege were popular with the masses, Andropov also attacked alcoholism, materialism, and lack of purposiveness among youth. He cracked down hard on absenteeism, shoddy work, and black marketeering. KGB and police checked lines at stores, people in the baths or at movies—if they were supposed to be on the job, they were fined and sent back to work. Unlike his predecessors, he avoided propagandistic rhetoric. Brezhnev's claim that the Soviet Union was a "developed socialist society" was replaced by the more sober view that the Soviet Union was building developed socialism but still had difficulties to overcome.

His major goal was to improve the performance of the Soviet economy. The economy in 1983 grew at the rate of about 3.2 percent, a substantial increase over the previous few years. This was, in part, attributable to the discipline campaign. In contrast to Khrushchev, Andropov was convinced that careful preparation and study were needed before major reforms should be introduced. On July 26, 1983, the leadership announced a major economic experiment would take effect in January. It called for greater independence for factories and enterprises in selected industries and for collective and state farms.

In regard to the nationalities issue, Andropov held that although fusion of nationalities remained a long-term goal, modernization and economic development were inevitably accompanied by the growth of national self-consciousness. He opposed extreme Russian nationalism and spoke out against disrespectful attitudes toward other nations and peoples. However, his campaign to improve labor discipline and reduce corruption had a disproportionate impact in Central Asia.

The Soviet's international situation deteriorated rapidly in the Andropov interval. The country was mired militarily in Afghanistan, deadlocked in negotiations with China, faced a crisis in Poland, and had problems in Lebanon, Central America, and the Caribbean. Relations with the United States worsened, hitting a new low after the Korean Air Lines incident of September 1, 1983. President Ronald Reagan's arms buildup put the weakened Soviet economy under enormous pressure.

Andropov moved rapidly, but he had little time. Within three months of his election as General Secretary, his life depended on regular kidney dialysis. He was last seen in public in August 1983, and he died February 9, 1984. His successor, the seventy-two-year-old Konstantin Chernenko, suffered from emphysema. His fifty-two years of party service were devoid of any accomplishments except loyalty to Brezhnev. His selection postponed the necessity of moving to a new generation of leaders and may have been intended to block Gorbachev, but Gorbachev got expanded responsibilities, particularly after Andropov's health began to fail in the fall of 1984. When Chernenko died on March 11, 1985, after thirteen months in office, Gorbachev was immediately elected as General Secretary.

Gorbachev inherited a country suffering from declining rates of economic growth, a widening gap between consumer expectations and the ability of the government to meet them, strain among class and ethnic groups, unfavorable demographic trends, and a serious health crisis. Despite Andropov's efforts, corruption was still pervasive. Perhaps most disturbing were the growing pessimism and disillusionment. The regime had implicitly asked to be judged on its ability to "deliver the goods," and the judgment seemed to be that it was failing to deliver. The international environment was increasingly hostile, especially relations with the United States under the Reagan administration. The costly, futile war in Afghanistan was taking its toll. Earlier, we noted that when Nicholas I bungled the Crimean War, it became evident that the regime was not only autocratic but inefficient, corrupt, and stupid. Although the Tsarist regime was to survive another sixty years, its legitimacy was shaken. The rot uncovered by the Crimean War was further exposed by Russia's humiliating performance in the Russo-Japanese War. In retrospect, it is clear that the Soviet Union was at the same juncture, but this was not apparent at the time either to Soviet leaders or American experts. Repeatedly, as we have noted, scholars stressed that the problems facing the Soviets, though serious, were not of crisis proportions. Colton, an acute analyst, stated: "An overall crisis of the political system does not exist. The regime has worries aplenty, but not so many that it will soon collapse beneath their weight."[52] It should then be no surprise that Gorbachev appears to have shared this view, moving to strengthen and reform the system, not to change its basic structure.

## NOTES

1. Timothy J. Colton, *The Dilemma of Reform in the Soviet Union* (New York: Council on Foreign Relations, 1984), 9.

2. (Cleveland) *Plain Dealer*, October 9, 1979, 17.

3. Zbigniew Brzezinski, *The Grand Failure* (New York: Collier, 1990), 34.

4. Leon Baradat, *Soviet Political Society*, 3d ed. (Englewood Cliffs, N.J.: Prentice Hall, 1992), 297–98.

5. Alec Nove, "Soviet Economy: Problems and Prospects," in *The Soviet Polity in the Modern Era*, ed. Erik P. Hoffmann and Robbin F. Laird (New York: Aldine, 1984), 453.

6. James R. Millar, "Post-Soviet Agriculture and Its Future," in *The Soviet Union Since Stalin*, ed. Stephen F. Cohen, Alexander Rabinowitch, and Robert Sharlet (Bloomington: Indiana University Press, 1980), 145.

7. Colton, *The Dilemma of Reform*, 15.

8. Ibid., 10.

9. Ibid., 17.

10. Henry Rowen, "CIA Briefing: Soviet Economy," in *The Soviet Polity*, ed. Hoffmann and Laird, 418.

11. Alec Nove, "Soviet Economy," 462.

12. Marshall I. Goldman, *USSR in Crisis* (New York: W. W. Norton, 1983), 97.

13. Ibid., 82–83.

14. David K. Shipler, *Russia: Broken Idols, Solemn Dreams*, rev. ed. (New York: Penguin Books, 1989), 171.

15. Goldman, *USSR in Crisis*, 97–98.

16. Alec Nove, "Soviet Economy," 454.

17. Literally, "on the left." The term implies illegal or semilegal transactions.

18. Hedrick Smith, *The New Russians* (New York: Avon Books, 1991), 24.

19. Goldman, *USSR in Crisis*, 55, 98.

20. Ibid., 99.

21. Gordon P. Smith, *Soviet Politics: Struggling with Change*, 2d ed. (New York: St. Martin's, 1992), 55.

22. Goldman, *USSR in Crisis*, 98–99.

23. Shipler, *Russia*, 172.

24. For reactions of middle-class citizens, see John Bushnell, "The 'New Soviet Man' Turns Pessimist," in *The Soviet Union Since Stalin*, ed. Cohen, Rabinowitch, and Sharlet, 179–99.

25. Alec Nove, "Soviet Economy," 464.

26. Bushnell, "The 'New Soviet Man,' " 187.

27. Ibid., 190.

28. Ibid., 194–95.

29. Ibid., 195.

30. David Lane, "Social Stratification and Class," in *The Soviet Polity*, ed. Hoffmann and Laird, 596.

31. Shipler, *Russia*, 202.

32. Nove, "Soviet Economy," 464.

33. The information on health care comes largely from Nick Eberstadt, "The Health Crisis in the USSR," *New York Review of Books*, February 19, 1981, 8.

34. Murray Feshbach, "A Different Crisis," in *The Soviet Polity*, ed. Hoffmann and Laird, 897.

35. Shipler, *Russia*, 217.

36. Ibid., 217–21.

37. Ibid., 199; Konstantin M. Simis, "USSR: The Corrupt Society," in *The Soviet Polity*, ed. Hoffmann and Laird, 296–98.

38. Goldman, *USSR in Crisis*, 101–4.

39. Smith, *Soviet Politics*, 57.

40. Simis, "USSR: The Corrupt Society," 305.

41. Robert G. Kaiser, *Russia: The People and the Power* (New York: Washington Square Press, 1984), 536.

42. On Russian nationalism, see Stephen K. Carter, *Russian Nationalism* (New York: St. Martin's, 1990).

43. Shipler, *Russia*, 326–36, 339–46.

44. Ibid., 336–39, 343–44.

45. Ronald Grigor Suny, "Transcaucasia: Cultural Cohesion and Ethnic Revival in a Multinational Society," in *The Nationalities Factor in Soviet Politics and Society*, ed. Lubomyr Hadja and Mark Beissinger (Boulder, Colo.: Westview Press, 1990), 242–45.

46. Jeremy Azrael, "Emergent Nationality Problems in the USSR," in *The Soviet Polity*, ed. Hoffmann and Laird, 619.

47. Ibid., 607–31.

48. Gertrude E. Schroeder, "Nationalities and the Soviet Economy," in *The Nationalities Factor*, ed. Hajda and Beissinger, 56–59.

49. Teresa Rakowska-Harmstone, "Nationalities and the Soviet Military," in *The Nationalities Factor*, ed. Hajda and Beissinger, 72–94.

50. Ibid., 91.
51. Ibid., 87–91.
52. Colton, *The Dilemma of Reform*, 58.

*Chapter 9*

# REFORM AND THE LOSS OF
# LEGITIMACY I

When Gorbachev was chosen as General Secretary of the party on March 11, 1985, the country faced a formidable array of problems. Although he was the first leader from the post-Stalin generation, not only was he surrounded by holdovers from the Brezhnev gerontocracy, but the system in which he operated had been formed in its essentials by Stalinism. The Khrushchev era had provided a short-lived and erratic thaw, but upon Khrushchev's removal in 1964 the regime reverted to a neo-Stalinist model, albeit one in which the implicit faith in the system had been shaken by Khrushchev's revelations of Stalin's crimes. Nevertheless, Khrushchev's successors, like Khrushchev himself, evidently believed that the structure of Stalinism was essentially sound and that their task was merely to remove the excesses of Stalinism while retaining its achievements. Foremost among the achievements of Stalinism was the economic transformation of Russia into a modern industrial power able to compete successfully with the United States as one of the world's two superpowers.

By the time Gorbachev came to power, it was clear that something had to be done about the declining efficiency of the economy. The dynamism that had characterized the economy under Stalin, Khrushchev, and even the first decade of Brezhnev's rule, had dissipated. Almost immediately, Gorbachev pushed the fight against corruption and inefficiency and for modernization of the industrial plant.[1] At the same Central Committee meeting at which he was named General Secretary, Gorbachev called for improving the management system, increasing the autonomy of enterprises, and reducing central control. But the approach was a continuation of Andropov's policies, not a bold new initiative, although it was undertaken with boldness. Gorbachev's campaign against alcoholism curbed the output and sale of alcoholic beverages. This resulted in huge lines outside liquor stores, the destruction of vineyards, shortages of sugar, which was used to produce home brew, and a sharp increase in cases of alcohol poisoning. Before the campaign began, revenue from the sale of alcohol amounted to approximately 20 percent of the national budget. The anti-alcohol drive may have cost 200 billion rubles.[2] The campaign was symptomatic of the fact that Gorbachev wanted to deal with the growing economic weaknesses of the Soviet Union but assumed that those weaknesses could be overcome within the framework of the existing system.

The economy was not the only problem facing Gorbachev, although a flourishing economy might well have provided him with the means to avoid, prevent, or delay the others. Furthermore, each of the other problems was intertwined with the problem of economic stagnation. The country was facing an ideological crisis, a crisis of faith. For much of the population, the ideology centered on the implicit promise of improving living standards and comprehensive social welfare, so that when the economy stumbled, their faith was shaken. Marxist-Leninism, even in its attenuated form, served to inhibit the leaders from looking for solutions outside its framework. Gorbachev might look back to Lenin, but he would not look elsewhere for alternative paths to modernity.[3] His efforts, at least initially, were in-system attempts at reform that could be justified in terms of the existing ideology.

Other problems, too, were related to the precrisis situation in the economy. The war in Afghanistan wasted resources, undermined morale, exacerbated relations among the nationalities, and stood in the way of improved relations with the West. Since much of the economic problem stemmed from the misdevelopment of the economy with its overemphasis on defense production and heavy industry, reduction of tensions with the West was essential in order to scale back military expenditures and redirect the economy into production for consumer needs. As early as April 7, 1985, Gorbachev announced a unilateral moratorium on medium-range missiles in Europe and called on the United States to respond with a similar freeze.[4] Although the United States rejected this approach, by the end of July Gorbachev announced that the Soviet Union was suspending the testing of nuclear weapons until the end of the year and called on the United States to halt testing. It is clear that Gorbachev understood the need to come to some arrangement with the West in order to concentrate resources and intelligence on the Soviet Union's pressing domestic problems.

Gorbachev's efforts to meet the economic challenge facing the country threatened the stability of the system. Although the challenge was not economic development, but rather redevelopment, much of the analysis of the disruptive effects of economic development in Third World countries applies to the situation Gorbachev faced. David Roth, Paul Warwick, and David Paul argue that in Third World countries, the problems and challenges of economic development often stimulate "cleavage-driven political instability."[5] Ethnic and racial cleavages are the most powerful sources of instability, but religion, ideology, and class cleavages can also be potent. Those who believe that their ideology prescribes the only true path will make every effort to block access to power by those who do not share the belief with equal fervor. Other cleavages come into play as economic development alters traditional social and economic structures. A newly emerging business class and the educated urban elite benefit from the new system, while traditional social classes feel threatened. In consequence, society is likely to become sharply divided between those who support and those who oppose socioeconomic change and development.[6] Development also enhances expectations of political participation. Roth, Warwick, and Paul point that the monopolistic political party is often used "to channel expectations of political participation and to direct economic development."[7] When, however, the single party proves unable to control social divisiveness or produce economic growth, pressures for pluralistic economics and politics will grow. Elements, at least, of the monopolistic party will inevitably oppose opening the political system to competing groups, thereby generating further cleavages and instability. When increasing numbers of citizens no longer accept the legitimacy of the system, the regime comes under increasing stress.[8]

Although the Soviet regime attempted to restore legitimacy by co-opting the liberal intellectuals and democratizing government, it was unsuccessful in the time available. The authority of the ideology and the control by the party weakened at a time when the regime had increasing difficulties in distributing sufficient patronage to maintain centralized authority. Linkages between the center and the nationalities on the periphery began to fray. Old forms of control were undermined before the regime was able to forge new patterns of interdependence.

*The Economist*, referring to Tsar Nicholas II, said: "Anyone crowned tsar in 1896 would have faced enormous difficulties. But the idea that Russia was doomed to become ungovernable over the next two decades is implausible." The article continues, "Led at this critical juncture by a man with vision and political skill, Russia would have stood a chance of joining the modern world."[9] Led in 1985 by Gorbachev, a man with vision and enormous political skill, the Soviet Union became ungovernable within six years. Machiavelli warns:

There is nothing more difficult to carry out, nor more doubtful of success, nor more dangerous to handle, than to initiate a new order of things. For the reformer has enemies in all those who profit by the old order, and only lukewarm defenders in all those who profit by the new order.[10]

## CONSOLIDATION OF POWER: INITIAL EFFORTS

For any new leader, especially one seeking to set a new policy direction, formation of a responsive leadership team is necessary. Faced with a gerontocracy of top Brezhnev-era officials, personnel changes were an essential first step for Gorbachev, and he moved rapidly. Three men who had risen to political prominence under Andropov's tutelage were promoted as early as April 1985. Viktor Chebrikov, the chairman of the KGB, moved from candidate to full member of the Politburo while Yegor Ligachev and Nikolai Ryzhkov, Central Committee secretaries, became full members of the Politburo without passing through candidate status. Ligachev was given responsibility for ideology and personnel matters, thus becoming second in command in the Politburo. Gorbachev came to rely heavily on Ligachev. Robert Kaiser stresses that all three were "tough-minded, independent, and relatively honest men . . . but they were not Gorbachev's clients, and owed him no special allegiance."[11]

Gorbachev began to gather his own team during his first year. He moved against his most formidable rivals, Grigori Romanov and Viktor Grishin, removing them from the Politburo. Andrei Gromyko was elevated to the ceremonial chairmanship of the Presidium of the Supreme Soviet, and Shevardnadze, a strong supporter of reform, replaced him as foreign minister. Shevardnadze was promoted from candidate to full member of the Politburo. Yeltsin, an obscure first secretary in Sverdlovsk, joined the Secretariat and then replaced Grishin as head of the Moscow party organization. Yakovlev, who had spent ten years as ambassador to Canada, was named head of the propaganda department of the Central Committee. It was from this position that he pushed *glasnost* and supported liberalization of the press. In September, Ryzhkov, who was charged with developing strategy for economic reform, replaced the eighty-year-old Nikolai Tikhonov as prime minister. At the Twenty-Seventh Party Congress, in March 1986, Yeltsin became a candidate member of the Politburo but left the Secretariat.

In his first year in power, Gorbachev replaced two-thirds of the country's top leaders, including eight of eleven members of the Secretariat, one-third of the government ministers, and one-third of the republican and regional leaders.[12] Gorbachev was not, however, able to pack the Politburo with people who owed their jobs to him. As General Secretary he had more leverage over the Secretariat, where the appointment of five new secretaries, including Yakovlev and Anatoli Dobrynin, the ambassador to Washington, established the Secretariat as Gorbachev's main base of support. Although Gorbachev's speed in gathering his own top team was impressive, in some ways it was chimerical. As his program became increasingly radical, his early appointees had to be replaced by figures more in tune with Gorbachev's new position. Furthermore, the *apparatchiki* in the party and the government, fearful of losing their privileges and power, stood in the way, resisting the implementation of reform policies. In an interview in May 1987 with *l'Unita*, the Italian Communist Party's newspaper, Gorbachev stated:

I want to emphasize that the restructuring is a long and difficult process. The new demands being placed upon the cause, upon people, and upon their duties at such a juncture are being realized quickly by some and more slowly by others.

What do we mean when we speak of resistance to the restructuring? It is a question of old approaches, of the inertia of old habits and of fear of novelty and responsibility for specific deeds. We are also being hampered by the bureaucratic layers.[13]

Gorbachev recognized the obstacles that Machiavelli warned about: the inertia of old habits, the fear of novelty, and the selfish interests of those who profit from the old order. Men do not give up power willingly.

## IDEOLOGY AND *GLASNOST*

Ideology was an essential element in legitimation of Soviet political rule. Although the doctrine was flexible, certain core beliefs were considered essential, and it was assumed that any Soviet government tampering with these would put its own survival in peril. These included support for the abolition of private ownership of the means of production and its replacement by common ownership and a planned economy; the belief that past sacrifices were justified by the fact that the Soviet Union had become one of the two most advanced world powers and was destined to emerge as the strongest; faith that the country was progressing toward a communist society characterized by a superabundance of goods; an assumption that wage differentials, while justified until the attainment of communism, should not be great—all should have some and none too much; the concept of the leading and guiding role of the Communist Party, which embodies the interests of the working class and is the definitive interpreter of the doctrine. There was faith in the righteousness of Lenin and the Bolshevik revolution he led. The Great Patriotic War was a central myth since it bound a suffering people together in a heroic war of good against evil. The extent to which Gorbachev would be driven to confront core beliefs and risk the very legitimacy of the system was not initially apparent even to him.

Almost immediately upon assuming power, Gorbachev proclaimed *glasnost*, the need for open release of information and trust in people. The purpose of *glasnost* was to encourage criticism of economic management in order to improve efficiency and expose corruption.[14] Gorbachev was convinced that the only way to pressure the entrenched bureaucracy was to use public opinion as a lever. In order for that to work, the public had to be encouraged to criticize openly and without fear of reprisal. Another aspect of *glasnost* was the need to improve the quality of public information. Basic information on the economy, life expectancy, infant mortality, and alcoholism had been suppressed, making meaningful assessment of Soviet conditions impossible. A third and related function of *glasnost* was to enlist the support of the cultural intelligentsia, who were viewed as an important constituency for reform.

On October 25, 1985, Gorbachev presented a new draft program to replace the Third Party Program, adopted under Khrushchev in 1961, which had confidently predicted that the present generation of Soviet citizens would live under communism. The new draft, in contrast, stated that attempts to move too fast to introduce communism without due account of the level of material and intellectual maturity of the society were doomed to failure. The program called for doubling production potential by the end of the century and increasing labor productivity by 150 percent in fifteen years but refrained from giving any dates by which communism would be achieved. Although the tone was more realistic, it was couched in party jargon, maintained the basic communist vision, and stated that while movement toward the goal of communism might be uneven, it was, nevertheless, inexorable.[15]

It was evident that Gorbachev was a more honest, determined, and dynamic leader than his predecessors, but his long-term objectives were unclear. Gorbachev evidently was a modernizer convinced that Stalinist economics led to a profligate use of human and material resources, but he seemed to be seeking an alternative to capitalist modernization.[16] He appeared to be seeking to eliminate the excesses of Stalinism and the negative effects of Brezhnevism and to return to Leninism. He moved toward an increasingly open society in the belief that *glasnost* would help to energize society and enlist the creative intelligentsia in support of economic restructuring.

On April 26, 1986, the Soviet Union suffered the world's worst nuclear disaster when one of the four reactors at the Chernobyl power station exploded. Swedish monitoring stations reported heightened levels of radiation traced to the Ukraine, but it was more than thirty-six hours after the explosion before the first official response, and then it was only a brief announcement that an accident had left a reactor damaged. A second statement the following day reported that two lives had been lost.[17] The failure to provide information promptly was met with worldwide criticism as a cloud of radioactive debris spread to Europe. It was two weeks before news of the disaster was printed on the front page of *Pravda*.[18] Gorbachev made no public comment until May 14, eighteen days after the explosion.

Chernobyl was an unspeakable disaster. Thirty-three deaths occurred in the immediate aftermath and several thousand subsequently. It was a severe blow to Gorbachev's plans for accelerating economic development. More significantly, the accident was, as Kaiser says, "a devastating blow to Gorbachev's hopes for building popular trust and enthusiasm."[19]

The failure to report fully and promptly led to worldwide skepticism about the likelihood that the Soviet Union was in fact moving toward a more open society. In the wake of Chernobyl, however, the campaign for *glasnost* was speeded up. The following years saw a constant expansion of the frontiers of the permissible, although there was considerable opposition from conservatives and occasional back-stepping by Gorbachev.

Hedrick Smith states that the "crucial symbolic gesture" was Gorbachev's phone call to Sakharov on December 16, 1986, inviting him to return to Moscow.[20] There were, however, earlier signs that Gorbachev was determined to enlist the liberal intelligentsia in his campaign for reform. In the summer of 1986, Vitali Korotich took over as editor of the weekly picture magazine *Ogonyok*. In four and one half years, its circulation rose from 260,000 to 4,600,000. It printed articles exposing excesses of the past, corruption within the party *nomenklatura*, and the futility of the war in Afghanistan. The Soviet military were a chief target.[21] Yegor Yakovlev took control of *Moscow News*, which became "one of the hottest newspapers of *glasnost*, full of juicy items and hard to find before it sold out."[22] Vladislav Starkov edited the provocative *Argumenty i Fakty*, whose weekly circulation jumped from 10,000 to 31.5 million copies.[23] These three were to play a vital role in widening the scope of the permissible.

Literary journals like *Novy Mir* began to publish long-banned books. Its circulation increased from 400,000 to 1 million between 1985 and 1988. Boris Pasternak's *Dr. Zhivago* appeared in *Novy Mir* in 1988. An article in the May 1988 issue argued that Stalin's terror had its roots in Lenin's suppression of opponents of the revolution.[24] Anna Akhmatova's *Requiem*, a poetic lament to the memory of her husband and son, was published in *Oktyabr* in 1987. Even the poems of Joseph Brodsky, who had emigrated in 1972 and won the Nobel Prize in 1987, were published. The serialization, beginning in the November 1989 issue of *Oktyabr*, of Vasily Grossman's novel, *Forever Flowing*, with its depiction of Lenin's intolerance, cruelty, and drive for power, caused a sensation and drew harsh criticism from hard-liners.[25]

The powerful anti-Stalinist film *Repentance* was shown to special Moscow audiences in October 1986 and then to millions of people throughout the Soviet Union. Other films also broke barriers, exposing aspects of Soviet society that had long gone unacknowledged. *Little Vera*, with its nude scenes, showed the depressing life of a provincial working-class family. Documentary films portrayed the impact of the Afghan war and the atrocities of Stalin's labor camps.[26]

Television had an extraordinary impact in the Soviet Union. The audience for prime-time nightly news was approximately 150 million, double the combined audience for all three network news broadcasts in the United States. "Twelfth Floor," monthly series in which teenagers throughout the country participated in lively discussions intermixed with rock music video, attracted tens of millions of viewers.[27] Leningrad's "Six Hundred Seconds" exposed crime, corruption, and incompetence. Battlefield coverage of the Afghanistan war became frequent.

Soviet television began to feature studio discussions with Western politicians and other important figures. Margaret Thatcher and George Shultz were interviewed live. Vladimir Pozner and Phil Donahue cohosted two "citizens' summit" programs in which American and Soviet audiences were linked by satellite. "Fifth Wheel," a Leningrad television program begun in 1988, was on the cutting edge, using investigative documentaries. It showed problems of returning Afghan veterans, dangers of a nuclear power station, problems of the poor and disabled, abuse of orphans, reminiscences of purge victims, and a program on the execution of the Tsar and his family.[28] Not surprisingly, "Fifth Wheel" came under repeated attacks from party leaders, Stalinists, and right-wing nationalists.[29] "Vzglyad" (View), the shocking Friday night magazine show, soon became the most popular television program reporting on crime, police corruption, prostitution, and drug addiction.[30]

Controls on the press and television were loosened further when Alexander Yakovlev took over responsibility for ideology from Ligachev. Jamming of Russian-language broadcasts of Radio Liberty and other Western stations stopped. CNN became available in early 1991. Television in the summer of 1989 presented a startling roundtable discussion by Germans and Russians on the Nazi-Soviet Pact of 1939 and its secret protocols. The full live coverage of the Congress of People's Deputies had the population riveted to their television sets. Even more startling was the fact that Soviet television showed the collapse of communism in Eastern Europe in 1989. "Vzglyad" showed film on the military's brutal suppression of the demonstration in Tbilisi in April 1989, broke the story when a right-wing group ran through a meeting of the Writers' Union in Moscow shouting anti-Semitic slogans, and presented evidence that Stalin's NKVD was responsible for the Katyn massacre of Polish army officers. It reported on acquired immunodeficiency syndrome (AIDS) in the Soviet Union, exposed the bloodshed in Afghanistan, criticized ethnic hazing in the army, and opposed the draft. Its proposal to remove Lenin's body from the mausoleum in Red Square and bury him beside his mother in Leningrad caused a stormy reaction. Censorship of the program was tightened. But "Vzglyad" soon became openly critical of Gorbachev's policies.[31]

Although Gorbachev initially was reluctant to reopen the issue of Stalin's crimes, believing that this had been dealt with sufficiently by Khrushchev and now could serve only as a tool for enemies to blacken the Soviet Union, by February 1987 he was insisting that there could be no blank spots in Soviet history. A Politburo commission was established to investigate the crimes of the Stalin era. School texts on the history of the Stalinist period were withdrawn and final history examinations were canceled. In 1988, Bukharin was rehabilitated posthumously and restored to Party membership. The rehabilitation of Kamenev, Zinoviev, and other old Bolsheviks followed in the same year. In total, about 1 million sentences were reviewed and repealed, and another 2 million were "given back their good names."

In 1989, some of Trotsky's works were published. Solzhenitsyn was readmitted to the Union of Soviet Writers, and in July 1989, after more than a year of pressure by its chief editor, *Novy Mir* began to serialize his *Gulag Archipelago*, an indictment not just of Stalin, but of Lenin, for establishing labor camps for political opponents. Finally, in August 1990, a presidential decree provided for the rehabilitation of all victims of repression in the

Stalinist period. Stalinist figures such as Andrei Vyshinsky, the chief prosecutor at the purge trials, and Andrei Zhdanov were denounced. The reassessment was not limited to individuals and their roles. The discovery of mass graves of victims of the Stalinist terror was reported. The existence of the secret protocols to the Nazi-Soviet Pact was acknowledged after years of denying their existence.[32] This was a devastating blow to the Russians' view of their role in the Great Patriotic War. Exposure of the secret protocols struck at the heart of the nation-binding myth and, of course, provided justification for the Baltic republics' drive toward independence.

The movement toward greater openness was not without setbacks. Gorbachev was under pressure from Right and Left, from those pushing for increased freedom of expression and from those who believed that irresponsible attacks on core beliefs were corroding the system. In January 1988 Defense Minister Dmitri Yazov appeared on television chiding writers for undermining respect for the military. *Ogonyok* was his principal target.[33] Furthermore, *glasnost* not only encouraged liberals but permitted the growth of the extreme right. Pamyat, originally a literary and historical society, fell under the control of extreme nationalists and anti-Semites. It proclaimed Russian superiority over other nationalities and opposed capitalism and the market. Although most were Orthodox Christians, some members of Pamyat regarded the Christianization of Kievan Rus as a Zionist plot to undermine the warrior qualities of the Slavs. *Nash sovremennik* and *Molodaya gvardiya* supported the Pamyat line, stressing patriotism and Russian nationalism.

The March 13, 1988, publication in *Sovetskaya Rossiya* of Nina Andreyeva's letter entitled "I Cannot Betray My Principles" alarmed liberals. Published while Gorbachev was visiting in Yugoslavia and endorsed by Ligachev, the letter attacked Gorbachev's reforms for threatening the basic concepts of socialism. It praised Stalin and attacked liberals for throwing "mud at our past and present." Party lecturers backed Andreyeva's views at meetings of communist activists and in the military. Liberals' fears were enhanced by the fact that no rebuttal appeared until three weeks had passed. *Pravda* then published an editorial on April 5 accusing Andreyeva of "whitewashing the past." Attacks on Andreyeva now appeared throughout the Soviet press, and *Sovetskaya Rossiya* itself reprinted the *Pravda* editorial. In the summer of 1989, Andreyeva published an article in *Molodaya gvardiya*, essentially reiterating her views. She soon became a symbol for unrepentant Stalinists and hard-core nationalists and the founder of a mass movement, Edinstvo, or Unity.[34]

In October 1989, Korotich, Starkov, Yegor Yakovlev, and a few other editors were summoned to a meeting with Gorbachev, who shouted at them and accused them of irresponsibility.[35] The regime had subtle means to rein in the press, particularly by limiting its supply of paper, deciding its salary levels, and determining whether it would receive computers. These devices limited the circulation of *Ogonyok, Argumenty i Fakty*, and, especially, *Mos-*

*cow News*. Although throngs of anticommunist protesters were permitted to march through Red Square at the end of the May Day parade, catcalls and taunts from marchers led the Soviet parliament to make it an offense publicly to insult or slander the president of the USSR. Nevertheless, in the spring of 1990 Gavriil Popov, the mayor of Moscow, criticized Gorbachev in the pages of *Ogonyok*. Criticizing Lenin was in style.[36]

In August 1990, after three years of pressure from reformers, a new press law came into effect, permitting the publication of journals free of party or state control.[37] The law eliminated censorship in principle, except for disclosure of state secrets, calls for the overthrow of the existing state or social system, and a limited range of other cases. However, state secrets were not defined. The president and the Supreme Soviet had the power under certain conditions to declare a state of emergency and impose controls over the media. Furthermore, in practice the ownership of media remained overwhelmingly in the hands of the Communist Party.[38] The censorship office, in fact, continued to function.[39] As Gorbachev himself came under sharp criticism from the media, he became increasingly impatient and accused the media of abuse of *glasnost*.

When Gorbachev moved to the right in the winter of 1990–91, the media suffered. "Vzglyad" was taken off the air. It was reinstated after strong lobbying by Yeltsin and others but was no longer broadcast live. Television coverage of the shootings by Soviet troops in Vilnius on January 13 presented the official line, denying that Soviet troops had been the first to open fire. Boris Pugo, the new Minister of the Interior, appeared on "Vremya, " the main television news program, to blame the Lithuanians for causing the violence. Official newspapers reiterated the same line. But *Moscow News*, *Literaturnaya gazeta*, and the new Russian radio station not only contradicted the official story but reported on attempts to reimpose censorship.[40] "Fifth Wheel" put footage collected by Lithuanians on the air, including bloody scenes of beatings and killing. Hundreds of thousands of people demonstrated in major cities across the Soviet Union. Yeltsin not only denounced Gorbachev but signed mutual assistance agreements with the three Baltic republics.[41] In May 1991, Russian Television went on the air, sponsored, protected, and financed by Yeltsin.[42]

The need to compete under market conditions raised serious difficulties for the press. Rising inflation led to price increases and falling circulation. *Pravda's* 9.5 million circulation in early 1989 fell to just over 2 million in 1991.[43] *Ogonyok*, which turned itself into a self-financing independent journal, was forced to increase its subscription price two and a half times. New journals and newspapers covering the entire political spectrum cut into the circulation of journals like *Ogonyok*.[44] There were publications for lesbians and gays, for Greens, for astrologers. Pornography made an appearance. There was more freedom of expression than ever before in the history of Russia.

The liberal cultural intelligentsia was no longer without power. The Congress of People's Deputies elected in March 1989 included important members of the intelligentsia—Yevtushenko, Sakharov, Roy Medvedev, Korotich, and others. Former dissidents had penetrated the political establishment and some had become part of the political leadership. The largest segment of the intelligentsia favored a more rapid transition to pluralist democracy and a market economy. They supported Gorbachev's liberal opponents. *Glasnost* not only opened the way to criticism of the past, of inefficiency, of bribery, of corruption but opened the way to criticism of the regime itself as the economy failed to improve and, in fact, deteriorated. Gorbachev himself came under increasing attack from all sides.

*Glasnost* had originally been intended as a tool that Gorbachev could use to strengthen the Soviet system. Gorbachev stressed Leninism as the basis of legitimacy, and although he wanted to push back the boundaries, he still wanted to limit the reform to what was ideologically acceptable.[45] *Glasnost*, however, undermined the legitimacy on which the entire political, social, and economic structure was based. Nothing was left untouched: "Things once held to be sacred were publicly profaned; matters long ago swept under the rug, openly exposed; the seeming unanimity of the country shattered; and . . . the future of the system placed in doubt."[46]

## NOTES

1. Bernard Gwertzman and Michael T. Kaufman, eds., *The Decline and Fall of The Soviet Empire* (New York: New York Times Company, 1992), 7–8.

2. Marshall I. Goldman, *What Went Wrong with Perestroika* (New York: W. W. Norton, 1991), 135.

3. Richard Sakwa, *Gorbachev and His Reforms 1985–1990* (New York: Prentice-Hall, 1991), 53–54.

4. Gwertzman and Kaufman, *The Decline and Fall*, 9.

5. David F. Roth, Paul V. Warwick, and David W. Paul, *Comparative Politics: Diverse States in an Interdependent World* (New York: Harper and Row, 1989), 392.

6. Ibid., 392–93.

7. Ibid., 394.

8. Ibid., 394–96.

9. *The Economist*, August 29, 1992.

10. Niccolo Machiavelli, "The Prince" in *The Prince and the Discourses* (New York: The Modern Library, 1950), 21.

11. Robert G. Kaiser, *Why Gorbachev Happened* (New York: Touchstone, 1992), 97.

12. Sakwa, *Gorbachev and His Reforms*, 13.

13. *Mikhail Gorbachev's Answers to Questions Put by l'Unita* (Moscow: Novosti Press Agency Publishing House, 1987), 33–34.

14. David Wedgewood Benn, " 'Glasnost' and the Media," in *Developments in Soviet & Post-Soviet Politics*, ed. Stephen White, Alex Pravda, and Zvi Gitelman (Durham, N.C.: Duke University Press, 1992), 182–83.

15. *New York Times*, October 26, 1985.

16. Sakwa, *Gorbachev and His Reforms*, 53–54.

17. *New York Times*, April 30, 1986.

18. *New York Times*, May 14, 1986.

19. Kaiser, *Why Gorbachev Happened*, 127.

20. Hedrick Smith, *The New Russians* (New York: Avon Books, 1991), 101. For a description of events surrounding this move, see Kaiser, *Why Gorbachev Happened*, 146–49.

21. John Newhouse, "Profile: Chronicling the Chaos," *The New Yorker*, December 31, 1990, 38, 52, 57–59.

22. Smith, *The New Russians*, 104.

23. John Newhouse, "Profile," 39.

24. Smith, *The New Russians*, 106–7.

25. Ibid., 102.

26. Ibid., 110–12.

27. For information on changes in Soviet television, see Ellen Mickiewicz, *Split Signals* (New York: Oxford University Press, 1988).

28. Smith, *The New Russians*, 155.

29. Ibid., 156–58.

30. Ibid., 165–67.

31. Ibid., 165–72.

32. Stephen White, *Gorbachev and After* (Cambridge: Cambridge University Press, 1991), 76–79.

33. *New York Times*, January 26, 1988.

34. Smith, *The New Russians*, 133–40; Kaiser, *Why Gorbachev Happened*, 204–13.

35. John Newhouse, "Profile," 39.

36. Ibid., 64.

37. Benn, "Glasnost" 190–94.

38. Ibid., 192–94.

39. John Newhouse, "Profile," 70.

40. Benn, "Glasnost" 192–93; Kaiser, *Why Gorbachev Happened*, 393–94.

41. Smith, *The New Russians*, 564; Kaiser, *Why Gorbachev Happened*, 395–97.

42. Smith, *The New Russians*, 571–73.

43. Benn, "Glasnost" 193–194.

44. Newhouse, "Profile," 48.

45. Sakwa, *Gorbachev and His Reforms*, 124.

46. Zbigniew Brzezinski, *The Grand Failure* (New York: Collier, 1990), 55.

*Chapter 10*

# REFORM AND THE LOSS OF LEGITIMACY II

In order to carry out his program of economic reconstruction, Gorbachev knew he would have to break the stranglehold of the party on the system. It was a question not merely of changing personnel but of altering the way the power structure operated, since everyone in the party had a vested interest in maintaining the status quo. This realization led Gorbachev to introduce *glasnost*, and this same realization led him to "democratization," the introduction of some elements of democracy into the existing political structure. He had no intention, however, of eliminating the party monopoly of power or permitting a competitive multiparty system.

## THE COMMUNIST PARTY

The Soviet political system was marked by parallel structures of party and government. While the structure of the government was defined in the constitution, the Communist Party of the Soviet Union (CPSU) was the focus of power in the Soviet system. Article 6 of the 1977 constitution stated that it was "the leading and guiding force of society and the nucleus of its political system, of all state organs and public organs." The party dominated the state, setting its course, supervising its operations, and selecting or approving its personnel. Supervision and control were essential party functions. The role of the state was primarily to administer the policies determined by the party.

Although Stalin deliberately created overlapping jurisdictions among the party, the state, and the police in order to enhance his own power, the supremacy of the party was reasserted after his death. The right of the party to rule received its justification from the ideology, and the party, in turn, provided the only true interpretation of the ideology. The mission of the party was to direct the course of Soviet development. The weakening of the ideology under *glasnost* ultimately undermined the justification for the

Communist Party's monopoly of power. Since the party was the central means of control over society, the weakening of its grip and the recognition of the legitimacy of other political organizations undermined the system and set centrifugal forces in motion.[1]

The party was structured hierarchically, with power flowing from top to bottom, from the Politburo and Secretariat at the apex to the primary party organizations at the bottom, in accord with the principle of democratic centralism. The essence of democratic centralism was "the absolutely binding character of the decisions of higher bodies upon lower bodies." Policy was determined at the top and the obligation of lower levels was to carry it out.[2] All communication was up and down the hierarchical ladder, and horizontal communication or structures were banned. Party secretaries at a given level in the hierarchy were not permitted to deal directly with one another, but could communicate only vertically through the hierarchy. This was intended to ensure tight control and discipline.

According to the party rules, the Party Congress of more than 5,000 delegates, meeting every five years, was the highest organ of power. In practice, from 1925 until 1986, it was largely ceremonial. It met at least every five years for intervals of two weeks, during which time delegates listened to interminable speeches and unanimously approved decisions reached by party leaders before the Congress met. Its delegates were approved by higher party organs, and when it elected the Central Committee, it approved a slate of candidates presented to it. Changes in its role occurred rapidly after Gorbachev came to power.

The Central Committee was charged with exercising the powers of the Congress when it was not in session. Party rules specified that the Central Committee had a broad range of responsibilities, including the power to appoint and remove members of the Politburo and Secretariat. The Central Committee played an important role at times, most notably in supporting Khrushchev in 1957 and in endorsing his removal in 1964. Although the Central Committee normally rubber-stamped decisions of higher bodies, membership was a sign of prestige. It included among its members the most powerful political figures in the country: high party officials; top leaders of the armed forces, police, state apparatus, and trade unions; and academic, cultural, and scientific leaders. The members represented the country's power elite, but since the Central Committee met only a few days every six months and since members had important outside responsibilities, they could not devote much time to the work of the Central Committee. Under Gorbachev the Central Committee met about twice as often as in the past and its role in the party increased.[3]

The Central Committee elected three committees: the Party Control Committee to oversee party discipline; the Secretariat to administer party affairs; and the Politburo, the key decision-making institution in the political system. The General Secretary headed the Secretariat and was first among equals in the Politburo. The Politburo included within its membership the top government and party leaders, including members of the Secretariat and the government Council of Ministers. It met every Thursday at eleven in the morning for five or more hours. The General Secretary usually chaired, but decisions were generally reached by consensus. Meetings received little or no publicity, although there might be brief accounts in the Soviet press. The size of the Politburo varied but ordinarily numbered eleven to twelve full members and eight or so candidate members. Yeltsin tells us that after the General Secretary entered the room, full members filed into the room in order of seniority. Candidate members and Central Committee secretaries were lined up in a row in the conference room, awaiting their appearance. Then all sat down in their assigned places. After initial opening remarks by Gorbachev, discussion of issues began. However, since materials were usually distributed only a day or two in advance, it was impossible for members to be grounded in the issues. Since the party bureaucracy (*apparat*) prepared the drafts for discussion, the *apparat* in reality controlled everything passed by the Politburo.[4]

The Secretariat was a key power center, second only to the Politburo. The most powerful leaders in the country sat on both the Secretariat and the Politburo. The Secretariat controlled a vast apparatus that administered and supervised the work of the party, government, and all key institutions of society to see they implemented plans and directives. It fulfilled an important control function through maintenance of the *nomenklatura* system, by which it verified, approved, or made all key appointments. These lists included all important positions in the government, large industrial enterprises, economic management, military, police, courts, press, trade unions, and academic institutions. Appointments to top positions were in the hands of the central Secretariat while less important jobs were under the control of lower-level secretariats. The Secretariat had direct control over the approximately 1 million full-time party functionaries. Each secretary supervised one or more of its 21 departments, which covered all aspects of society.

Beginning in 1988, the size of the apparatus was cut, the number of departments drastically reduced, and a series of commissions established. In August 1990, the party declared it was abandoning the *nomenklatura* system and would retain control only over party positions. Since loss of this control would weaken their positions, many *apparatchiki* obstructed transfer of personnel appointments to the electorate or government organs.[5]

## Party Reform

The Twenty-Seventh Party Congress in February and March 1986 took place when Gorbachev had been in power almost a year. In that year he had taken initial steps to alter the composition of the inner circle of party leaders, firing opponents and incompetents and rejuvenating the leadership. The Congress was anticipated with great excitement at home and abroad. Gorbachev called for radical reform of the system of economic management, support for *glasnost*, and socialist democracy. Although the Congress approved what Gorbachev called "truly revolutionary changes," proposals for implementation were vague.[6] Yeltsin, the new Moscow party chief, openly assailed the party leadership for failing to deal with problems of corruption and attacked the perquisites of party officials.[7]

The concept of "democratization" was introduced at the January 1987 plenum of the Central Committee. Gorbachev criticized the party for contributing to the country's stagnation and attacked the Stalinist system of rigid central controls and ideological inflexibility. A competitive secret ballot and term limitations were introduced for party offices. Opportunities for rank-and-file participation in party affairs were widened through establishment of advisory commissions.[8] Gorbachev defended *glasnost*, criticized abuses of power, and called for personnel changes. Breaking with all precedent, Gorbachev broadcast his closing speech on national television.[9]

Tension began to build up in the Politburo with clashes between Yeltsin, then a candidate member of the Politburo, and Ligachev, the number two man. Yeltsin wrote to Gorbachev on September 12, outlining his objections to the conduct of the Politburo and, more especially, his objections to Ligachev. He asked to be released from the duties of first secretary of the Moscow City Committee and from his responsibilities as a candidate member of the Politburo. The October 1987 meeting of the Central Committee was called to celebrate the seventieth anniversary of the revolution. Gorbachev asked Yeltsin not to mar the celebration by bringing the dispute to public attention. Yeltsin ignored the plea. He attacked Ligachev for holding up needed changes. He complained about "adulation of the general secretary" and warned of the dangers of a revived cult of personality. Yeltsin said, "I must put before you the question of my release from the duties and obligations of a candidate member of the Politburo."[10] Gorbachev was angered by Yeltsin's defiance of the party leadership.

In February 1988 Yeltsin was officially removed from his position as candidate member of the Politburo, but he remained on the Central Committee. Soon after, Gorbachev gave Yeltsin a ministerial post as first deputy chairman of construction. This was the first incident in what would become an embittered rivalry between Gorbachev and Yeltsin. Time and time again, as Gorbachev sought to free himself from the conservative forces in the party, he would be attacked by Yeltsin and his supporters for not going far enough. Although for a time Gorbachev was able to balance the Right against the Left, the constant attacks from Right and Left eventually undermined the legitimacy of Gorbachev's rule. Ultimately this loss of control over a disintegrating political system and the division between these two powerful personalities emboldened the Right to attempt a coup d'état.

Gorbachev persuaded and pressured the Central Committee to approve a package of reforms limiting the terms of party and government officials to ten years, expanding the authority of popularly elected legislatures, and requiring competitive elections by secret ballot for deputies. The reforms were intended to remove the party from involvement in day-to-day management.[11] Mary McAuley points out that the underlying assumption of Gorbachev's strategy was that the structural arrangements of the system were sound. What were needed was good leadership and the right people to run the system. The problem was that party involvement in everyday administration was a consequence of the structural arrangements. Since the party was responsible for state institutions, it was driven to control them by interfering with management responsibilities.[12]

Gorbachev took the step of convening the Nineteenth Party Conference, the first since 1941, in order to secure broad party support for reforms. Expectations were high, but local party organizations chose conservative delegates.[13] Several of Gorbachev's strongest supporters were not selected, and others were added only after public protests and intervention by Gorbachev and his top aides. Despite a ban on demonstrations in the city center, political activists with a variety of demands held demonstrations in the days leading up to the conference, which opened June 28, 1988.[14]

Gorbachev called for a shift of power from the party to elected government bodies and from the center to localities. He recognized that his economic reforms had been unable "to break the stranglehold of central government ministries" and "had become tangled in bureaucratic resistance."[15] He now presented a plan that called for a thorough restructuring of government.[16] There was contentious debate before the 4,991 delegates approved the package in a divided vote. Philip Taubman states, "The conference shattered the stifling political customs of the Soviet system, making candor, pointed debate, even public confrontation between party leaders acceptable."[17]

Yeltsin and Ligachev openly opposed each other at the conference. Bill Keller described Ligachev as "a weighty presence . . . and a figure of integrity. . . . the voice of patriotic duty and discipline, the scourge of self-pity and negativism." Yeltsin "looked tired and sickened by the pressure of his disgrace, by his disbelief that the party could spurn a man who believed in it so strongly. By the end of the night he had heard his plea for dignity rejected by the crowd and by Mr. Gorbachev."[18] This incident fueled Yeltsin's strong resentment against Gorbachev. After the unsuccessful coup three years later, Yeltsin reminded Gorbachev of the humiliation he felt had been visited upon him at this time.

Although Gorbachev was moving power from the party to the state structure, the party remained a formidable power structure over which he was not willing to surrender control. Gromyko, the veteran party stalwart, resigned from the Politburo, and three others were dismissed. Four new members were elevated to the Politburo. Ligachev remained on the Politburo, but instead of being the number two man, in charge of ideology, he now headed a new commission supervising agriculture.[19]

In April 1989 Gorbachev persuaded 110 inactive full and candidate members of the Central Committee to resign en masse. These so-called dead souls had already been retired from the key government and party positions that had won them their places. Twenty-four candidate members were promoted to full status, but the purge reduced the size of the Central Committee to 251 full and 108 candidate members. Only the Party Congress had the power to replace those who resigned.[20] Although the resignations appeared to go smoothly, many regional party officials were clearly angered at Gorbachev for undermining the authority of the party and the military, for tolerating nationalism and the undermining of the ideology, and for failing to solve economic problems. They felt threatened by the state structures that were exerting power that had been the exclusive domain of the party. The publication of their speeches in *Pravda* revealed a deep division in the party and "an unmistakable sense that Mr. Gorbachev had betrayed the party regulars."[21]

Gorbachev warned that another shake-up might be necessary to strengthen the party's ability to deal with the economy, rising nationalism, and loss of faith in the party's own future. On September 20, three of the twelve voting members of the Politburo, including Vladimir Shcherbitsky, the longtime Ukrainian leader, were removed by the party Central Committee. Vladimir Kryuchkov, the new KGB chief who had been campaigning to improve the image of the KGB, was chosen to fill one of the Politburo voting seats.[22]

After the collapse of communism in Eastern Europe, conservatives were even more fearful that Gorbachev would betray the party at home. Gorbachev insisted that he supported the party monopoly of political power and described his goal as humane socialism.[23] Nevertheless, it was apparent that the Soviet Communist Party was beginning to splinter along national and ideological lines. The legislatures of Lithuania and Estonia abolished the party's monopoly of power and legalized multiparty systems. The Lithuanian Communist Party declared its independence from the CPSU. Communists in Latvia declared their intention to form a party independent of Moscow. Democratic Platform, a group of reformers in the party, called for an end to the party monopoly on power, an end to democratic centralism, and abolition of the rule against organized factions in the party. Conservatives who opposed Gorbachev's economic and social reforms prepared alternative platforms.[24] On the eve of the February 5–7 meeting of the Central Committee, 100,000 Soviet citizens staged a six-hour parade and rally in the center of Moscow demanding that the Central Committee forgo its monopoly of power. Many, emboldened by the fall of communism in Eastern Europe, shouted "Resign! Resign!" at the Central Committee.[25]

The Central Committee, after heated debate, agreed to surrender the party's monopoly of power and to support the creation of a powerful presidency.[26] Despite the radical nature of this move and its departure from

Leninist principles, reformers within the party believed the Central Committee did not go far enough. Yeltsin, who cast the only vote against the platform, said he would favor formation of an independent party if the forthcoming Party Congress failed to expel hard-liners and adopt a more radical program.[27]

Hard-liners pushed for creation of a separate Russian Communist Party, which they were confident they would be able to control. At the founding Congress of the Communist Party of the Russian Republic in Moscow on June 19, a large number of the delegates were *apparatchiki*. Clearly shaken by the loss of Eastern Europe, the right-wing brutally assailed Gorbachev. Andreyeva praised Ivan Polozkov, the leading contender for leadership of the Russian party, who called for a return to orthodox Marxism. Polozkov's election led thousands of reformers to resign from the party.[28]

The Twenty-Eight Party Congress met on July 2, 1990. On the eve of the Congress, *Moscow News* published a poll showing that less than half the respondents believed that the party could solve the country's problems.[29] In previous Congresses, delegates had been chosen by the leadership to represent various constituencies. For this Congress, delegates were elected by local party organizations. This move, intended to increase democracy within the party, resulted in a delegation heavily weighted with party officials, industrial managers, bureaucrats, and representatives of the armed forces. About half of the 4,683 delegates were party officials.[30] However, the Congress could not be controlled by the leadership. Not only were there clear differences of view, but they were openly expressed. Although factions were still not permitted, "platforms" were allowed.[31] Delegates cross-examined individual Politburo members, one after the other. Gorbachev and other leaders were openly criticized.[32] Gorbachev was elected party leader after he delivered a blistering attack on hard-liners.[33]

In a contested election, Vladimir Ivashko, the centrist leader of the Ukrainian Communist Party, defeated Ligachev for the newly created post of deputy party leader. Since Gorbachev would be concentrating on the state structure, the deputy party leader was expected to conduct the day-to-day affairs of the party. If Ligachev, the most formidable conservative rival of Gorbachev, had won, he might have been able to wrest control of the party from Gorbachev and then set the still powerful party organization against the newly formed state organs in a bitter contest. As it was, the conservatives were humiliated.

The Politburo was restructured and removed from control over the government. It doubled in size from twelve to twenty-four full members, including Gorbachev and Ivashko, the party leaders of all fifteen republics, the Moscow party leader, the editor of *Pravda*, and five party secretaries. Gorbachev was the only one with a top post in the party and the government. All other top government officials lost their positions on the Politburo in a measure intended to reflect the fact that the Politburo was no longer supposed to have a role in government decisions. The new makeup was an attempt to curb pressures from several republican parties to break ties with the Moscow party by giving their leaders direct representation on the highest organ of the party. It also cut down on Russian ethnic domination. Seventeen of the twenty-four members were now non-Russian while previously the twelve-man Politburo had only three non-Russians. The Politburo had clearly been weakened with the creation of the new presidency and the overall strengthening of the government. It was no longer the key decision-making body. It became, instead, an internal policy board running the party, not the country.

The Congress elected a sixteen-member Secretariat, including eleven responsible secretaries and five new positions for ordinary members chosen from the party's general membership.[34] Efforts were made to weaken the power of the *apparatchiki*, but they had formidable powers, were hard to dislodge, and did much to block reform.

Gorbachev spoke of his commitment to democratic government, to pluralism of opinion, to a market-oriented economy, and to humane democratic socialism. But the mass of the delegates were confused, feared the future, and blamed party officials, the press, and the Politburo for the loss of party prestige and the failure to arrest the economic decline. In a dramatic move toward the end of the Congress, on July 12, Yeltsin quit the party. This was a direct slap at Gorbachev. The following day two of the most popular reform leaders, Gavriil Popov, head of the Moscow government, and Anatoly Sobchak, the leader of Leningrad, also left the party.[35]

The Central Committee became more conservative as reformers resigned from the party in late 1990 and 1991. The April 1991 Central Committee meeting was the scene of a direct confrontation between Gorbachev and the conservatives. Prior to the meeting, rumors were rife that the Central Committee might vote no confidence in Gorbachev. Gorbachev was subjected to attack after attack by speakers, led by Polozkov. When Gorbachev offered to resign, the Central Committee recessed while the Politburo met. Clearly, enormous pressure was exerted behind the scenes, since the Politburo soon announced its unanimous support for Gorbachev. The conservative opposition collapsed for the time being, and the Central Committee overwhelmingly confirmed its confidence in Gorbachev's leadership.[36]

Gorbachev came to recognize that his efforts for fundamental economic reform were being frustrated by the party itself. In an effort to generate backing for his policies, he shuffled and reshuffled the membership of the Politburo and Secretariat and the senior administrative apparatus. However, the republic, regional, city, and district party organizations remained resistant to change. Each had a party organization essentially modeled after the central organization, headed by a powerful secretary. Gorbachev's reforms directly challenged their privileges, threatening removal of their access to special stores and medical clinics. Perhaps even more important was the threat to their power to supervise government, factories, collective farms, and other institutions and to make appointments through the *no-menklatura* system. Removing party leaders was difficult: "Replacing a regional party leader can mean dismantling an entire network in which dozens of officials have a stake in the survival of the leader."[37] These Soviet versions of patron-client relations proved exceedingly difficult to control from the center.

Further resistance to change could be found in the primary party organizations (PPOs) at the base of the hierarchy. More than 425,000 of these were organized at every workplace and in some residences. But these PPOs were not intended to serve as vote-getting machines. They were the main point of contact with the party and a crucial means by which the party served as the "guiding force of Soviet society." They supervised the workplaces where they were situated and ensured that party directives were carried out. They controlled the key day-to-day levers of political and economic power and, like the party layers above them, had everything to lose if Gorbachev's reforms took root. They, too, became centers of resistance.[38]

In 1988, when the party was cautioned not to interfere in government and management, their oversight functions began to decline. In July 1990, a decision was made to switch emphasis from the workplace to residential areas as the party prepared to alter its role from an instrument of control to one of building support to compete in contested elections. In July 1991, Yeltsin ordered party committees out of offices, factories, the armed forces, and KGB units in Russia. After the failure of the coup in August 1991, PPOs were banned in workplaces throughout the Soviet Union.

The loss of faith in the party and the loss of privileged status for its members led to a falling off in party membership. At the end of the 1980s, the party had numbered almost 20 million members, about 10 percent of the adult population. To govern effectively and to ensure loyalty of elites through the exertion of party discipline, the party included those in positions of power throughout society. For control purposes, the party also had representatives in all social groups and organizations. During the 1980s, approximately 45 percent of the total members were listed as workers or those of worker background. Probably only 30 percent were real workers. About 12 percent were listed as peasants and about 43 percent as white-collar employees. The higher one's occupational or educational level, the greater was the chance of being in the party. One-third of party members had partial or complete higher education as compared with 8 percent of the general population. About one-half of all university graduates were party members. In 1989, membership declined for the first time in thirty years. In 1990 resignations reached an unprecedented level, as 3 million members left the party. The Komsomol lost about one-quarter of its members in 1990. In early 1991, an additional 12 percent indicated their intention of resigning from the party. Over 1 million members were behind in their dues.[39]

Although it was still by far the largest organization in the country, its membership was down to 15 million in 1991.

### Political Pluralism

Soviet society had been characterized by the absence of autonomous voluntary associations articulating genuine public interests. Instead, groups acted as transmission belts. The government itself established mass organizations in every area of economic and social life as a means of control and to mobilize members for centrally determined purposes. The country lacked institutions and groups independent of the party.

*Glasnost* created the space necessary for the emergence of autonomous groups and the beginnings of civil society. At the Twenty-Seventh Party Congress, Gorbachev called for creation of women's councils and veterans' associations. Hundreds of new groups were formed by sports fans and stamp collectors, lawyers, cooperative associations, peasant farmers, supporters of peace and nuclear disarmament. Afghan War veterans lobbied for better health care and recognition from the public. By 1988 there were more than 30,000 informal groups or *neformalny* organizations.

In terms of the development of a civil society, the emergence of a range of political movements from 1987 on was of more significance. Several groups, including the Democratic Perestroika Club, Elections '89, and the Federation of Socialist Clubs, wanted to speed up reform. The Democratic Union opposed the Communist Party and the entire socialist system.[40] Popular front organizations supporting sovereignty or independence sprang up in non-Russian regions. Sajudis, the Lithuanian popular front, won control of the Lithuanian parliament. Communist parties split into independent and loyalist branches.

By 1991, at least 20 "political parties" were operating at the national level and about 500 at the republican level.[41] Democratic Platform was a loose alliance of reform communists and noncommunist radicals. Its program called for transforming the Communist Party into a parliamentary party that would oppose other parties in competitive elections. After the Twenty-Eight Party Congress, its leaders announced that they were leaving the Communist Party to form their own party, Democratic Russia.[42] It rejected the government's economic policies, pushed for early popular elections for the presidency, and called for sovereignty of the Russian republic. Democratic Russia was responsible for organizing mass demonstrations in support of Yeltsin.[43] The Democratic Party of Russia, founded by Nikolai Travkin in May 1990, was the largest and best-organized noncommunist party with 50,000 members. Standing closer to the center of the political spectrum, it supported a democratic Russian state within a voluntary union of republics, market relations, and multiparty elections. The Republican Party, which stood somewhere between the Democratic Party and the Communist Party, was the second largest party with about 20,000 members.[44] These parties, however, existed only in nascent form. The future of democracy in Russia depended in large measure on whether these organizations could be forged into strong, stable political parties able to connect public concerns with the conduct of government, offer coordinated programs of action, and present candidates for office.[45]

## THE GOVERNMENT

The Communist Party had been the focus of power in the Soviet system. The government bureaucracy basically carried out party policy. The 1977 constitution, the country's fourth, set forth an elaborate federal structure based on the nationality composition of the country, included a bill of rights, and made explicit the institutional structure. Article 6 of the constitution called the Communist Party the "leading and guiding force" and the "nucleus of the political system." The Nineteenth Party Conference set in motion a shift from the party to new governmental structures.

According to the constitution, the bicameral Supreme Soviet was the highest authority in the Soviet state. The 750-member Soviet of the Union was based on population while the seats in the 750-member Soviet of Nationalities were apportioned to nationality-based territorial units. The legislature met twice a year, with each session lasting only two days. All votes were unanimous. Although some of the most powerful people in the Soviet Union served as deputies, a broad cross-section of the population was represented. The body was a rubber-stamp institution, although the sixteen standing commissions of each chamber may have provided an arena for some bargaining and compromise.[46] The Supreme Soviet formally elected the Presidium and the Council of Ministers.

Deputies of the Supreme Soviet were elected every five years from single-member constituencies. Nominations were made by public organizations such as trade unions, the Komsomol, and work collectives, but all were controlled by the party. It always ended up that only one candidate was nominated for each seat. Nominations were followed by a nationwide campaign, lasting about six weeks, in which candidates were publicized and voters were urged to come to the polls. During the campaign, voters "instructed" candidates about removing local grievances. Election Day was a national holiday on which people got dressed up in their best clothes. Almost every citizen eighteen or over voted on Election Day, with turnouts reported as exceeding 99 percent. The ballot had the name of only one candidate: voters voted for a candidate by folding and putting the unmarked ballot into a box; they voted against a candidate by crossing out the name. It was possible to step into a voting booth, but the assumption was that only those voting negatively would do so. There were about 2 million negative votes election after election, but no candidates at the national or republic level were ever defeated.

The thirty-nine-member Presidium chosen by, and supposedly account-able to, the Supreme Soviet included a chairman, a first deputy chairman, a secretary, and the chairs of the Presidiums of the fifteen union republics serving as deputy chairmen. The Presidium served as a steering committee and collective head of state. Its chairman, serving as titular head of state, was frequently referred to as the president of the Soviet Union. Brezhnev took over the position of chairman of the Presidium in 1977. Andropov and Chernenko assumed this position shortly after becoming General Secretary. Under Gorbachev, as we have seen, Gromyko initially held this position. When the Supreme Soviet was not in session, the Presidium could issue edicts and decrees, amend laws, and alter the membership of the Council of Ministers. Although these actions had to be approved subsequently by the Supreme Soviet, they went into effect immediately. The Presidium also had the authority to ratify and denounce treaties. In practice, since the Presidium met infrequently, most of its power was exercised through its chairman and secretary.

A Defense Council, responsible for national security, was formed by the Presidium. Although this very important council had previously been headed by the chairman of the Presidium, Gorbachev chaired the Defense Council beginning in 1985. Its membership included the ministers of for-eign affairs and defense and the chairman of the KGB.

The Council of Ministers and its chairman (prime minister) were for-mally elected by, and accountable to, the Supreme Soviet. The size of the council was not fixed but numbered about 115 in the 1980s. Because of its unwieldy size, a smaller body, the Presidium of the Council of Ministers, formed an inner executive body that exercised most of government's administrative powers. The Council of Ministers was composed of minis-tries and state committees. The position of Chairman of the Council of Ministers was extremely powerful.

In addition to ministries found in the cabinets of parliamentary democ-racies, the Council of Ministers included ministries for such things as machine building, shipbuilding, electronics, and chemicals. State commit-tees were set up to deal with issues across sectors, such as planning (Gosplan), science and technology, prices, and state security (KGB). The ministries were responsible for vast bureaucracies stretching from Moscow down to the local level. In 1985, the government bureaucracy employed 17.7 million people, not including the Ministries of Defense and Interior and the KGB.[47] All-union ministries controlled operations directly while union-republic ministries operated through corresponding ministries in the Council of Ministers of the Union-Republics.

### Reform of the Legislature

By the late 1980s, there was a consensus that a new constitution was needed. Since the leadership was unwilling to wait for the long process of drafting and achieving overall agreement, changes were made by constitutional amendment. A major structural change created two legislative bodies, an entirely new Congress of People's Deputies that elected from its membership a smaller bicameral Supreme Soviet. The system of soviets at lower levels was strengthened as a means of cutting down on the entrenched powers of the party apparatus. The package also created a strengthened president to oversee domestic and foreign policy.[48]

New institutions were created, altered, and re-created in rapid succession, but none was able to sink roots and create a sense of legitimacy. For a time there was a sense of exhilaration but it was short-lived. The setup was complex and hard to understand. Furthermore, these new, untested institutions were required to deal with a deteriorating economic situation and ethnic cleavages in a country in which there was no consensus on democratic values.

The Congress, which was to meet for only a few days at least once a year, was a large representative body of 2,250 members. One-third were elected from units based on population and one-third from national-territorial units. They were chosen from single-member districts by universal, equal, direct suffrage by secret ballot. The last one-third were elected by social organizations such as the CPSU, the Komsomol, trade unions, artistic organizations, and the Academy of Sciences. People had multiple votes, depending upon the number of organizations they belonged to. Campaign expenses were covered from state funds, though some candidates got additional funds from supporters.

The procedure for election of members of the Congress was new and untested. Nominations were made by officially recognized organizations in a cumbersome procedure that filtered out many reformers.[49] In some constituencies, the party had considerable influence over the nomination process. Sakharov was at first maneuvered out of a seat allocated to the Academy of Sciences, but his supporters fought back, and he finally won the seat. The CPSU nominated exactly one hundred candidates for its one hundred seats. Since most senior party leaders were included on this list, they were not subject to competitive election.[50]

Two-thirds of the deputies were chosen in multicandidate elections. Candidates were encouraged to issue platforms so voters could know their views. In Leningrad, a group of democratic activists formed Election '89, which supported its own candidates in contested elections and targeted the party's unopposed candidates.[51] In races with three or more candidates, runoffs were required if no candidate received a majority. If there were one or two candidates, and none received a majority, the process started over from the nomination stage. Even unopposed candidates could be defeated by crossing their names off the ballot. More than 172 million voters or 89 percent turned out for the election.

Yeltsin, who had been nominated in almost 200 constituencies, ran from the largest constituency in the country, the all-Moscow national territorial district of 9 million people. He campaigned calling for an end to special privileges for the elite, for direct popular election of the new president, and for a nationwide debate on a multiparty system. Yeltsin won with 89 percent of the vote despite opposition from party leaders.[52]

Many other liberals won. Popular front candidates won in the Baltics. There were stunning upsets of senior party officials, including the Leningrad party chief, a candidate member of the Politburo, who ran unopposed. The mayor and second-ranking communist leader of Moscow, the commander in chief of the Moscow military region, the commander of the Northern Fleet, the chairman of the Moscow and Kiev city councils, the president and prime minister of Lithuania, and the Estonian KGB chief were among those defeated.[53] Of the 399 candidates who had run unopposed, 195 were rejected. This was not an unadorned victory for liberals, however. The vast expanses of Central Asia and the dark villages of Russia had little in common with Moscow and Leningrad or the Baltics. The proportion of party members, in fact, increased as compared with previous elections, from 71 percent to 87 percent. Furthermore, over 65 percent were paid administrators of some kind, compared with 43 percent in the outgoing Supreme Soviet.[54] Although the election itself was far from being fair and democratic, it nevertheless served to challenge the party's monopoly on control.[55]

The Congress, shown on live television, transfixed the population, who watched outspoken deputies raise issues never before raised in public. People could not believe what they were seeing and hearing. The eight hours of live coverage were seen by 200 million viewers across twelve time zones. Francis X. Clines called it "the biggest television hit in Soviet history."[56] Every day after the Congress session huge rallies at Olympic Stadium cheered on the liberals. Approximately 400 of the deputies, reformers and nationalists from the Baltics and other republics, worked together informally. They were a minority, but large enough to have an impact on debate especially when they were backed by the Moscow demonstrations in support of their popular hero, Yeltsin.

Immediately following the opening of the session, a Latvian deputy called a moment of silence to honor those killed in Tbilisi. Medvedev and others demanded to know who was responsible for sending the troops to Georgia when Gorbachev was out of the country. The implication was that Ligachev was responsible and should resign. An unknown deputy from a town north of Leningrad nominated himself to run against Gorbachev for chairman of the Supreme Soviet, but the deputies voted more than two to one against allowing a contested election.[57] Gorbachev was then elected after a televised cross-examination by the Congress in which several deputies questioned whether he should be leader of both the party and the government. As a result of his election, Gorbachev became the presiding officer.

When elections were held for the Supreme Soviet, Yeltsin was at first denied a seat. After thousands of demonstrators rallied in protest, a legislator agreed to forfeit his seat, and the Congress then voted to give it to Yeltsin. However, other Moscow insurgents were denied seats in the Supreme Soviet.[58] Anatoly Lukyanov, Gorbachev's legal adviser and friend, was overwhelmingly approved as vice president after intense questioning. When Gorbachev later became president of the Soviet Union, Lukyanov was elected chairman of the Supreme Soviet, winning 64 percent of the voted in a multicandidate election.

The Congress sessions were chaotic, with booing, hissing, clapping, and shouting. The limits on public discussion seemed to disappear as deputies attacked government policies, opposed the Afghan War, and criticized the KGB. The Congress set up a commission to investigate the Nazi-Soviet Pact and another to look into the Tbilisi killings. Sakharov assailed the Congress for failing to end the party's monopoly of power. He called for direct election of top officials, limits on the KGB, a smaller, professional army, and a looser federation. He warned of impending economic catastrophe and ethnic violence. Gorbachev, who had given Sakharov the floor, finally lost patience and turned off Sakharov's microphone.[59] However, "the party's ability to pronounce upon the one, correct policy for the country had been publicly challenged. Political authority began to slip away from the leading party bodies to the Congress of Deputies."[60]

Members of the redesigned Supreme Soviet of 542 full-time legislators were elected by the Congress for five-year terms with up to 20 percent rotating each year. As with the old Supreme Soviet, there were two houses, the Soviet of the Union and the Soviet of Nationalities, of equal size and power. The Supreme Soviet was smaller than in the past, and it was to have at least two sessions each year, three to four months in length. It was the working legislative body, with the power to adopt legislation and the state budget. Although 86 percent of the deputies were party members, there were fewer party officials than in the past. Eight permanent commissions, four attached to each house, and fourteen committees of the Supreme Soviet as a whole included not only Supreme Soviet deputies but deputies from the Congress. The commissions and committees could conduct hearings on legislation, but they lacked adequate staff, experts, and information. They were denied detailed budgetary control. There were provisions for voting no confidence in the government by a two-thirds vote. The Supreme Soviet adopted a question period for which deputies could submit written or oral questions to the chairman or individual ministers and agency heads. They had difficulty, however, in gaining access to information to which they were entitled since government ministers were reluctant to make it available.

The first session of the new Supreme Soviet began on June 10, 1989, the day after the Congress ended. After the first day, live television coverage gave way to evening rebroadcasts since so many people had stayed home from work to watch. There were verbatim reports in the press and reporters had access to deputies and legislative leaders. The Supreme Soviet considered candidates for the Council of Ministers on an individual basis. Prime Minister Nikolai Ryzhkov had to defend his choices under a barrage of criticism. Three ministers were rejected, the nominations of six others were withdrawn by Ryzhkov, and two others quit when it was clear they would be defeated. There was tough debate over the confirmation of Yazov as defense minister. Gorbachev defended him as a progressive. After changing the requirement for a majority vote of the membership, Yazov was confirmed by a majority of those present. Robert Kaiser notes, "By saving Yazov's job, Gorbachev appeared to create a special bond with his senior military commander."[61]

At the end of July, after Yeltsin called for establishing a left-radical group to push reform, 316 Congress deputies, 90 of whom were on the Supreme Soviet, formed the Inter-Regional Group. Its support came both from Russian reformers in Moscow, Leningrad, Volgograd, and other urban centers and from nationalists from the Baltics, Ukraine, Moldavia, and Georgia. Politically, it was divided among those who wanted to confront Gorbachev head-on and those who wanted to support Gorbachev while pressing him to take bolder action. Despite divisions among its membership, it was united in its opposition to the power of the party apparatus and to the arbitrary power of the armed forces, the KGB, and the MVD. In September, it called for an end to the Communist Party's monopoly on power and demanded that Gorbachev recognize it as a parliamentary opposition.[62]

### The Presidency

The euphoria produced by the elections, the Congress, and the first days of the Supreme Soviet soon wore thin in the face of mounting economic difficulties, demands for national sovereignty, a strike by half a million miners, and rising crime. Party conservatives were blocking reform while Gorbachev was finding it increasingly difficult to exert any power. After achieving Central Committee approval of his proposals, Gorbachev convoked an extraordinary session of the Congress on March 13, 1990, to amend the constitution to eliminate the monopoly of the Communist Party and approve creation of the position of president of the USSR. Gorbachev was convinced of the need for a strong executive to circumvent the party bureaucracy.

The post was modeled after the American and French presidencies but was closer to the French since it was grafted onto a parliamentary structure. The proposal was highly controversial. The nearly 400 members of the Inter-Regional Group feared that the position could become the base for future dictatorship, if not by Gorbachev, then by a successor. Deputies from the Baltics and Transcaucasia opposed limitations on their sovereignty.

Since approval of a constitutional amendment required a two-thirds vote of the entire membership of the Congress, Gorbachev had to agree to some of the reformers' demands. Amendments limited the president's power to issue decrees and to declare a state of emergency. The Congress was given the power to impeach the president by a two-thirds vote if he violated laws or the constitution.

Many wanted direct popular election of the president, but Gorbachev apparently feared the divisiveness of an election campaign and wanted to be in office as president before the Party Congress met at the end of June. He just barely got the two-thirds vote authorizing the Congress to elect the first president. In the future, the president was supposed to be elected for a five-year term by direct and secret ballot. In the election for the presidency, Gorbachev got 1,329 votes, with 495 opposed. But this was less impressive than it might seem, since he received the votes of only 59.2 percent of the total membership.[63] His election by the Congress meant he had no popular mandate. The creation of the presidency produced a strong executive leader in theory, but by this time republics were increasingly unwilling to obey any central authority.

Two bodies were appointed by the president to assist him. The Council of the Federation, to coordinate the activities of the republics and deal with nationality problems and policies, consisted of the heads of union republic Supreme Soviets. From the beginning, the Baltic republics accepted only observer status. The Presidential Council, appointed by the president, was a consultative committee to advise on major foreign and domestic policy. It included the chairman of the Council of Ministers ex officio. Gorbachev appointed fifteen members, including important government and party officials and public figures. Two nationalists were included: Valentin Rasputin and Venjamin Yarin, a blue-collar populist. Gorbachev's attempt to balance different interests in his appointments made the council unworkable.

## Republic Elections

Elections were held in several republics in February and March 1990 for regional, district, and city councils, republic Supreme Soviets, and, in the Russian Federation, a Russian Congress of People's Deputies.[64] These were multicandidate elections, but the Communist Party was still the only organized political party. Although names of parties did not appear on the ballot, Lithuania in fact had a two-party competitive election in which the People's Front defeated the Communist Party. The elections to republican legislatures produced majorities in favor of independence in all three Baltic republics and Moldavia. On March 11, the Lithuanian Supreme Soviet voted to declare the republic independent.

In Russia, three associations or coalitions emerged to nominate and campaign for candidates. A Democratic Russia Bloc called for a new federal structure of sovereign states and nations and the abolition of government control of the means of production. The bloc opposed not only the official communists but the Patriots as well. The rightist nationalist Patriots, who waged a nasty campaign characterized by smears and anti-Semitism, suffered a huge defeat when not one of the candidates they backed was elected to the Russian Congress. In Leningrad, the Democrats won 80 percent of the city's seats in the Russian Congress and 65 percent in the Leningrad city soviet. In Moscow, Democrats won 55 of 65 seats in the Congress and 263 of 465 seats in the Moscow city soviet. Although the Democrats did extraordinarily well in Moscow and Leningrad, they did less well in the smaller cities, towns, and villages. Altogether, the Democratic Bloc won about one-third of the 1,000 plus seats in the Russian Congress of People's Deputies. The Congress elected a bicameral Supreme Soviet from its membership. This legislature became embroiled in controversy with Yeltsin after the dissolution of the Soviet Union.

The election of Yeltsin to the position of chairman of the Supreme Soviet of the Russian Republic over Gorbachev's strong opposition was a severe challenge to Gorbachev's authority. The Russian Congress voted on June 8 that its laws took precedence over all-union laws and recognized the Baltic states. Yeltsin and the Russian legislature confronted Gorbachev and the union in a "war of laws" over whether the laws of the republics or the laws of the center took precedence. It was one thing for a small republic to demand sovereignty, but Russia contained a majority of the population of the union and the largest share of its industry and natural resources. For Russia to assert that its laws took precedence over the laws of the union was, in effect, to set up a second governing power directly challenging the legitimacy of the first. By this time it was becoming clear that Russia was governed by two rival governments, that of Gorbachev and that of Yeltsin.

### Political Crisis

Gorbachev was having increasing difficulty in implementing policies. In September 1990, he was granted emergency powers for eighteen months to put into effect economic policies and to strengthen law and order. Republics, regions, factories, and farms were bypassing the central government to make deals with each other. The underground economy was siphoning off goods from the state system, crime was increasing, and nationalism was on the upswing. Hard-liners in the army were increasingly hostile, demanding firmer control at the center.[65]

Gorbachev soon found his decrees being countermanded by republic and local governments and ignored by the government bureaucracy. Public confidence in his ability to solve economic problems and prevent chaos was falling rapidly. On November 17, he received parliamentary approval for enhanced presidential power. The executive branch was put under his control to calm rumors of a military coup, control hard-liners, and reassure Western governments and investors.

In an attempt to reassert control over a disintegrating country, Gorbachev moved to the right in the winter of 1990–91. On December 2, he fired the moderate Vadim Bakatin as minister of the interior, replacing him with Boris Pugo, the former party leader and KGB chief in Latvia. Just over a week later, Kryuchkov, the KGB head, stated on television that the KGB was prepared to fight "with all the means at their disposal" those inside the country and abroad who threatened the state.[66] Gorbachev became obsessed with fear of spreading ethnic conflicts.

By the December 1990 session of the People's Congress, disillusionment had set in. It was evident that the Congress was too large and clumsy to be effective. The Inter-Regional Group of reformers had lost members while the hard-line Soyuz (Union) bloc was gaining. Gorbachev was acting dictatorially, bullying the Congress into following his dictates. Further moves were taken toward presidential control. The Council of Ministers was replaced by a Cabinet, headed by a prime minister, nominated by, and accountable to, the president. The president headed a new Security Council responsible for defense and public order. The Presidential Council was eliminated, and the Council of Federation, headed by the president, became the primary decision-making body.[67]

Shevardnadze, the foreign minister, stunned the Congress and the world by his resignation and his warning that the country was moving toward dictatorship.[68] Kryuchkov, the head of the KGB, warned that Western businesses and governments were endangering security, cheating Soviet partners, and imposing an alien capitalist ideology. He called for decisive measures to end ethnic violence.[69] In an attempt to placate the Right, Gorbachev chose Gennadi Yanaev, a relatively obscure, convinced communist who had spent his career in the Komsomol, to serve in the new post of vice president. Yanaev failed to win the election on the first try, but Gorbachev pushed him through.[70] By the close of the Congress, Gorbachev was isolated from reformers and surrounded by hard-liners. Despite reformers' fear of presidential prerogatives, Gorbachev was "politically, the least powerful leader the Soviet Union had yet experienced."[71]

After Soviet armed forces stormed into Lithuania, killing fourteen people on January 13, reformers denounced Gorbachev. Thousands came out into the streets of Moscow to protest. On January 20, Riga, Latvia, was attacked by forces under the control or influence of the MVD chief Pugo, who had formerly headed the Latvian KGB. Yeltsin called on Soviet soldiers to disobey orders to shoot civilians and joined in a call for the United Nations (UN) to investigate the shootings in Lithuania. Gorbachev gave the KGB power to investigate private enterprises to combat economic espionage.[72] Armed soldiers joined the police in patrolling streets in more than 400 cities, and the media were reined in. Valentin Pavlov, who had been minister of finance, replaced Ryzhkov as prime minister on January 14, after Ryzhkov suffered a heart attack.

The question of the future form of the Soviet Union became the paramount issue before the country. Although a Gorbachev referendum for "renewed union" won with about three-fourths of the vote, divisive forces continued unabated. The Baltic republics, Armenia, Georgia, and Moldavia, refused to even participate in the referendum. Ukrainian voters endorsed maintenance of the union but also voted in favor of sovereignty. The Russian electorate supported a question Yeltsin had added to the referendum, calling for direct election of the Russian president.

Amid growing unrest, Gorbachev issued a ban on public demonstrations in Moscow during a special session of the Russian Congress called by conservatives to censure Yeltsin. It was obvious that Moscow demonstrators would support Yeltsin. Gorbachev put the Moscow police under the national Ministry of the Interior. Approximately 50,000 MVD and army troops entered the city to prevent demonstrators from reaching the Kremlin, where the Congress was to meet. More than 100,000 turned out in defiance of the ban to demonstrate for Yeltsin. The deputies voted to reject the ban on rallies and declared Gorbachev's takeover of the Moscow police illegal. Parades cheered Yeltsin and called for Gorbachev's resignation.[73] Rather than censoring Yeltsin, the Congress granted him extraordinary powers to rule by decree.[74] Essentially, Yeltsin received from the Russian Congress the same powers that he had tried to deny Gorbachev. The popular election for president was scheduled for June 12.

At the end of April, Gorbachev moved to the Left, as he came under renewed attack from communist hard-liners. On April 24, Gorbachev and the leaders of nine republics met and signed the "nine-plus-one" agreement, calling for a power shift from the center to the republics, a new union treaty, a new constitution, and new elections. Perhaps as significant was Gorbachev's agreement to turn over control of half the nation's coal mines to Russia.

Yeltsin, with Alexander Rutskoi as his running mate, campaigned vigorously for the Russian presidency. He was opposed by Ryzhkov, the candidate of the party establishment; Bakatin, who ran as a supporter of Gorbachev; and Vladimir Zhirinovsky, a rabid nationalist. Gorbachev did not oppose Yeltsin. Yeltsin won more than 57 percent of the vote, becoming the first popularly elected leader in Russian history. Unlike Gorbachev, he now had a direct mandate from the people. Popov and Sobchak, reform allies of Yeltsin, swept to victory as mayors of Moscow and Leningrad, with more than 65 percent each. Yeltsin issued an edict directed at the Communist Party banning political activity in places of employment. In a nonbinding referendum, the voters of Leningrad supported restoring the city's original name, St. Petersburg.[75]

In June 1991 Pavlov, backed by the heads of the army, KGB, and MVD, went around Gorbachev and appealed to the Supreme Soviet for expanded powers. Gorbachev fended off this attack from the Right but did nothing to reprimand or punish Pavlov. Gorbachev became immersed in trying to get agreement on a new Union treaty to preserve the country. The right-wing was vehemently opposed to the concessions he was prepared to make.

Gorbachev was desperately trying to get Western economic aid to prevent a crisis. On July 17, he met with the leaders of the G-7 industrial nations (United States, Japan, Britain, Canada, France, West Germany, and Italy) in London but came home nearly empty-handed. Many Russians, even liberals, felt embarrassed that Gorbachev had gone to London to beg. His failure to win a promise of assistance was considered humiliating.

On July 23, *Sovetskaya Rossiya*, a right-wing paper, printed an angry denunciation of Gorbachev and his policies. It called on the people to rise up and defend the country against those who were destroying it. The deputy minister of the interior and the deputy minister of defense were among the twelve signatories. At a Central Committee meeting two days later, Gorbachev presented a party program that envisaged the transformation of the Soviet Union into a democratic federation of sovereign republics with a market economy. Despite the fact that it departed radically from traditional communist beliefs, it passed overwhelmingly, with little opposition being voiced.[76] On August 2, Gorbachev announced that the union treaty would be ready for signature on August 20. On August 18 the coup began.

Theodore Draper presents a highly perceptive analysis of the fall of the Soviet Union, in which he hones in on the loss of control by the Communist Party. He states, "Whatever ups and downs the Party had . . . it alone kept the centrifugal forces of this immense, mosaic country from breaking apart."[77] He points out that Gorbachev's reforms were inspired by Lenin's NEP, but when Lenin introduced limited economic experimentation, he tightened political controls. When Gorbachev originally moved to avert economic paralysis through *perestroika* (restructuring), he wanted economic reform and political liberalism within the framework of socialism and the one-party state. When he found that the party stood in the way of innovation and reform, he attempted to shift power from the party to the state, but since the party permeated and controlled the institutions of government, this proved ineffective. Gorbachev then attempted to establish a new system of state institutions parallel to the party organization, with Gorbachev himself heading both structures. He hesitated too long in destroying the party's monopoly of power and the party bureaucracy. Draper concludes:

Gorbachev's structural reforms divided and demoralized the party so it could no longer function as the only political bonding that held the country from flying apart. But he delayed for so long in "abolishing the Party's monopoly of power" that he left a confused legacy of communists without a party and a state weighed down with remnants of the Stalin-Brezhnev-Gorbachev past.[78]

## NOTES

1. Theodore Draper, "Who Killed Soviet Communism," *New York Review of Books,* June 11, 1992, 12.

2 Merle Fainsod, *How Russia Is Ruled* (Cambridge: Harvard University Press, 1963), 209–10.

3. Leon P. Baradat, *Soviet Political Society,* 3d ed. (Englewood Cliffs, N.J.: Prentice-Hall, 1992), 115.

4. Boris Yeltsin, *Against the Grain,* trans. Michael Glenny (New York: Summit Books, 1990), 143–45.

5. Joan DeBardeleben, *Soviet Politics in Transition* (Lexington, Mass.: D. C. Heath, 1992), 126; Baradat, *Soviet Political Society,* 118.

6. Serge Schmemann, "Gorbachev on the Soviet Economy: A Flock of Innovative Ideas," in *The Decline and Fall of the Soviet Empire,* ed. Bernard Gwertzman and Michael T. Kaufman (New York: New York Times Company, 1992), 29–31.

7. Serge Schmemann, "Taking Off the Rose-Colored Glasses in Moscow," in *The Decline and Fall of the Soviet Empire,* ed. Gwertzman and Kaufman, 31–33.

8. Stephen White, *Gorbachev and After* (Cambridge: Cambridge University Press, 1991), 242.

9. Robert G. Kaiser, *Why Gorbachev Happened* (New York: Touchstone, 1992), 151–55.

10. Yeltsin, *Against the Grain,* 126–28, 145–46, 177–96. The text of the letter can be found on pages 178–81.

11. *New York Times,* May 27, 1988.

12. Mary McCauley, *Soviet Politics: 1917–1991* (New York: Oxford University Press, 1992), 93.

13. For the system devised by the *apparat,* see Yeltsin, *Against the Grain,* 218.

14. *New York Times,* June 26, 1988.

15. *New York Times,* June 29, 1988.

16. McCauley, *Soviet Politics,* 96.

17. *New York Times,* July 2, 1988.

18. *New York Times,* July 3, 1988. For Yeltsin's description, see Boris Yeltsin, *Against the Grain,* 222–37.

19. *New York Times,* October 1, 2, 1988.

20. *New York Times,* April 26, 1989.

21. *New York Times,* April 28, 1989.

22. *New York Times,* September 21, 1989.

23. *New York Times,* November 27, 1989.

24. *New York Times,* December 6, 8, 21, 1989.

25. *New York Times,* February 5, 1990.

26. The Congress of People's Deputies abolished Article 6 in March 1990.

27. *New York Times,* February 9, 1990.

28. Kaiser, *Why Gorbachev Happened,* 336–39.

29. Ronald J. Hill, "The Communist Party and After," in *Developments in Soviet & Post-Soviet Politics,* ed. Stephen White, Alex Pravda, and Zvi Gitelman (Durham, N.C.: Duke University Press, 1992), 79.

30. Baradat, *Soviet Political Society,* 111; Kaiser, *Why Gorbachev Happened,* 340.

31. White, *Gorbachev and After,* 242.

32. *New York Times,* July 4, 1990.

33. *New York Times,* July 11, 1990.

34. DeBardeleben, *Soviet Politics in Transition*, 121.

35. *New York Times*, July 14, 1990.

36. Baradat, *Soviet Political Society*, 115.

37. *New York Times*, April 17, 1988.

38. Ibid.

39. White, *Gorbachev and After*, 243.

40. Ibid., 40–41.

41. Ibid., 57.

42. DeBardeleben, *Soviet Politics in Transition*, 83.

43. White, *Gorbachev and After*, 58.

44. Timothy J. Colton, "Politics," in *After the Soviet Union*, ed. Timothy J. Colton and Robert Legvold (New York: W. W. Norton, 1992), 37; White, *Gorbachev and After*, 57–59.

45. White, *Gorbachev and After*, 66–67.

46. Philip G. Roeder, *Soviet Political Dynamics* (New York: Harper and Row, 1988), 184.

47. Stephen F. Cohen and Katrina vanden Heuvel, *Voices of Glasnost* (New York: W. W. Norton, 1989), 15.

48. *New York Times*, June 30, December 2, 1989.

49. For a description of the three stage process of elections, see Jeffrey W. Hahn, "Soviet Institutions in Transition," in *Developments in Soviet & Post-Soviet Politics*, ed. White, Pravda, and Gitelman, 93–97.

50. *New York Times*, March 16, 1989; Kaiser, *Why Gorbachev Happened*, 256.

51. Hedrick Smith, *The New Russians* (New York: Avon Books, 1991), 445–46.

52. For a description from Yeltsin's perspective, see Yeltsin, *Against the Grain*, which is mostly devoted to a description of his campaign.

53. *New York Times*, March 28, 1989; Kaiser, *Why Gorbachev Happened*, 260–66.

54. White, *Gorbachev and After*, 48–49.

55. Smith, *The New Russians*, 444.

56. *New York Times*, May 31, 1989.

57. Smith, *The New Russians*, 451–58, 464.

58. For a description of the process by which deputies were elected to the Supreme Soviet, see Hahn, *Soviet Institutions in Transition*, 99–100.

59. *New York Times*, June 10, 1989.

60. McCauley, *Soviet Politics*, 101.

61. Kaiser, *Why Gorbachev Happened*, 290.

62. Smith, *The New Russians*, 475–77.

63. Kaiser, *Why Gorbachev Happened*, 326–27.

64. *New York Times*, March 20, 1990.

65. Smith, *The New Russians*, 594–600.

66. Kaiser, *Why Gorbachev Happened*, 378–79.

67. White, *Gorbachev and After*, 61–62.

68. Kaiser, *Why Gorbachev Happened*, 385–88.

69. *New York Times*, December 21, 23, 1990.

70. *New York Times*, December 27, 28, 1990.

71. White, *Gorbachev and After*, 62.

72. Smith, *The New Russians*, 609–612.

73. *New York Times*, March 29, 1991.

74. *New York Times*, April 6, 1991.

75. *New York Times*, June 14, 1991.

76. Kaiser, *Why Gorbachev Happened*, 416–18.
77. Draper, *Who Killed Soviet Communism*, 12.
78. Ibid., 14.

# Chapter 11

# THE ECONOMIC CRISIS

When Gorbachev came to power, he recognized that the Soviet economy was badly crippled and in danger of becoming much worse: "As we address short-term . . . issues, we must never forget that the most profound problems of our economy are longer-term and structural. . . . Many of the problems did not develop overnight. We cannot expect to solve them overnight."[1]

These words, which might have been spoken by Gorbachev, were in fact spoken by Bill Clinton as he was preparing to take over the American presidency. Both men were aware of profound structural problems, but both assumed that incremental changes would suffice and that they had time to solve the problems facing their countries. On April 23, 1985, at a Central Committee plenum, Gorbachev announced his program of *perestroika*. In contrast to the stagnation of the recent past, Gorbachev's proposals seemed revolutionary. But, in reality, he sought change within the existing framework of state socialism.[2]

Gorbachev supported economic decentralization and some increased autonomy for enterprises, but he had no intention either of giving up state ownership of the means of production or of converting to a market economy. He spoke of economic acceleration and intensification, stressing the need to increase investment in heavy industry, especially the machine-building sector. At the same time, he wanted to increase the availability of consumer goods. His first approach was to attack corruption and inefficiency and, influenced by Ligachev, to launch an antialcohol campaign.[3] He created new superministries to streamline control and to carry out strategic planning. A huge superministry, Gosagroprom, was created to deal with agriculture. In an effort to improve the quality of production, an independent agency for state quality inspection was introduced on January 1, 1987.[4] Teams of outside inspectors were placed in factories and told to reject defective output and cut performance bonuses.[5] Gorbachev, however, failed to realize fully the seriousness of the economic crisis facing the Soviet Union. Although expectations were raised, the 1986 economic performance fell below expectations. The Chernobyl disaster of April 1986 undermined the Five-Year Plan, which called for doubling the percentage of electricity generated by nuclear power.[6] Economic costs associated with the disaster amounted to more than 9 billion rubles. As a result of the antialcohol campaign, the sale of alcoholic beverages fell 37 percent, depriving the government of an estimated 16 billion rubles in revenue. Severe weather in the winter of 1986–87 disrupted the economy and the new quality control program shut down numerous manufacturing lines.[7] The government severely underestimated the budget deficit, which had long been hidden by supplying credits to state enterprises and then counting the credits as revenue. As a result of the underestimation, rather than cutting state expenditure, the government took on new social and investment commitments.[8] Gorbachev's emphasis on investment in heavy industry and machine tools contributed to the deficit. To offset increased imports of Western machine tools, he cut back on imports of consumer goods. This not only frustrated consumers but led to lost sales tax revenue.[9] Although Gorbachev had raised people's expectations by talking of more and better consumer goods, increased agricultural output, better health care, and more housing, little progress was made. Gorbachev had no feasible plan by which he could reach his goals. By late 1986, Gorbachev realized that his first attempt at economic reform would not work and that more radical proposals were needed.

At the end of June 1987, two years after coming to power, Gorbachev presented the Central Committee with a proposal for radical reorganization of economic management and partial dismantling of centralized controls.[10] Abel Aganbegyan, his economic adviser, spoke of building an economy in which central planning withered, unneeded workers were dismissed, companies were measured by their profits, and bad companies would go bankrupt.[11]

The Law on State Enterprise of January 1, 1988, was the principal effort to put Gorbachev's proposals into effect. The new system of *khozraschyot*, economic accountability, was to be applied initially to firms producing about 50 percent of the country's industrial goods and was to expand to include almost all enterprises by 1990. Gosplan was to issue long-term guidelines, not detailed instructions. Enterprises would be permitted to engage in trade with each other and set their own prices. Managers would no longer be allocated machinery and raw materials by Moscow but would have to negotiate for supplies with other firms or territorial supply agencies. Instead of obligatory targets imposed from above, enterprises would enter contracts with buyers. To ensure that the country's needs for essential goods and services would be met, enterprises would still have to fulfill "state orders," or *goszakazy*, for the delivery of goods specified by their ministries. The percentage of output subject to state orders was supposed to shrink to 86 percent of production in 1988 and to 25 percent in 1989, the rest being sold on the open market.

Investment was to come from profits and repayable credits. New independent banks were to be created. Enterprises were supposed to be self-financing. Unprofitable departments and enterprises would be able to cut staff and reduce wages. Those that failed to meet a minimum standard of profitability were to face bankruptcy and be closed down. Because fewer bureaucrats would be needed, the staff of central ministries was cut by one third. Since 25 percent of the enterprises were operating at a loss or with only marginal profits, a period of hardship was anticipated. To offset a backlash by workers, Gorbachev planned to introduce the system gradually, with safety nets to prevent workers from facing unemployment.[12]

Problems arose in implementing the new system. Because it was introduced during an economic crisis, the leadership was unwilling to tolerate a drop in current production while the transition was effected. State orders were used to ensure that firms met the targets set in the 1986–90 Five-Year Plan, thereby undermining enterprise independence. Furthermore, although enterprises were supposed to be able to keep their profits to reward productive workers and managers and for capital investment, up to 80 percent were taken by the ministries. The staggered approach, with some industries switching to the new plan immediately and others shifting later, added confusion. Since there were no wholesalers from whom managers could purchase needed supplies or to whom they could sell their products, manufacturers had to create their own trading relations with suppliers and customers. Managers often sought high levels of state orders to ensure sources of supply. Gross output, rather than market-based success indicators, therefore continued to determine the pattern of production. Without a price reform that would have doubled or tripled prices, it made little sense to pressure firms to be self-financing.

When managers exercised their authority to alter their product mix, they increased the share of expensive goods they produced. This raised their profits but created shortages of cheaper basic products. Production of children's goods and breakfast cereals fell. The shortages led to long lines and in some areas a system of rationing was introduced. People traveled tens of miles to wait on lines for food in Moscow, since it was better-supplied than other areas. Outsiders, who saw the better supplied stores of Moscow, resented Muscovites, while Moscow residents resented their stores being raided by outsiders. People had no more goods than before but had to pay more. Ordinary people saw no gain from *perestroika*.[13]

In an innovation borrowed from the Yugoslav experience, factory workers were to elect their managers. Since managers' jobs were dependent on workers, wages rose rapidly without improvements in productivity or corresponding price increases. Janos Kornai warns that in state-owned firms where employees elect the management, the manager seeks popularity with the workers, which he can attain easily by raising wages. The most effective way to dissolve tensions in an enterprise is to announce a pay increase. Neither the constraints of the command economy where wage discipline is enforced by bureaucratic means nor the constraints of a genuine market economy where private ownership stimulates discipline are present. The result is wage inflation.[14] In 1988 the average monthly income of workers and staff in the state sector rose by 7 percent, but productivity rose by only 5.1 percent. In 1989 wages rose by 9.5 percent, but labor productivity by only 2.3 percent.[15] There was little restraint on managers since they were aware that the state would not really let them go bankrupt. In June 1990, the workers' right to elect managers was eliminated. By this time, Goldman argues, the damage was done.[16]

In order to increase the availability of consumer goods and services, planners turned increasingly to private cooperatives independent of state regulation. On May 1, 1987, for the first time since Lenin's NEP, individual farming and cooperatives were legalized. Given the fact that Gorbachev was surrounded by conservatives reluctant to see the jettisoning of cherished beliefs and practices, it is not surprising that this measure was hedged with restrictions. Regular state workers could participate in cooperative ventures only outside regular work hours. New cooperative restaurants, taxis, beauty parlors, and auto repair and other services were soon set up. Although there were strict limits on size, access to bank loans, and ability to hire labor, by 1988 more than 14,000 cooperatives had been created, primarily in the Baltics, Georgia, Moscow and Leningrad.[17]

A new Law on Cooperatives in late May 1988 gave cooperatives equal rights with the state sector of the economy. They were allowed to hire and dismiss workers, own machinery used in production, engage in foreign trade, own and expand capital assets, file lawsuits, and organize joint ventures with state enterprises. They were permitted to set up banks and sell stocks and bonds. Cooperatives were even encouraged to compete directly with state companies in light industry, consumer goods, food processing, and construction.

Despite the efforts at economic reform, at the party conference in late June 1988, Gorbachev expressed disappointment with the state of the economy. He warned that state budget expenditures had exceeded revenue for many years, raising the danger of inflation. He called for a more radical approach. The practice of price setting and government distribution of supplies needed to be replaced by enterprises competing in the marketplace for energy and raw materials. He promised to impose limits on the power of the central ministries to issue state orders for products, a power that had enabled the central ministries to continue to run the economy much as they had in the past. Prices of consumer goods would need to be raised, although consumers would be compensated. Local governments would be permitted to tax the earnings of companies in their jurisdictions, thus freeing them to some extent from financial dependence on Moscow and making producers more sensitive to local needs. He urged managers to use their new powers to reward better workers with higher wages.[18]

Despite Gorbachev's urging, attempts by managers to operate under *khozraschyot* were sabotaged by the economic and party *apparat*. Directors were called on to provide workers to clear snow, clean streets, or distribute vegetables. The local party committees still made hiring and firing decisions, making it impossible for a factory to be truly self-financing.[19]

By the end of July, Gorbachev was speaking of a farm leasing program and the transfer of failing factories to private entrepreneurs. He seemed willing to move from half-measures to more radical initiatives to overcome the problem of a sagging economy.[20] Despite strong opposition from conservatives who viewed joint ventures as a form of capitalist exploitation, legislation permitting joint venturing with foreign firms was approved in December 1988. Reformers argued that if the Soviet Union was to become competitive in world markets, it would need not only Western technology but Western capital and management skills.[21]

Efforts to improve the economy were partially derailed by a number of factors, only some of which were subject to Gorbachev's control. The Armenian earthquake in December 1988 led to nearly 25,000 deaths and 8,500 million rubles in damages.[22] As a result of the fall in the world price of oil, petroleum export sales fell. This loss amounted to a drop of 10 billion rubles, one-third of the country's export earning capacity.[23] The 1988 grain harvest was the worst in three years, necessitating increased grain imports.[24] In October 1988, the minister of finances suggested for the first time approving a deficit budget for the coming year. He calculated the deficit at 36 billion rubles, but the Supreme Soviet lowered the figure to 35 billion. Many economists put the actual deficit at more than 100 billion.[25]

Deficits and debts were financed by printing more money. The Soviet Union had long suffered from suppressed inflation, since the money paid in wages exceeded the value of available goods and services. However, in the past, with controlled prices, the inflationary forces were not apparent to the consumer. In 1988, with the increasing size of the budget deficit and the legalization of cooperatives, prices began to rise for the first time since World War II.[26] To counter the inflationary pressures, in February 1989 the leadership reduced capital investment of state funds in heavy industry and reduced arms expenditures. A decision was made to convert part of the armaments industry into consumer-oriented light industry. These decisions, though, were implemented slowly and inconsistently.[27]

In mid-March 1989 Gorbachev called for a new agrarian policy. He recognized that massive investments to revive collective agriculture had failed. Insistence on maintaining collective farms and state ownership in the face of evidence that private initiatives were far more productive has long been taken as evidence of the influence of ideological imperatives on Soviet policy. In mid-1988, fifty-year leases had been introduced for families and other groups, but there were few takers. Peasants were unsure of the permanence of the policy and feared that, with a shift in policy, they might be labeled *kulaks*.[28] Now Gorbachev indicated that almost half of the country's 50,000 farms were operating at a loss or barely breaking even while receiving billions of dollars in subsidies. He proposed that state and collective farms be restructured into amalgamations of relatively independent units rented on long-term lease agreements to leaseholders with real power. Families or groups of farmers would be given equal legal and financial footing to compete with large state farms. He called for abolition of the huge state agricultural superministry he had created in November 1985 since, instead of streamlining operations, it had proven to be a bureaucratic impediment. Gorbachev said he wanted new legal guarantees to ease the fears of private farmers, a new system of cooperative banks and stock markets to finance them, and more flexible prices. Farms would still be required to deliver set amounts to the state before disposing of the surplus on the market. For the future, after a major easing of price controls, he proposed granting farmers complete freedom in marketing their produce. However, free markets were seen as still several years away. In an effort to reassure consumers, Gorbachev said retail prices on staples such as bread, meat, and dairy products would not rise for two to three years.[29]

The proposals, more far-reaching than previous moves, soon encountered serious resistance. Three million bureaucrats had a vested interest in the collective farm system as did millions of peasants who feared that market economics would send the state and collective farms into bankruptcy, leaving them in worse poverty than before.[30] Collective farmers preferred a system in which their livelihood was guaranteed, they did not have to work very hard, and they faced no risks.

The most visible evidence of *perestroika* was the growth of cooperatives. By June 1989, the number had increased to 133,000, employing nearly 3 million people. Ordinary citizens did not look at these as an unalloyed success. High prices caused resentment. The prices in an Estonian co-op that offered foreign cosmetics were so high that people called it "the hysterical shop." Some "entrepreneurs" bought in the state sector and sold in high-priced cooperatives. In 1989, after it was estimated that about 3 billion rubles had been taken out of retail trade and resold at higher prices, the Supreme Soviet banned cooperatives that merely bought items and resold them without adding in any way to their value. New enterprises were strong-armed into paying protection money to the Soviet "Mafia." The growing differential between earnings of successful cooperative members and state salaries fostered increasing envy. Some cooperatives paid their members twice as much in a day as an ordinary worker earned in a month. People became indignant at the money being made by shady characters who seemed to contribute nothing to society. High percentages of those engaged in cooperative enterprises had criminal backgrounds. Muscovites resented Georgian "businessmen" making fortunes and flaunting their wealth in expensive cafés in Moscow. Workers called for the disbanding of cooperatives. Gorbachev himself spoke of "open money grubbing" by some who exploited shortages to enrich themselves.[31]

Nevertheless, in early March 1990, for the first time since NEP, individuals were permitted to own small factories and even hire workers. Then, in May, a Gorbachev decree encouraged private ownership, construction, and sale of housing.[32] By the middle of 1991, 4.5 million people, 8 percent of the work force, were employed as private individuals, and a similar number worked full-time in cooperatives. Restaurants, cafés, pay toilets, and repair shops were no longer the only cooperatives. Cooperatives were engaged in textile and consumer goods manufacturing, scientific research and development, and provision of technical goods and services. However, the most successful cooperatives, in construction or industrial supply, were heavily dependent on state enterprises. Huge state enterprises broke off entire factories, which operated as cooperatives with several hundred workers. Factories leased their buildings and equipment to cooperatives, which planned to purchase the facilities as they prospered. Furthermore, cooperatives were still viewed with deep suspicion from many quarters. Ideological opponents viewed them as a dangerous step toward abandonment of the socialist system. Some state enterprises were angered at the competition while state planners saw them as a threat. Many ordinary citizens resented what they viewed as profiteering and blamed cooperatives for shortages in state stores.[33]

By the summer of 1989, even supporters of Gorbachev had grown disillusioned with the results of economic reform. He was subject to increasing attacks from both the Right and the Left. Siberian coal miners staged a coal strike protesting food shortages, working conditions, and lack of soap. The strike spread to the Donbass in the Ukraine, to southern Russia, and then to Central Asia and the Arctic North. Although the miners feared retaliatory violence, neither Ryzhkov nor Gorbachev contemplated the use of force. Instead Gorbachev tried to ally himself with the miners. Even though he was aware that it would further destabilize the economy, Gorbachev met the miners' demands.[34]

None of the efforts to produce benefits for consumers were paying off. People no longer believed that things would get better. Prices at cooperatives were beyond what state workers could afford, lines outside state stores remained, and shelves were often empty. There was little motivation to work harder since there was nothing to buy. Corruption and semilegal markets were spreading. Expectations had been raised, but in fact the economy had worsened. With *glasnost*, people were free to express their frustrations. Gorbachev recognized the need for more thorough economic reform but wavered on how far to go. A team of economists under Leonid Abalkin, a Gorbachev adviser, devised a plan to dismantle the central planning system and abolish price controls. Prime Minister Ryzhkov presented his own far more conservative program, which was rejected by the Supreme Soviet. The Abalkin team came up with a new radical proposal for "shock therapy," but Gorbachev rejected it as irresponsible. On May 23, 1990, Ryzhkov presented a plan for a gradual transition to a "regulated" market that proposed tripling the price of bread on July 1 and raising prices of food, clothing, and consumer goods on January 1, 1991. People reacted with panic buying across the country. Moscow announced only residents with proper identification would be allowed to shop in Moscow stores. Other regions of the country responded in kind. Gorbachev distanced himself from the plan, leaving Ryzhkov to defend it. Reformers called it all shock and no therapy. It was met with outrage on all sides and was rejected by the Supreme Soviet on June 14.[35] The Supreme Soviet called on the government to submit a comprehensive economic program by September 1.

During the summer of 1990, teams of Soviet and Western economists began drafting proposals for the economy. Gorbachev seemed to be moving toward radical reform. In June, Stanislav Shatalin, a radical economist and adviser to Gorbachev who was then working for Yeltsin, came up with a 500-day plan.[36] Gorbachev and Yeltsin agreed at the beginning of August to appoint a joint team under Shatalin to devise a compromise plan for the painful transition to a free market economy. They invited representatives from the republics to join the effort. They also agreed on the need for a new union treaty altering the relationship between the center and the republics. Work on the plan was completed in early September. Ryzhkov, however, supported an alternative plan taking a slower, more cautious approach to a free market. He argued that the Shatalin plan would lead to a precipitous fall in living standards and engender unrest. After months of indecision in which the economy floundered, Gorbachev seemingly endorsed the 500-day plan, stating, "If you ask me, I am more impressed by the Shatalin program."[37] On September 12, Yeltsin engineered approval by the Russian Supreme Soviet, 251 to 1.

Gorbachev wavered. The Shatalin plan was completely unrealistic in assuming that a transition to a market economy could occur in 500 days. It called for large-scale privatization, increased delegation of powers to republics, and creation of a banking system and stock markets at the same time that it promised to protect low-income people. Selected wage and price controls were to continue in the early stages, and consumer goods were to be imported to absorb cash. Next, subsidies to industry and agriculture would end, most industrial ministries would be abolished, most price controls would end, and farmland, housing, and businesses would be extensively privatized. The state planning bureaucracy, the industrial ministries, the vast agricultural apparatus, the military, and regional and local party officials all opposed the plan. Many argued that it would lead to the dissolution of the Soviet Union.[38] Bill Keller points out, "Even some ardent proponents of change worried that the 500-day timetable in Mr. Yeltsin's plan was unrealistic, risking runaway inflation, unemployment, and popular upheaval. . . . The surrender of power to the republics meant the accelerated disintegration of the union."[39]

The Soviet Union and Gorbachev were soon engaged in a direct confrontation with Yeltsin and Russia. On September 24, the USSR Supreme Soviet supported a Gorbachev proposal to work out a compromise between the Ryzhkov and Shatalin plans by October 15. It also granted Gorbachev emergency economic powers for eighteen months to pull the country out of its economic crisis. The resolution, approved by a vote of 305 to 36, gave Gorbachev authority to put into effect policies on wages, prices, finances, and the budget and to strengthen law and order. Yeltsin opposed the request for special powers, warning that Russia would not tolerate any infringement of its sovereignty.[40] On October 1, the Russian Supreme Soviet decided to implement the Shatalin plan without waiting for the Soviet Union.[41]

In mid-October, Gorbachev sent the Soviet parliament a compromise economic plan. He called for an economy based on free enterprise, private ownership, the phasing out of state controls on prices, and an open door for foreign investors. He proposed drastic cutbacks in government spending. Most state-owned enterprises, farms, and housing would be sold to individuals and cooperatives. The republics would have considerable leeway to tax, spend, and determine their own pace of privatization. The center, however, would retain control over vast deposits of oil, natural gas, gold, and diamonds, as well as hard currency earnings. The stabilization was estimated to take not 500 days, but eighteen months to two years. The compromise satisfied no one. Yeltsin denounced the Gorbachev plan as a tactical retreat. The military and the KGB were alarmed by the potential breakdown of central authority.

On November 17, Gorbachev was given strong presidential powers to strengthen his control, rein in hard-liners, and reassure Western governments and investors. However, his decrees were often countermanded by republic and local governments or ignored by the central bureaucracy. As the Soviet food distribution system neared collapse, Western governments provided emergency food supplies to help the Soviet Union get through the winter.[42]

The country faced a major crisis at the end of December, when the Russian Republic voted to contribute only 23.4 billion rubles to the next Soviet budget, less than one-tenth of the amount expected. Russia in the past had contributed one-half of the total union budget, which was projected at 261 billion rubles for 1991. Under the Soviet system, republics collected the revenue and passed it on to the central government, which then sent each republic a share for its budget. The inability of the center to force the republics to transmit tax revenue gave republics the ability to bankrupt the center. Because Russia and other republics withheld funds, federal receipts in 1991 were only 40 percent of the planned level. This endangered the maintenance of the army, state factories, hospitals, education, and pensions.[43] Republics refused to obey orders from the center.

In the winter, Gorbachev moved further to the Right as the country seemed to spin out of control. He and Yeltsin faced each other in an increasingly bitter battle. In January 1991 economic results for 1990 were published. Although they do not seem bad in comparison to 1992, at the time they seemed to indicate the failure of reform and lack of hope for improvement. GNP had fallen by 2 percent, labor productivity had dropped by 3 percent, and national income was down 4 percent. Industrial output, agricultural production, and foreign trade were all down. Incomes, however, had risen by 11 percent and inflation had reached an annual level of 19 percent.[44] The government moved to reduce the excess money supply or "ruble overhang" by suddenly removing fifty- and one hundred-ruble notes from circulation. People were given three days to exchange notes up to a maximum of 1,000 rubles unless they could prove the money was obtained legally. The manner in which this was done fueled resentment.

In April, Gorbachev introduced a package of anticrisis measures calling for strict discipline and an accelerated transition to a market economy. As a first step toward convertibility, the tourist exchange rate for the ruble was set close to the black market rate. Anyone holding hard currency was suddenly rich. Ten dollars bought a banquet for eight with champagne, caviar, and sturgeon, all presumably siphoned off from state supplies. Since black marketeers had the easiest access to dollars, resentment climbed. All sorts of "businessmen" offered fabulous deals to Americans. To cut budget deficits and encourage production, subsidies were cut drastically. Price increases amounting on average to 180 percent were implemented on a wide range of consumer goods. A 5 percent sales tax, referred to as "the president's tax," was imposed on many basic goods. Workers were compensated with a sixty-ruble monthly supplement, but this came nowhere near making up for the increases. Furthermore, hoarding prior to the increases had depleted goods, so shelves were empty. Gorbachev's demands for a moratorium on strikes and demonstrations were met by defiance as workers demonstrated in Byelorussia and the Ukraine, Georgian leaders called for a strike, and Siberian coal miners, already on strike, sharpened their demands. The coal miners won a 25 percent wage increase, further straining the budget. After a secret meeting with leaders of nine republics, Gorbachev agreed to rescind the unpopular price increases and taxes while the republics agreed to support emergency economic measures and call for an end to strikes.[45]

Gorbachev's relations with Yeltsin improved, especially after the Soviet Union transferred control of the Siberian coal industry to Russia and when, on May 11, Gorbachev signed an agreement with nine republics for economic planning and power sharing. All republics except Georgia and Estonia then agreed on an emergency economic plan.[46] Gorbachev, Yeltsin, and the other republic leaders sought trade concessions and credits from the United States and other Western countries to cushion the enormous costs of economic transformation so the process could proceed without social upheaval. However, the finance ministers of the G-7 industrial nations were opposed to any large-scale assistance to the Soviet Union until it had demonstrated its commitment to thoroughgoing reform. The problem was that Gorbachev was afraid of embarking on the course of rapid transition without some assurances of financial aid to prevent catastrophe. In mid-July, Gorbachev flew to London where he made a plea for help from the G-7. Although he received pledges of special association with the International Monetary Fund and the World Bank and technical assistance, essentially he came away empty-handed.[47]

By mid-1991, the Soviet had begun a downward spiral that would accelerate with the fall of the Soviet Union. What privatization had taken place was essentially *nomenklatura* privatization, with managers retaining control. Almost all sectors experienced a massive fall in output. In the first nine months of 1991 the prices of industrial goods rose at an annual rate of 164 percent, retail prices rose 103 percent, and agricultural procurement prices rose 56 percent. Peasants responded by refusing to sell grain to the state, hoping that procurement prices would be increased. In 1990, more than 2,000 new "commercial" banks had been set up, mostly controlled by industrial firms and primarily involved in interfirm lending. As a consequence, credit issues rose 36 percent. The USSR State Bank and the Russian Central Bank were soon engaged in a struggle to control them.[48]

The country's budget deficit was increasing. Since the Russian turnover tax rate was below the union's rate, firms increasingly chose to pay the tax to Russia rather than to Union authorities. Republican and local budgets were also experiencing deficits. Enterprises were retaining profits, increasing wages, and cutting payments to the state. They ignored output plans and refused to pay taxes. The value of the ruble began to plummet. Food subsidies and measures to strengthen the safety net were a major drain on the budget.[49]

The country also faced an international debt crisis that would continue to burden the post-Gorbachev years. At the end of 1992, $22 billion was due in interest and capital repayments on the $58 billion hard currency debt. The gold reserves had shrunk from 1,340 million tons in 1989 to 240 million tons at the end of 1991. Foreign trade was down 37 percent over the previous year. While food imports rose, imports of everything else were cut drastically.[50]

Despite the initial optimism when Gorbachev came to power, he left the economy in worse shape than when he took over. He started out with no overall plan or blueprint. Although he was willing to take bold measures to improve the economy, his intent was not to transform the socialist economy into a free market economy. When he is criticized for taking half measures, this presumes that in fact he wanted to go all the way. What he intended was to borrow from the experience of the outside world to work within the framework of socialism. Over time, circumstances forced him to adopt more and more of the free market, but Gorbachev proclaimed himself a democratic socialist, not a free marketeer. Even after the putsch Gorbachev said, "I am a confirmed supporter of the idea of socialism." He went on to add, "We must recognize that it was the model of socialism that we had in our country which proved a failure, and not the socialist idea itself."[51]

His problem was that as he created some market conditions, he had to break down the old economic structures. The old structures had at least worked minimally, enabling the economy to muddle along, going from bad to worse but still functioning. Richard Ericson notes that *perestroika* destroyed the institutions of the command economy but failed to create functioning market institutions.[52] As the old structure broke down, the center lost control over production and distribution. Factories failed to respond to state orders. Republics, regions, and cities threw up trade barriers or resorted to barter arrangements. Retail prices, which had been subsidized to keep costs on basics down, would shoot up if prices were freed from state control. The prices of bread, milk, meat, gas, and electricity failed even to cover the costs of production. By 1990, food subsidies alone absorbed 15 percent of the Soviet budget. When the government took tentative steps to eliminate subsidies by raising prices, it met strong opposition. The fear of public reaction to soaring prices and the dangers of setting off inflation led Gorbachev to postpone price reform in the hope of first achieving a balance between demand and supply of consumer goods. When wages rose faster than productivity, the situation worsened.[53]

The Soviet economy was built on large monopolies that had never had any incentive for efficient use of capital, labor, or material resources. If prices were freed of government control, these monopolies could simply charge higher prices. There would be no reason for them to respond to higher prices by producing more, since added production would simply cause a drop in price. The way to maximize their own benefit was to restrict production and keep prices high. The only way to introduce the discipline of the market would be to create competition through breaking up existing state monopolies or encouraging joint ventures. As republics and regions began to declare sovereignty, foreign firms became increasingly reluctant to invest. Furthermore, the ruble needed to be made convertible if foreign investors were to be able to repatriate their profits. Efficiency would require cutting back on work forces, creating unemployment. It would also mean that inefficient enterprises would have to be allowed to go bankrupt, further increasing unemployment.

Peasants had no experience as independent farmers, nor was there any tradition in Russia of independent farming. Hedrick Smith speaks of the "collective instincts, born in the countryside of prerevolutionary Russia, embedded in the peasant psyche" and of hostility toward those who rise above the herd.[54] Russians themselves said, "In Russia most people want everyone to be equal, even if that means that everyone is equally poor."[55] Peasants were reluctant to take the risk of becoming farmers with no assurance of what would happen to them if the crop failed or government policy changed. The most skilled rural residents were trained as tractor drivers or mechanics, rather than as farmers. Young men, who might have been expected to welcome the challenge, had been leaving backward rural Russia for years, moving to urban areas. Furthermore, farm equipment was designed to serve large *kolkhozes* and giant state farms. Independent farmers had no assured access to seed, fertilizer, or feed grain. Managers of state and collective farms, often hostile to individual and family farming, threw up roadblocks, refusing to make machinery available when it was needed. Although a February 1990 law allowed private ownership of tractors and other farm machinery, making it possible for farmers with sufficient capital to buy the machinery to lessen dependence on the collective farms, no system of credit was available. Farmers had the right to lease land for life and to pass the land on to their children. They were not, however, permitted to sell it, give it away, or hire others to work it. Whether these measures could entice peasants to become individual farmers was problematic.[56] Sobchak reported that peasants smashed the machinery and burned the barns of other peasants who tried to work their own land.[57]

Workers met Gorbachev's reforms with resistance and cynicism. They were disillusioned with change as nothing seemed to come of it, except disappearance of goods from the shops. Even goods regulated by rationing were hard to find. There were inexplicable shortages of soap, razor blades, and even bread. They saw black market profiteering and growing inequalities in what was supposed to be a workers' state. Workers began to resist attempts to solve the country's economic problems at the expense of living standards and social welfare. A coal miners' strike that broke out in July 1989 spread to all major coal-mining areas in Russia and the Ukraine. At its peak, some half million miners were on strike. Demands centered on pay, food and soap supplies, safety and pensions, managerial and union structures, and pollution. The government conceded most of the strikers' demands, but strikers retained a high level of distrust of government. The strike committees were turned into permanent workers' committees to ensure that the promises were kept. Although the Supreme Soviet in October 1989 banned strikes for fifteen months, the number of strikes increased, leading to shortages of fuel and raw materials. In the first three months of 1990, an average of 100,000 workers were on strike each day. In June 1990 an independent miners' trade union was established.[58]

Factory managers feared the consequences of failing to make the grade under competition. There were no real banks to turn to for credit, there were no wholesalers from whom to purchase supplies or to whom products could be sold, there were no accountants trained to keep true profit-and-loss books, there was no commercial law, and there were no lawyers trained to handle commercial relations. A transition to a market economy would leave hundreds of thousands of bureaucrats stranded. Each had everything to lose and nothing to gain.

Any transition would inflict real pain on many ordinary people, but the poor would suffer most. In June 1989 Ryzhkov revealed that 40 million Soviet citizens lived below the poverty line. The numbers included pensioners, some peasants who worked poor-quality land, and unskilled workers. As long as the state had subsidized rent, food, and other basics, they were able to survive. When prices began to rise, pensions were raised an average of 15 percent.[59] In the future, however, the huge budget deficit would make it increasingly difficult for the government to provide an adequate safety net for the unemployed, the sick, the disabled, and pensioners.

Richard Sakwa argues, "The government miscalculated in believing that in conditions of democratization the Soviet population would be willing to tolerate yet more short-term sacrifices on the premiss [*sic*] that the future would be better."[60] Only a popular political leader could command sufficient support to risk undertaking such a transition. By the time Gorbachev understood the complexity and risks involved, he had lost his popularity and was besieged on all sides.

## NOTES

1. *New York Times*, December 15, 1992.

2. Mikhail Gorbachev, *Perestroika* (New York: Perennial Library, 1988), xii, 17, 22–23.

3. Richard Sakwa, *Gorbachev and His Reforms 1985–1990* (New York: Prentice-Hall, 1990), 269–72.

4. Gorbachev, *Perestroika*, 39, 77; Marshall I. Goldman, *What Went Wrong with Perestroika* (New York: W. W. Norton, 1991), 87–90; Hedrick Smith, *The New Russians* (New York: Avon Books, 1991), 211.

5. Peter Rutland, "Economic Crisis and Reform," in *Developments in Soviet & Post-Soviet Politics*, ed. Stephen White, Alex Pravda, and Zvi Gitelman (Durham, N.C.: Duke University Press, 1992), 209–10.

6. Robert G. Kaiser, *Why Gorbachev Happened* (New York: Touchstone, 1992), 128.

7. *New York Times*, March 24, 1987.

8. Sakwa, *Gorbachev and His Reforms*, 272.

9. Goldman, *What Went Wrong with Perestroika*, 131.

10. Gorbachev, *Perestroika*, 19–20, 70–72.

11. *New York Times*, June 27, 1987.

12. *New York Times*, January 2, 1988; Rutland, "Economic Crisis and Reform," 209–10; Sakwa, *Gorbachev and His Reforms*, 279; Gorbachev, *Perestroika*, 72–78.

13. Rutland, *Economic Crisis and Reform*, 209–11; Gorbachev, *Perestroika*, 74–76; Goldman, *What Went Wrong with Perestroika*, 118–20, 139–42; Sakwa, *Gorbachev and His Reforms*, 270–80; Stephen White, *Gorbachev and After* (Cambridge: Cambridge University Press, 1991), 118, 121–23.

14. Janos Kornai, *The Road to a Free Economy* (New York: W. W. Norton, 1990), 98–99.

15. White, *Gorbachev and After*, 126.

16. Goldman, *What Went Wrong with Perestroika*, 142.

17. *New York Times*, January 2; March 9, 22, 1988.

18. *New York Times*, June 29, 1988.

19. Gavriil Popov, "Perestroika and the Primacy of Politics," in *Chronicle of a Revolution*, ed. Abraham Brumberg (New York: Pantheon Books, 1990), 182–84.

20. *New York Times*, August 1, 1988.

21. Goldman, *What Went Wrong with Perestroika*, 117–18.

22. White, *Gorbachev and After*, 118.

23. Goldman, *What Went Wrong with Perestroika*, 131.

24. *New York Times*, January 17, 1989.

25. Otto Latsis, "The Deep Roots of Our Problems," in *Chronicle of a Revolution*, ed. Brumberg, 176.

26. Goldman, *What Went Wrong with Perestroika*, 136–37.

27. Latsis, "The Deep Roots of Our Problems," 176–77.

28. Sakwa, *Gorbachev and His Reforms*, 288.

29. *New York Times*, March 16, 1989.

30. Smith, *The New Russians*, 213–15.

31. *New York Times*, March 9, 1988; Barbara B. Green, "Moscow and Tallinn Under Gorbachev," *The Gamut: A Journal of Ideas and Information* 28 (Winter 1989): 36–64; Sakwa, *Gorbachev and His Reforms*, 294; White, *Gorbachev and After*, 124.

32. Smith, *The New Russians*, 290–91.

33. Rutland, "Economic Crisis and Reform," 212; Smith, *The New Russians*, 270–87.

34. Kaiser, *Why Gorbachev Happened*, 292–94.

35. Rutland, "Economic Crisis and Reform," 216; Kaiser, *Why Gorbachev Happened*, 333–34; Smith, *The New Russians*, 259–61.

36. Rutland, "Economic Crisis and Reform," 217. This was a revised version of a 400-day plan devised by Grigorii Yavlinsky, another radical economist.

37. *New York Times*, September 12, 1990; Kaiser, *Why Gorbachev Happened*, 359–63.

38. Kaiser, *Why Gorbachev Happened*, 363–64.

39. *New York Times*, October 18, 1990.

40. *New York Times*, September 25, 1990.

41. *New York Times*, October 2, 1990.

42. *New York Times*, November 24, 1990.

43. *New York Times*, December 27, 1990.

44. White, *Gorbachev and After*, 127.

45. *New York Times*, April 25, 1991.

46. *New York Times*, May 6, 12, 17, 1991.

47. *New York Times*, July 17, 18, 1991.

48. Rutland, "Economic Crisis and Reform," 219–22.

49. Ibid., 222–24.

50. Ibid., 224.

51. Mikhail Gorbachev, *The August Coup* (New York: HarperCollins, 1991), 47.

52. Richard E. Ericson, "Economics," in *After the Soviet Union*, ed. Timothy J. Colton and Robert Legvold (New York: W. W. Norton, 1992), 52.

53. Sakwa, *Gorbachev and His Reforms*, 274.

54. Smith, *The New Russians*, 203.

55. Green, "Moscow and Tallinn," 47.

56. Sakwa, *Gorbachev and His Reforms*, 288–90.

57. Smith, *The New Russians*, 204.

58. Sakwa, *Gorbachev and His Reforms*, 211–14.
59. Ibid., 298.
60. Ibid., 302.

*Chapter 12*

# DISSOLUTION OF THE SOVIET UNION

When Gorbachev came to power, his first priority, we have seen, was to improve economic efficiency. In the process, national sensitivities were largely ignored. Since many of the minority nationalities had cultures that encouraged or tolerated nepotism, favoritism, and corruption, they were hit hard. The draft party program in October 1985 emphasized the steady drawing together of nationalities and the need for non-Russians to master the Russian language in order to achieve this goal.[1] *Glasnost*, with its loosening of censorship, enabled reformers to expose the terrors of Stalinism as well as the corruption and privilege of the Brezhnev era. Nationalists soon took advantage of the same freedom to articulate their concerns about the preservation of their national cultures and languages. This cultural nationalism soon evolved into political nationalism with demands for sovereignty and independence. Without a supranational ideology able to serve as a focus of loyalty or an economy enabling the center to distribute patronage or a party able to maintain centralized control, the empire, first put together by the Russian Tsars, could have been held together only by force. But neither Gorbachev nor the men surrounding him had the will to use the necessary force.

Leaders of the Soviet Union had believed that they could create a new Soviet national identity in which ethnic groups and nationalities would retain their culture and customs but all would recognize a higher loyalty as Soviet citizens. The assumption, not restricted to Marxists, was that national-political identity did not have to coincide with ethnicity. Political scientists have argued that "the chief political problem of . . . new states is . . . national integration, . . . forging a single nation from two or more distinct peoples."[2] This is not, of course, a problem restricted to new states. It has been a central function of political socialization in the United States and has become increasingly salient in Europe. One problem with the implementation of this goal in the Soviet Union was that Soviet national identity was confounded with Russian identity. The common language, common history, and common culture were in fact Russian. Appeals to Soviet nationalism were, in practice, appeals to Russian nationalism.

The second major problem arose from the federal nature of the state. Territorial divisions were based on ethnic-nationality communities. The USSR was divided into fifteen union republics; twenty autonomous republics (ASSRs); eight autonomous regions, or *oblasts*; and ten national districts, or *okrugs*. Each union republic and most lower-level units had their own language, cultural facilities, and schools, but Soviet nationalities were expected to subordinate their political and national activities to higher political goals.

Philip Roeder shows how federalism shaped the mobilization of ethnic communities. Within each ethnic-national territory, the regime had created a cadre of party and state officials drawn from the indigenous nationality but dependent on the center. A major task of the indigenous elite was to prevent the emergence of a counterelite that could challenge the Soviet system. To this end, they were given a monopoly over resources that could be used to mobilize the ethnic community, thus preventing independent ethnic protest. Independent associations were banned and dissident intellectuals were denied access to means of communication. Since the cadres received material rewards and status from the center, it was in their interest to support existing central institutions. They served as channels to articulate national interests and to bargain with the center for political, economic, and cultural concessions. But any local leaders who challenged central authority could be removed from their positions. Affirmative action policies favoring indigenous nationalities reinforced their loyalty to the center.[3]

In time, these federal institutions and ethnic cadres became the instruments of ethnic assertiveness in what Roeder calls ethnofederalism.[4] As terror abated, these cadres felt freer to press their own agendas. They built institutional and even popular support as their patronage opportunities expanded and began to take more assertive stands in dealing with the center. With declining economic growth, it became increasingly difficult for the center to provide the material rewards necessary to assure their loyalty. With fewer resources, competition among ethnic communities grew. Resentment by the more developed republics of the regime's redistributive economic policies grew as the economic pie shrank. Increased autonomy was seen as a way to keep their resources at home. The cadres mobilized ethnic pressure to secure additional resources, using nationalist popular fronts to support them in negotiating with Moscow. In some cases they even encouraged communal violence as a way of pressuring Moscow. In some republics the cadres lost control over the popular movements and political power passed into the hands of counterelites. Roeder states, "The policies of *demokratizatsia* and *glasnost* . . . undermined the ability of cadres to contain the protest they . . . mobilized."[5]

The problem was further complicated by the wide variations among republics in levels of education, urbanization, and material well-being. The Slavs dominated politically. The Baltic states, particularly Latvia and Estonia, had the highest standard of living, but they compared themselves with Finns and Swedes. The Central Asian republics were the poorest, but they had benefited from the Soviet system, which had poured vast capital investment into developing natural resources and building industrial plants and irrigation projects. The Soviet Union was remarkably successful in raising the educational and economic level of underdeveloped areas.[6] The redistributive policy came under attack as economic conditions worsened. The more developed republics opposed draining of their resources for the benefit of Central Asia, while the Central Asians were convinced that they were exploited by the center and resented the fact that their standard of living was far below that of the western and northern republics.

Ethnic groups within republics also differed considerably in occupation, income, and educational levels. Large numbers of Russians and Ukrainians had moved into the Baltics and Central Asia. They were more urbanized than the indigenous population, usually more highly educated, made up the industrial sector, and predominated in positions of control. Socioeconomic stratification largely overlapped stratification by ethnicity. This, combined with the expectation that the indigenous people were expected to learn Russian while local Russians did not have to learn the language of the republic, fostered resentment against Russians.[7] This was particularly true in the Baltic republics where the small native populations feared loss of their national identity as a result of a steady in-migration. The indigenous nationalities came to view the local Russians as agents of a colonial power headquartered in Moscow.

Arguing that it was essential that all republics put the common interest of the Soviet Union above their own, Gorbachev called for a struggle against national narrow-mindedness and arrogance, nationalism and chauvinism. Nevertheless, non-Russians soon began to use *glasnost* to press for rehabilitation of their cultures, histories, and national languages. The Chernobyl disaster in April 1986 raised awareness of environmental problems. It was assumed that environmental degradation was a consequence of centralized controls that ignored the well-being of local populations. Non-Russians protested displacement of their languages by Russian and attacked Moscow's control over their cultural life. In the Baltics, Russians were assailed for not learning the local language. Gorbachev remained almost oblivious to the rising cultural nationalism.[8]

The first explosion of nationalism occurred in December 1986, not in the European part of the union, but in Alma-Ata, the capital of Kazakhstan. In an attempt to clean out corruption, Gorbachev replaced Dinmukhhamed Kunaev, a Kazakh who had been party chief of Kazakhstan for a quarter of a century, with Gennadii Kolbin, a Russian from outside the republic. The intent, clearly, was to bring in someone who was not implicated in the pervasive patron-client relationships. Kunaev's removal was seen by Kazakhs as a blow to their national pride. Thousands of young people, mostly students, engaged in anti-Russian rioting, which was suppressed by troops who killed dozens and seriously wounded hundreds. Martha Brill Olcott states that the violent repression was seen as another instance in a long series of Russian retaliations against Kazakh efforts at political self-expression.[9]

## THE BALTICS

Although the Baltic peoples had long-standing grievances against the Soviet Union, it was not until *glasnost* that they were given political expression. In the summer of 1987 the Latvian Helsinki Group honored victims of the June 1941 deportations. All three Baltic republics held peaceful demonstrations on August 23, the anniversary of the Nazi-Soviet Pact.[10] Local party leaderships showed some sympathy with nationalist demands, supporting increased status for the national languages, limitations on immigration, and increased economic autonomy. In April 1988 the Estonian Popular Front was organized by nationalists and Communist Party members who supported political and economic change.[11] Lithuanian party and nonparty intellectuals established the Lithuanian Movement for Reconstruction, Sajudis, in June, and a Latvian Popular Front soon followed. These popular fronts grew into movements with mass followings articulating nationalist goals. They championed ecological causes, demanded the truth about the Nazi-Soviet Pact, called for increased language rights, and insisted on an end to immigration.[12]

The communist parties cooperated with the popular Fronts. On October 1, with the approval of the Communist Party, the Estonian Popular Front held its first Congress, and, with the encouragement of the head of the Estonian Communist Party, it announced its intent to run candidates in elections.[13] When the Latvian Popular Front at its first Congress on October 8–9 called for sovereignty and statehood, the Latvian Communist Party responded positively. Latvian was designated the state language and the flag and national anthem of the interwar republic were legalized.[14] The founding Congress of Lithuania's Sajudis on October 22–23 was broadcast live on the state television network. A Catholic mass, celebrated in front of the cathedral, was also televised. Algirdas Brazaukas, the newly appointed head of the Lithuanian Communist Party, spoke to the Congress and reported that Gorbachev considered Sajudis a positive force for reform.[15]

All three Baltic republics opposed Gorbachev's 1988 constitutional amendments, believing that the changes would limit their autonomy. They especially opposed the power given to the Congress to declare republic laws unconstitutional. Estonia adopted a Declaration of Sovereignty on November 16, 1988, asserting the right to veto all-union laws on Estonian territory. The Estonian Communist Party's support for this enabled it to maintain credibility and contain the challenge of the popular front. Latvia and Lithuania had initially supported Estonia, but, under pressure from Moscow, their Communist Parties backed down.[16] Gorbachev denounced Estonian policies as political adventurism and warned that national discord could jeopardize *perestroika*.[17]

Sajudis and the Lithuanian Communist Party competed for seats in the March elections to the new Congress of Deputies. Both supported sovereignty, but Sajudis declared that its ultimate goal was "an independent and neutral Lithuanian state" and declared that Lithuania had been occupied by the Soviet Union against its will. Brazaukas warned that direct defiance of the Soviet Union and calls for separatism risked possible imposition of a state of emergency.[18] Although Sajudis decided not to challenge Brazaukas or his deputy in the election, they won thirty-six of the forty-two seats. In permitting multicandidate elections, Gorbachev had recognized the legitimacy conferred by the ballot box. It was now difficult for Gorbachev to deny the legitimacy of the Sajudis victory. Brazaukas could govern only with the toleration of the moderate wing of Sajudis, which set the agenda.[19] On May 18, 1989, with the backing of both the Communist Party and Sajudis, the Lithuanian Supreme Soviet formally declared sovereignty and proclaimed the goal of complete independence. On July 29, the Latvian Supreme Soviet declared Latvian sovereignty.

The Baltics, encouraged by support from Yeltsin, Sakharov, and others, now pushed for independence. In early August, the Estonian Supreme Soviet introduced a residency requirement for voting and for election to office. In response, Russian workers went out on strike. Gorbachev declared that the law violated the Soviet constitution. The level of tension increased.[20] In a dramatic move that received worldwide television coverage, the fiftieth anniversary of the Nazi-Soviet Pact was marked by a 400-mile human chain of 2 million people linking Estonia, Latvia, and Lithuania in a united demand for independence. The three popular front organizations formed an alliance. The CPSU Central Committee condemned the nationalist movements in the Baltics, warning the republics that if the situation continued, their "very existence could wind up in question."[21]

Leaders of the popular fronts of the three Baltic republics condemned the warning. The three governments supported an antidraft movement, called for local militias, and spoke of introducing their own local currencies. The Lithuanian Supreme Soviet approved a referendum on secession and supported separate Lithuanian citizenship. Latvia asserted the right to veto all-union laws, while Estonia denounced the 1940 annexation.

Gorbachev's tolerance of revolutionary changes in Eastern Europe and his declaration that the Soviet Union had no moral or political right to intervene there led nationalist leaders in the Baltics to claim that their situation was no different from that of Poland, Hungary, or Czechoslovakia. Gorbachev feared that however strong the claims of the Baltics might be, to grant them independence would be only the first step in the dissolution of the union. In an attempt at compromise, Gorbachev persuaded the all-union Supreme Soviet to grant economic self-management to Latvia, Lithuania, and Estonia. But neither compromise nor efforts at persuasion dampened the drive for independence. In early December, Lithuania kept the pressure up by abolishing the Communist Party monopoly of power and legalizing rival political parties. Then, on December 20, the Lithuanian Communist Party voted to break away from the Soviet party to become an independent Communist Party. It endorsed the creation of "an independent democratic Lithuanian state."[22]

Gorbachev's response was not to use force but to plead with the Lithuanians to remain in the union. He promised greater freedom within a restructured federation while warning that any republic's decision to secede would have repercussions throughout the Soviet Union. A quarter of a million people rallied in Cathedral Square where they cheered nationalist calls for an independent Lithuania and rejected Gorbachev's plea.[23]

In a multicandidate election in Lithuania at the end of February, Sajudis and its allies, running on a platform urging rapid independence, won more than two-thirds of the seats in the Lithuanian Supreme Soviet. On March 11, 1990, Vytautas Landsbergis, the leader of Sajudis, was elected president, defeating Brazaukas. The Lithuanian Supreme Soviet then voted 124 to 0, with nine abstentions and absentees, to proclaim the restoration of the independent statehood, which had been ended by Soviet annexation in 1940. It changed the name of the Lithuanian Soviet Socialist Republic to the Lithuanian Republic and replaced the hammer and sickle with the old Lithuanian coat of arms.[24] Gorbachev felt that the declaration of independence was a direct slap in the face since the Congress of People's Deputies, opening on March 12, was scheduled to approve a new law on secession. The Lithuanians enacted laws directly opposed to national legislation. Republic border guards and security forces were created. Conscription into the Red Army was halted and Lithuanians in the army were encouraged to desert.

Gorbachev declared the Lithuanian actions a violation of the Soviet constitution. The Soviet government began what Francis X. Clines called "the slow war of nerves . . . to keep Lithuanian rebellion from becoming a precedent for other dissatisfied republics to challenge Moscow's sovereignty."[25] Military forces moved through Vilnius in an attempt at intimidation. Soviet troops arrested a group of army deserters who had taken refuge in a hospital, occupied the state prosecutor's office and Communist party buildings, and seized the printing plant.[26] After issuing an ultimatum, Moscow cut off energy supplies and the shipment of goods. On July 2, after two and a half months of behind-the-scenes maneuvering and pressure, the embargo was lifted when Lithuania agreed to suspend its declaration of independence for one hundred days.[27] The moratorium did not resolve the issue of sovereignty but cooled down the conflict.

Estonia and Latvia tried to avoid provoking a direct confrontation with Moscow but continued to move steadily toward independence. In February 1989 the Estonian Citizens' Committees organized elections for an unsanctioned alternative legislature, the Estonian Congress, which claimed descent from the prewar body. Only citizens of the prewar republic and their descendants could vote, thus disfranchising all those who had moved to, or been born in, Estonia after 1940. Some 500,000 people, almost 90 percent of those eligible, took part. Extreme nationalists then urged cancellation of elections for the Estonian Supreme Soviet and transfer of power to the Congress. The extremists were overridden, and on March 18, 1990, Estonians and Latvians elected Supreme Soviets in multiparty elections. The popular fronts won in both. The new Estonian Supreme Soviet decreed that the Soviet constitution had no force in the country since Estonia had been an occupied country since 1940 and was legally independent. It declared the beginning of a transition period to full independence and chose the popular front leader Edgar Savisaar as prime minister.[28] On May 4, the Latvian Supreme Soviet proclaimed independence but, like the Estonians, referred to a transitional stage toward full independence.

## THE TRANSCAUCASUS

In Transcaucasia, nationalist activity focused primarily on the conflict among nationalities, rather than against the Soviet Union or Russians. Robert Cullen notes, "in the mountainous republics of the Transcaucasus . . . reform has . . . permitted the resumption of old feuds between people who no longer have to pretend that they and their neighbors belong to the same Soviet family."[29] In late 1987, the Armenians of the Nagorno-Karabakh Autonomous Region, an enclave in the mountainous area of western Azerbaijan, began to agitate for unification of the territory with Armenia. Although 95 percent of the population were Armenian Christians, Stalin had turned over the region to the Azerbaijan Republic in 1921. Both the Azeris and the Armenians claimed that the region was historically theirs. On February 20, the regional soviet of Nagorno-Karabakh voted formally to seek unification with Armenia. Hundreds of Armenian demonstrators poured into Yerevan's main square to campaign for unification with Nagorno-Karabakh. The demonstrators, who carried portraits of Gorbachev, believed that under *glasnost* a historic wrong could be righted. The demonstrators were not hostile to central authority or anti-Russian.[30] But for the first time a nationalist movement challenged existing borders.

Gorbachev appealed to Armenians to end the protests as he sought a way out of the crisis. He feared that altering existing territorial arrangements would set a precedent for innumerable claims over contested borders throughout the Soviet Union. He therefore rejected the Armenian demands, condemned extremism and disturbances of public order, promised reforms in Nagorno-Karabakh, and sent officials to try to calm the situation.

Believing that Moscow was acceding to Armenian demands, Azeris now went on a rampage through Armenian neighborhoods in the city of Sumgait, Azerbaijan, burning houses, torturing, and killing residents. Troops had to be used to restore order. Azerbaijani intellectuals in Baku founded a club that grew into the Azerbaijani Popular Front, committed to retention of Nagorno-Karabakh.[31] Demonstrations continued in Armenia and Azerbaijan. In May, Moscow sent troops and dismissed the party first secretaries of both Armenia and Azerbaijan.

In early July, Soviet troops intervened against Armenian demonstrators occupying the Yerevan airport, killing one Armenian and injuring several. Protesters voiced increasing disenchantment with Gorbachev.[32] The Karabakh Committee, a group of Armenian intellectuals with mass support, issued the manifesto of the Armenian National Movement. A petition demanded that the Armenian Supreme Soviet defy Moscow and declare Nagorno-Karabakh part of Armenia.[33]

The USSR Supreme Soviet rejected Armenia's demand for the return of Nagorno-Karabakh in July. Armenians, who had historically turned to Russia for protection and support now lost faith in the Soviet Union. Their reaction was anger and frustration. Demonstrations became an everyday event. In September troops and armed vehicles were sent to Yerevan, but demonstrations and strikes continued.

Azeris began to mobilize to defend the territorial integrity of Azerbaijan. In late November, protests in Baku became violent, and a state of emergency was declared. When counterrallies took place in Yerevan, emergency rule was imposed, and the city was put under virtual military occupation. Violence in both republics escalated. About 200,000 Armenians fled to Armenia and about 130,000 Azeris fled to Azerbaijan.

A major earthquake struck Armenia on December 7, 1988, killing about 25,000 and leveling cities. Gorbachev cut his visit to the United Nations short in order to hurry back but was taken by surprise when, amid the devastation, he was confronted with arguments over Nagorno-Karabakh. Authorities arrested leaders of the Armenian Karabakh Committee, sending them to jail in Moscow.[34] Opera Square, where nationalists had been gathering regularly, was ringed with troops, who broke up any public gathering.[35]

In January 1989, the Soviet Union dissolved the local organs of government and imposed direct rule over Nagorno-Karabakh. The Soviets in Karabakh opened Armenian schools and took other measures to meet the demands for cultural expression. The government released interned members of the Karabakh committee in May 1989.[36]

In August, Azeri militants blockaded transportation routes to Armenia and Nagorno-Karabakh, preventing delivery of food, fuel, and construction supplies to earthquake-damaged areas. It took two direct ultimatums from Gorbachev before the blockade was eased. At this point radicals took control of the Azerbaijani Popular Front. Supported by thousands of Azerbaijani refugees who had fled Armenia, they held mass demonstrations and staged a large-scale protest strike in Baku.[37] The communist-controlled Azeri Supreme Soviet called for full restoration of its control over Nagorno-Karabakh and for economic sovereignty. The Armenian Supreme Soviet, for its part, repeated claims to Nagorno-Karabakh. Both sides organized private armies. Stores of weapons and munitions were stolen from military bases. In October Azerbaijan declared that Nagorno-Karabakh was an integral part of Azerbaijan, insisted on sovereignty within the USSR, and reserved the right to secede after a referendum. At the end of the year, Nagorno-Karabakh was restored to Azeri control.

In January 1990, Azerbaijan erupted in violence as mobs broke away from a rally in Baku and rampaged through the streets for days, driving Armenians out of their homes and beating and killing them. Nearly all of the 200,000 Armenian inhabitants of Baku fled. The Armenians received no help from the Azerbaijani police or Interior Ministry troops. Russians, fearing they might be in danger, began to flee. The headquarters of the Central Committee of the Azerbaijan Communist Party was surrounded by the crowd. A week after the violence, on the night of January 19–20, columns of Soviet tanks and soldiers crashed barricades erected by Azeri nationalists, shot at buses, and crushed cars. A hundred and fifty people were killed, and more than six hundred were injured.[38]

Gorbachev claimed that the military assault was necessary to prevent a coup by the Azerbaijani Popular Front. Azeris tore down the barbed wire on the borders with Iran and crossed the frontier. The Azerbaijani province of Nakhichevan, a popular front stronghold on the border with Turkey and Iran cut off from Azerbaijan by Armenian territory, declared its independence from the Soviet Union. Soviet troops arrested insurgents and broke a blockade of Baku Harbor using warships, tanks, and artillery. The city remained under military occupation, but those who died under Soviet tanks and gunfire were honored by schoolchildren, black flags draped buildings, photographs were circulated showing the bullet-ridden bodies of Azerbaijani men, and thousands visited the grave site. Much of the city's industry was halted by strikes.[39] The Soviet government drew back from using the force necessary to assert control over Azerbaijan but used enough to inflame Azeri nationalism and turn it against Gorbachev, Moscow, and the Soviet Communist Party.

The Baku pogrom and subsequent occupation served to discredit the Azerbaijan Popular Front. Ayaz Mutalibov, the first secretary of the Communist Party, took advantage of the opportunity to pose as a nationalist by taking a strong stand against Armenian claims to Nagorno-Karabakh. The Communist Party did well in the elections in the fall of 1990. By contrast, the Communist Party of Armenia was discredited. In August 1990, Levon Ter-Petrosyan, the leader of the National Movement, was elected president of the republic.[40] Both Armenia and Azerbaijan declared sovereignty. Repeated Soviet efforts at a truce failed. The struggle over Nagorno-Karabakh turned into a seemingly endless war.

Although most of the attention was focused on the Armenian-Azeri conflict, Georgian nationalism also grew. At the end of 1987 prominent dissidents formed a society that raised cultural and linguistic demands while declaring that its ultimate aim was Georgian independence. In early 1988, radical groups that rejected compromise broke away to form a popular front. About a dozen different opposition groups were organized along ethnic and generational lines. Although the party made concessions, a series of demonstrations broke out in September 1988. As the size and frequency of demonstrations accelerated, party leaders were unable to control the situation. Georgians began to complain about discrimination against Georgians in the Abkhaz Autonomous Republic in northwest Georgia and about Azeri settlers in the Southwest. Hundreds of thousands of demonstrators massed outside the Georgian Supreme Soviet in November, demanding the right to secede.[41]

In early spring 1989, 15,000 protesters called for Georgian independence while denouncing efforts by Abkhazians to secede from Georgia. Although the demonstration was denounced by Moscow, the Georgian popular front was strongly supported by Georgians. In April, more than 100,000 demonstrators in Tbilisi again demanded Georgian independence from the Soviet Union and the complete integration of Abkhazia into Georgia. Since Abkhazians were only 17 percent of the population of Abkhazia while Georgians were 45 percent, Georgians had difficulty seeing any justice in the Abkhazians' call for cutting ties with Georgia. Strikes closed factories and stores while tensions rose. On April 9, 1989, Soviet troops armed with sharpened spades and toxic gas broke up the demonstration, killing nineteen. The event, labeled "bloody Sunday," sent waves of protest throughout Georgia, strengthening demands for independence. A state of emergency was declared and tanks patrolled the streets. Shevardnadze, the foreign minister and former Georgian party leader, flew to Tbilisi to appeal for calm. Hunger strikers set up tents, strikes disrupted industrial production, and resistance movements and parties sprang up. Although the independence move was fragmented, composed of feuding political groups, all were united in opposition to Soviet rule.[42]

Nationalist and reform groups in the Baltics and elsewhere reacted with alarm to the killings. Many took the event as evidence that the Gorbachev regime was no better than its predecessors. The Congress of People's Deputies, which opened on May 25, honored the dead and condemned the killings. It established a commission to look into responsibility for the Tbilisi killings.

Demonstrations, boycotts, and blockades of railroads in Georgia in August 1989 forced the authorities to permit multiparty elections. On March 20, 1990, the Georgian Supreme Soviet abolished the Communist

Party's monopoly of power. The election resulted in victory for a coalition led by the nationalist dissident Zviad Gamsakhurdia. The legislature called for full restoration of sovereignty as it had existed up to 1921. After a referendum in which 98 percent voted for independence, Georgia declared independence on April 9, 1991.[43]

In December 1990, South Ossetia, an autonomous republic in Georgia, stated that it wanted to remain in the Soviet Union. Gamsakhurdia declared South Ossetia dissolved and sent in troops. The conflict by March 1991 led to more than 51 killed and over 13,000 refugees.[44]

## CENTRAL ASIA

Mass political movements spread to the Muslim republics of Central Asia.[45] Under Brezhnev, corrupt republic leaders had been given wide latitude in running their republics in exchange for their support of central authority. Moscow had used economic patronage to weld loyalty. In the interest of efficiency, Gorbachev eliminated the affirmative action policies that had favored indigenous nationalities for jobs, promotions, political appointments, and admission to higher education. He replaced all five first secretaries in Central Asia.[46] As he moved to clean up corruption and improve efficiency, he weakened ties to the center and raised resentment at Slavic domination of the union. Although there was talk about an Islamic union of Soviet Muslim peoples, based on shared religion and mutual economic dependence, there were strains among the peoples that made this unlikely.[47] Moreover, the republics are ethnically divided. The percentage of the titular nationality in each republic ranges from 40 percent in Kazakhstan to 72 percent in Turkmenistan. In Kazakhstan, Russians account for 38 percent and Ukrainians for another 5 percent. Russians are also a major presence in Kirghizia, where they account for 22 percent of the population. One million Uzbeks live in Tajikistan and one million Tajiks in Uzbekistan.[48]

As noted earlier, Kazakhstan, a republic bigger in size than all of Western Europe, had the first major nationalist riot in Alma-Ata. After cleaning up many abuses and reforming the administration, Kolbin, a Russian, was replaced by a Kazakh, Nursultan Nazarbaev, in 1989. Informal groups took shape, concerned with environmental issues, the status and future of the Kazakh language, and the right to their own history.[49] They were angered by contamination from the nuclear weapons testing ground at Semipalatinsk and played a major role in getting the testing grounds moved to the far north. There was also concern over rumors that a German homeland would be created in Kazakhstan and opposition to the influx of non-Kazakh laborers. The groups formed a loose coalition with the Adilet (Justice) Association, which dedicated itself to the rehabilitation of Stalin's victims.[50] Kazakhstan, however, remained a strong supporter of the union.

Uzbekistan, the third largest republic in population with almost 20 million people, was a sinkhole of corruption. Ruling cliques found at every level of society were tied into local networks of power. The level of health care, housing, disease, malnutrition, and infant mortality was shocking.[51] Government and party leaders embezzled billions of rubles. Brezhnev had required the Uzbeks to increase the amount of cotton they picked each year. This was impossible, especially since previous years' statistics had been inflated. The party leaders, however, assured Moscow that all had gone according to plan or even exceeded it. Moscow then paid for the record crop. After paying farms for what had actually been harvested, the republic leaders pocketed the rest. Gifts were then sent to Brezhnev. The system was able to distribute sufficient rewards to bind the center and the periphery with ties of mutual corruption. Although Gorbachev tried to clean up the corruption, in 1988 regional party officials pardoned 675 people who had been sentenced for their role in the Brezhnev era "cotton scam."[52] New rackets and swindles followed.

As central controls loosened, ethnic disputes broke out. Border skirmishes with Kirghizia resulted in hundreds of deaths. In 1989, in the Ferghana Valley of Uzbekistan, several hundred Meskhetians were killed as Uzbek youth rampaged through their villages.[53] MVD special forces had to be called in to restore order.

The Uzbek popular front movement, Birlik, founded in November 1988 by a group of Uzbek intellectuals, was stimulated by rural poverty and environmental issues associated with the republic's cotton monoculture. Modeled on Sajudis, the movement was instrumental in having Uzbek recognized as the state language of the republic.[54] Uzbekistan in June 1990 became the first republic in Central Asia to declare its sovereignty. There were, however, a recognition of Uzbekistan's economic dependence on Moscow and no movement for secession. In the elections of March 1990, the communists prevailed.

Tajikistan, the smallest and poorest of the Central Asian republics and the most distant from Moscow, owed its existence to Stalin's decision to carve a separate republic out of Uzbekistan. Sizable numbers of Tajiks, the only non-Turkic people in the region, live in Uzbekistan and Afghanistan. One-quarter of Tajikistan's population is Uzbek.[55] Serious problems developed when a resurgent Islamic movement, backed by the Muslim clergy and the Islamic Renaissance Party, opposed communists and secularists. Youth gangs rampaged through streets, attacking nonbelievers and women who did not wear traditional Muslim clothes. When rumors spread that Armenian refugees were being given preference for scarce housing, riots broke out in which about twenty Armenians were killed. Moscow had to send troops to end the fighting. About 23,000 Russians were forced to flee as anti-Russian feelings soared.[56] Political leadership, while favoring increased economic autonomy, opposed separatism.

Kirghizia, on the Chinese border, was one of the poorest republics. It accounted for less than 1 percent of the Soviet GNP and had only 4.4 million people, many of them nomads breeding horses. Like other Central Asian republics, it suffered from nepotism, cronyism, and corruption. Local elites were purged after Gorbachev came to power. There was a revived interest in Kirghiz culture and history, but there was no attempt to give the language official status. Interethnic clashes seemed a major form of nationalist expression.[57] In 1989 a serious clash occurred with the Tajiks over water rights. In 1990 a fight with Uzbeks broke out over land use when a Kirghiz party boss transferred land from an Uzbek-populated *kolkhoz* to landless Kirghiz. At least 250 were killed and some estimates put the deaths at over a thousand. Angry young demonstrators then surrounded the Communist Party headquarters, blaming the party for mismanaging the crisis and causing needless bloodshed.

Hunger strikes and a campaign by a new Democratic movement forced the leadership to permit the parliament to elect a new president. In October 1990, Askar Akayev, a physicist who had spent twenty years in Leningrad, was chosen. The parliamentary groups that supported him organized a political party, Democratic Kyrgyzstan, with a hierarchy of local and regional leaders and dues-paying members. Kirghizia became the first Central Asian republic to break with communist dictatorship. By the end of 1990, Kirghizia had declared sovereignty and dropped both "Soviet" and "Socialist" from the name of the country. Akayev promised a multiparty system and changed the name of the capital from Frunze, after a Soviet military hero, to the original Bishkek. During the August putsch, Kirghizia was the only republic besides Russia to experience an attempt to overthrow its government. When the local KGB chief tried to arrest the president, Akayev arrested him, sent loyal troops to surround Communist Party headquarters, broadcast Yeltsin's appeal for resistance, and banned the Communist Party from government bodies. When the coup collapsed, the power of the local Communist Party was broken.[58]

Turkmenistan was relatively peaceful, with some demands centered around environmental issues, the language question, and the need to reexamine history. Its land is 90 percent desert while its capital, Ashkhabad, is a Russified oasis. Annette Bohr notes that the Turkmen "constitute more of a tribal confederation than a modern nation."[59] Not only is the level of social and economic development low, but the intelligentsia is small and finds it difficult to articulate the interests of Turkmen society or mobilize the population. Further, the republic was desperately dependent on Moscow for subsidies and for imports of food and textiles.[60]

Central Asian nationalism was fed by the belief that the area had been exploited economically by the Soviet Union, which had used it as a source of cotton, gold, and oil without providing fair compensation. In reality, these areas were dependent upon the center for financial assistance. In 1991, the union subsidized between 20 and 45 percent of each republic's government spending.[61]

## THE SLAVIC CORE

Byelorussia, the most Russified nationality, was assumed to have little sense of national consciousness. During the 1980s Byelorussia became one of the leading economic growth regions of the Soviet Union, with a concomitant improvement in the standard of living. As the economic situation improved, it was accompanied by a rise in nationalism. Informal groups sprang up advocating increased use of the Byelorussian language and strengthening of its culture. The Chernobyl explosion activated environmental concerns, and there was a movement to uncover the crimes of the Stalin era, in particular the uncovering of mass graves. When an independent youth movement tried to arrange a conference in Minsk in January 1989, its plans were obstructed. It then moved to Vilnius, where it was welcomed by Sajudis. This contact radicalized the Byelorussian movement. In February 1989, the Renewal Byelorussian Popular Front for Perestroika, a confederation of informal organizations, staged a rally in Minsk with 50,000 in attendance.[62] Byelorussian ethnic consciousness was spurred by modernization, growing ethnic awareness, and a desire to emulate other republics. In 1990, its Supreme Soviet declared sovereignty and claimed its laws supreme over union laws.

Ukraine, the second most important republic with 52 million people, produced one-quarter of the union's food and one-third of its industrial products. The Chernobyl disaster raised fears about environmental disaster and raised questions about the model of industrial development and political control that had permitted the tragedy to occur. Soon a large number of informal groups began pressing cultural, political, and ecological issues. Intellectuals questioned whether the Ukrainian famine of 1932–33 might have been artificially created. Demands came for publication of banned literary works and the rehabilitation of writers. A major concern was for the future of the Ukrainian language. An amnesty of political prisoners in 1987 led to the return to the Ukraine of well-known dissidents, who then encouraged nationalist activities. The monopolization of the celebration of the millennium of the Christianization of Kievan Rus by the Russian Orthodox church fed Ukrainian nationalism. The Ukrainian Helsinki Union, reestablished in 1988, called for transformation of the Soviet Union into a confederation of independent states.[63] Rukh, the Popular Movement of the Ukraine for Perestroika, was formed in November 1988. At its inaugural Congress in September 1989, Rukh called for greater political and economic autonomy from Moscow, the ouster of the long-term party boss Shcherbitsky, and the revival of Ukrainian language and culture.

Nationalism in the Ukraine could not be ignored. Gorbachev flew to the Ukraine on September 28. Shcherbitsky, the longtime leader, was replaced by his deputy, Vladimir Ivashko, a cautious pragmatist who had called for tougher measures to suppress nationalism. Although Rukh sought full sovereignty of Ukraine, including eventual secession, it was much more cautious than Sajudis in Lithuania. Nationalist sentiments were far stronger in the western Ukraine than in the Russified eastern part, and it was questionable whether ordinary citizens shared the strong sentiments for independence.[64] Furthermore, unlike the Baltics or Transcaucasia, the Ukraine was part of the Slavic heartland. It seemed inconceivable that Gorbachev would allow the secession of the Ukraine. Nevertheless, in March 1990, Rukh and its allies won about one-quarter of the seats in the election to the Ukrainian Supreme Soviet. The Supreme Soviet then declared Ukraine sovereign and voted to create its own armed forces, remain neutral in foreign affairs, end deployment of Ukrainian troops outside the Ukraine, and demand their recall. It claimed complete control over its industry, agriculture, and natural resources.[65]

## MOLDAVIA

Moldavians, the most rural and least developed of the European republics, began to express nationalist demands in mid-1988. The overwhelming majority of the population is Romanian, speaks Romanian, and considers itself Romanian. Initially, Moldavians focused on cultural issues, reasserting their ethnic identity as Romanians. The Moldavian popular front, created in January 1989, called for the establishment of Moldavian as the official language of the republic and the restoration of the Latin alphabet, restrictions on immigration, restoration of the pre–World War II flag, recognition of the Moldavian Orthodox church, a change in leaders, and full sovereignty. The reintroduction of the Latin alphabet was accepted, but adoption of Romanian as the state language was rejected on the basis that the republic was multinational. The Romanian flag began to appear as a symbol of dissent. On November 7, 1989, a mass demonstration in Kishinev blocked the traditional Revolution Day parade, and the party first secretary was chased from the reviewing stand. The demonstrations were finally dispersed forcibly.[66] In the aftermath, Moldavian was recognized as the official language. The popular front demanded reinterpretation of Moldavian history, particularly the secret protocols to the Nazi-Soviet Pact, the incorporation of Moldavia into the Soviet Union, and the treatment of Moldavians under Soviet rule.[67] In southern Moldavia the Gagauz, a Turkish minority, declared its own republic in December 1989, and in eastern Moldavia 300,000 Russians and Ukrainians declared establishment of an independent Dniester republic.

As long as Nicolae Ceaucescu was in power in Romania, Moldavians had no desire to come under Romania's control. After Ceaucescu was forced out in December 1989, Moldavians began to push either for independence or for unification with Romania. In the spring of 1990, border crossings into Romania became common. In the summer of 1990, Moldavia declared sovereignty, with control over all its land and resources. The name was changed to Moldova.

## THE DISSOLUTION OF THE SOVIET UNION

As the economy worsened and ethnic conflicts flared, Gorbachev was subjected to attacks from Right and Left, and it became increasingly difficult to hold the Soviet Union together. Gorbachev's decrees were ignored by republics that were asserting sovereignty over all natural resources on their territories. Every republic except Kirghizia declared some form of self-rule. Dozens of ethnic enclaves claimed sovereignty. All republics except Lithuania were prepared to sign the Shatalin 500-day plan which would have created an economic commonwealth and given almost complete economic independence to the republics. Gorbachev backed away, unwilling to surrender that much power to the republics. It would not be long before Gorbachev would regret not making the concessions at this juncture, although it is questionable if any such commonwealth could have survived.

Although Gorbachev was granted emergency economic powers, this failed to resolve the question of the distribution of power between the center and the republics. His demands that republics fulfill the central economic plan's contracts for delivery of goods and services were countermanded by republic leaders. Republics refused to enforce decrees they did not approve. On November 17, Gorbachev announced a new government structure in which the Federation Council, made up of the leaders of the fifteen republics, would become the country's chief executive agency subordinate to the president. Gorbachev, assisted by a new Security Council, would oversee the army, the police, and the KGB, and a network of presidential representatives around the country would enforce his orders. Gorbachev proposed that the new scheme remain in force until a new union treaty was enacted. The Baltic republics and Georgia immediately asserted they would refuse to participate in the Federation Council. Yeltsin, too, rejected the plan, asserting that Russia's laws had precedence over Soviet laws. He insisted on recognition of the full sovereignty of the republics. Instead of a union treaty, he called for a union of sovereign states.[68]

Gorbachev, insisting that the union could not be divided, denounced Yeltsin's views and outlined a union treaty that would allow republics the right of self-determination and secession, but only after a process of referendum, consensus, and approval. He again asserted that allowing republics to secede could mean bloodshed. The debate over the future of the union continued, but none of the republics supported Gorbachev's Union of Sovereign Soviet Republics. Bargaining centered on ownership of natural resources, taxes, and control over the army and police. The three Baltic republics, Georgia, and Moldavia declared they would not sign any union treaty. Lithuania refused even to send a delegation to the Congress of People's

Deputies, which was debating the future of the country. Armenia and Azerbaijan, embittered by their recent experiences with Moscow, were reluctant to endorse Gorbachev's proposals. Ukrainian leaders supported a union treaty but were hesitant because of nationalist sentiment, particularly in the western Ukraine. The Asian republics and Byelorussia seemed likely to go along but maneuvered to see what they could gain from the bargaining process. Russia was the key. Although popular support was strong in Russia for the maintenance of the union, Yeltsin had gone around the center by signing two-way agreements with other republics. In an effort to bypass uncooperative leaders, Gorbachev demanded a popular referendum in every republic on the concept of a union treaty. The struggle pitted the immensely popular Yeltsin against the increasingly unpopular Gorbachev.[69]

In the winter of 1990–91, faced with the breakdown of the economic and political ties that bound the republics into a common union, Gorbachev shifted to the Right. On January 10, he called on Lithuania to end its defiance of Soviet rule. The army and KGB, using a Committee for National Salvation, tried to overthrow the Lithuanian government. Soviet troops, plowing through a crowd of civilians, seized the Vilnius radio and television center on January 13. Fifteen civilians were killed and more than one hundred were wounded. The Lithuanian government blockaded itself inside the parliament building. On January 16, hundreds of thousands of mourners came out into the streets of Vilnius. Yeltsin sent representatives and parliamentary deputies came from Latvia, Estonia, Georgia, Armenia, Azerbaijan, and the Ukraine to show support for the Landsbergis government.[70]

Over 100,000 protesters demonstrated in Moscow in opposition to the military crackdown in Lithuania; Gorbachev said he was unaware of the attack until it was over but made no effort to show disapproval. Yeltsin flew to Riga and denounced the decision to use force. He signed mutual assistance agreements between Russia and the three Baltic republics.[71] When, on January 20, Soviet Black Berets attacked and took over the Ministry of the Interior building in Riga, Latvia, killing four, Gorbachev said he knew nothing about it and called for an investigation. Gorbachev lacked the stomach to use the force that would have been necessary to restore central control. Stalin would not have hesitated, but neither would Khrushchev or Brezhnev. Gorbachev had undermined belief in the ideology and the party, and without that legitimacy he could no longer justify the use of force to hold the system together. To use force without the legitimation of the ideology and the party meant reliance on naked brutality alone. This he could not do. The force that was used created political martyrs, strengthened the determination of those republics committed to secession, and drove others to seek greater independence. The summit meeting between the United States and the Soviet Union was postponed.

Gorbachev scheduled a March 17 nationwide referendum on continuing the Soviet Union in a renewed democratic form. The citizens voted either yes or no to the question "Do you support the preservation of the union as a renewed federation of sovereign republics in which the rights of a person of any nationality are fully guaranteed?" Moldavia, the three Baltic republics, Georgia, and Armenia did not participate. Over 77 percent of the population supported the preservation of some kind of union. The vote, however, did not resolve the confrontations between the center and the increasingly assertive republics.

Gorbachev presented a revised treaty for a Union of Sovereign Republics that increased the authority of the republics while the center retained control over defense, security, foreign policy, and foreign economic activities. It was promptly attacked by Yeltsin.[72] Toward the end of April 1991, Gorbachev began to move closer to reformers as he came under increasing attack from conservatives. He met with the leaders of nine republics (the three Slavic republics, the five Central Asian republics, and Azerbaijan) in an attempt to create a framework for a loose federation.[73] On July 24, Gorbachev announced that an agreement had been reached with the nine on a draft treaty for a decentralized union.[74] The leaders of republics were to sign the new union treaty on August 20.

The organizers of the putsch of August 19, 1991, believed they had to act to prevent the signing of the treaty, which they felt spelled the end of the Soviet Union. The State Emergency Committee put Gorbachev under house arrest in the Crimea and announced that his responsibilities were being assumed by Vice President Yanaev. The committee was composed of the most formidable power holders in the Soviet Union, including Defense Minister Yazov, KGB Chairman Kryuchkov, Interior Minister Pugo, Prime Minister Pavlov, Vice President Yanaev, and three others. All were men who had been trusted by Gorbachev. They announced that the country had become ungovernable, extremist forces were attempting to break up the state, and the economy was in crisis. They promised to restore the greatness of the Soviet Union. What became clear was that they were unable to command the loyalty of the Soviet people or of considerable elements of the armed forces. Geoffrey Hosking points out that the tanks "moved in such a half-hearted manner that a barricade of trolleybuses and a handful of gasoline bombs were sufficient to restrain them."[75] The coup collapsed in three days.

Not only were the plotters unable to take power, but their attempt to do so hastened the dissolution of the union. Yeltsin became the hero and the dominating political figure. Although Gorbachev initially refused to hold the Communist Party responsible for the putsch and asserted his intention to remain as party leader, he owed his rescue to Yeltsin and his allies. Power had clearly shifted to Yeltsin, who shut down the Communist Party in Russia and forced Gorbachev to replace his cabinet with appointees loyal to Yeltsin. Anticommunist sentiment spread as it became clear that the top organs of the party had not opposed the coup. On August 24, Gorbachev resigned as head of the Communist Party, disbanded its leadership, and banned the party from any role in governing the country. As Yeltsin seemed to be moving into a power vacuum, assuming many of the powers and functions of the center, other republics became alarmed.[76] Georgia and the three Baltic republics had previously declared independence. Now Ukraine, Byelorussia, Moldavia, and even the Central Asian republics declared their independence. The Ukrainian declaration on August 24 was most significant, since it was clear there could be no agreement on a confederation without Ukraine.

In response to the Ukrainian declaration, Yeltsin threatened to review borders of any republic besides the Baltics that seceded. Both Ukraine and Kazakhstan reacted with furor, which was calmed only with great difficulty.[77] Agreement was reached in early September by eleven of the twelve remaining republics to set up a transitional government controlled by the republics, which would try to work out a loose confederation. When the Congress of People's Deputies approved the new arrangement, it acknowledged the end of central authority. Although Gorbachev was assigned a coordinating role, it was without any real power. The new ruling council recognized the independence of the three Baltic states. Both Gorbachev and Yeltsin now tried to persuade the republics that it was in their interests to form a unified economic sphere. A majority of the republics reached agreement on a loose economic community, but Ukraine refused to sign.[78] Nine republics signed the agreement in November, but after Yeltsin moved to take control over Russia's oil, diamonds, gold, and other precious metals and took over the Soviet Foreign Ministry and all Soviet embassies abroad, republics refused to initial a new union treaty. Following a December 1 Ukrainian referendum in which more than 90 percent voted in support of independence, Russia promptly recognized Ukrainian independence.

On December 8, the leaders of the three Slavic republics met in Minsk, where they agreed to form a Commonwealth of Independent States open to all members of the former Soviet Union. Gorbachev was, in essence, stripped of his authority. Although Gorbachev declared the Slavic leaders' action illegal and dangerous, they carried out a successful, peaceful coup.[79] On December 21 all of the republics except the Baltic states and Georgia joined in the loose arrangement, and all agreed that the Soviet Union had ceased to exist. On December 25 Gorbachev resigned as president. The next day the Supreme Soviet of the USSR declared an end to the union. Yeltsin took over Gorbachev's office in the Kremlin. The failed coup of August sped up the dissolution of the Soviet Union, but the process had already been set in motion. There was a fundamental incompatibility between retention of the empire and the reforms that Gorbachev had initiated. *Glasnost*, market reform, and democratization had undermined the legitimacy of the communist system and the Soviet empire. Gorbachev permitted popular fronts to displace the Communist Party, he pulled back centralized state power, and he was reluctant to use force to maintain the regime. The old bases of legitimacy had been destroyed, but new ones that could hold the country together had not been created. The leaders of the coup pictured themselves as patriots trying to rally the country to hold the union together. When the country failed to respond, even the leaders of the coup proved irresolute, unwilling to use the necessary force.

## NOTES

1. Bohdan Nahaylo and Victor Swoboda, *Soviet Disunion* (New York: Free Press, 1990), 236.

2. David F. Roth, Paul V. Warwick, and David W. Paul, *Comparative Politics: Diverse States in an Interdependent World* (New York: Harper and Row, 1989), 32.

3. Philip G. Roeder, "Soviet Federalism and Ethnic Mobilization," in *The Soviet Nationality Reader*, ed. Rachel Denber (Boulder, Colo.: Westview Press, 1992), 148–55.

4. Ibid., 149.

5. Ibid., 156–70. The quotation is from 169.

6. Leon P. Baradat, *Soviet Political Society*, 3d ed. (Englewood Cliffs, N.J.: Prentice-Hall, 1992), 331.

7. Gabriel Almond and G. Bingham Powell, Jr., *Comparative Politics Today*, 5th ed. (New York: HarperCollins, 1992), 363–64.

8. Nahaylo and Swoboda, *Soviet Disunion*, 248–49.

9. Martha Brill Olcott, "*Perestroyka* in Kazakhstan," *Problems of Communism* 39 (July-August 1990): 66–67.

10. Nahaylo and Swoboda, *Soviet Disunion*, 276–79.

11. *New York Times*, June 21, 1988.

12. Although 80 percent of the population of Lithuania were Lithuanians, only 62 percent of Estonia's population were Estonians, and 51 percent of Latvia's population were native Latvians.

13. *New York Times*, October 2, 1988.

14. Graham Smith, "Latvians," in *The Nationalities Question in the Soviet Union*, ed. Graham Smith (New York: Longman, 1990), 64–65.

15. V. Stanley Vardys, "Lithuanian National Politics," in *The Soviet Nationality Reader*, ed. Denber, 460–61.

16. Ibid., 461–64.

17. Nahaylo and Swoboda, *Soviet Disunion*, 317.

18. *New York Times*, March 10, 1989.

19. Hedrick Smith, *The New Russians* (New York: Avon Books, 1991), 353–62.

20. For a description of the mood in Estonia in the summer of 1989, see Barbara B. Green, "Moscow and Tallinn Under Gorbachev," *The Gamut: A Journal of Ideas and Information* 28 (Winter 1989): 51–64.

21. *New York Times*, August 27, 1989.

22. *New York Times*, December 21, 1989.

23. *New York Times*, January 12, 1990.

24. *New York Times*, March 12, 1990.

25. *New York Times*, April 14, 1990.

26. Ibid.

27. *New York Times*, June 30, 1990.

28. Richard Sakwa, *Gorbachev and His Reforms 1985–1990* (New York: Prentice-Hall, 1990), 234–35.

29. Robert Cullen, "A Reporter at Large: Roots," *The New Yorker*, April 15, 1991, 55.

30. Ronald Grigor Suny, "Nationalism and Democracy in Gorbachev's Soviet Union: The Case of Karabagh," in *The Soviet Nationality Reader*, ed. Denber, 486.

31. Cullen, "A Reporter At Large," 67.

32. Suny, "Nationalism and Democracy," 495.

33. *New York Times*, September 5, 1988.

34. Cullen, "A Reporter at Large," 68.

35. *New York Times*, December 12, 21, 1988.

36. Cullen, "A Reporter at Large," 68.

37. Ibid., 69.

38. Ibid., 70.

39. *New York Times*, February 17, 1990.

40. Cullen, "A Reporter at Large," 72–73.

41. Robert Parsons, "Georgians," in *The Nationalities Question in The Soviet Union*, ed. Smith, 189–91.

42. *New York Times*, April 9, 1990.

43. Baradat, *Soviet Political Society*, 343; Stephen White, *Gorbachev and After* (Cambridge: Cambridge University Press, 1991), 165.

44. White, *Gorbachev and After*, 165.

45. Four of the republics speak Turkic languages: Uzbekistan, Kazakhstan, Kirghizia, and Turkmenistan. The fifth, Tajikistan, speaks Persian.

46. Zvi Gitelman, "Nations, Republics and Commonwealth," in *Developments in Soviet & Post-Soviet Politics*, ed. Stephen White, Alex Pravda, and Zvi Gitelman (Durham, N.C.: Duke University Press, 1992), 138–41.

47. The Islamic Renaissance Party or IRP was initially banned by all five Central Asian republics. Uzbekistan outlawed all religious parties and clergy were not permitted to run for parliament. See Robin Wright, "Report from Turkestan," *The New Yorker*, April 6, 1992, 57.

48. *The Economist*, December 26, 1992, 44–46.

49. Ingvar Svanberg, "Kazakhs," in *The Nationalities Question*, ed. Smith, 206–10.

50. *New York Times*, August 27, 1989.

51. Shirin Akiner, "Uzbeks," in *The Nationalities Question*, ed. Smith, 220.

52. David Remnick, "Dons of the Don," *The New York Review of Books*, July 16, 1992, 47–48.

53. The Meskhetians, a Turkic people, were forcibly relocated to Central Asia from Georgia in 1944.

54. Smith, *The New Russians*, 318.

55. John Payne, "Tadzhiks," in *The Nationalities Question*, ed. Graham Smith, 267–71.

56. Baradat, *Soviet Political Society*, 347–48; Wright, "Report from Turkestan," 67.

57. Simon Crisp, "Kirgiz," in *The Nationalities Question*, ed. Smith, 250–54.

58. *The Economist*, October 19, 1991; Wright, "Report from Turkestan," 69–70.

59. Annette Bohr, "Turkmen," in *The Nationalities Question*, ed. Smith, 228–29.

60. Ibid., 229–30.

61. *The Economist*, December 26, 1992, 45.

62. Ralph S. Clem, "Belorussians," in *The Nationalities Question*, ed. Smith, 115–20.

63. Peter J. S. Duncan, "Ukrainians," in *The Nationalities Question*, ed. Smith, 100–105.

64. *New York Times,* September 29, 1989.

65. Baradat, *Soviet Political Society,* 349.

66. Ibid., 342–43.

67. Jonathan Eyal, "Moldavians," in *The Nationalities Question*, ed. Smith, 135–36.

68. *New York Times,* November 18, 20, 1990.

69. *New York Times,* November 24; December 19, 1990.

70. *New York Times,* January 17, 1991.

71. Robert G. Kaiser, *Why Gorbachev Happened* (New York: Touchstone, 1992), 396.

72. *New York Times,* March 10, 1991.

73. *New York Times,* April 25, 1991.

74. *New York Times,* July 25, 1991.

75. Geoffrey Hosking, "The Roots of Dissolution," *The New York Review of Books,* January 16, 1992, 34.

76. *New York Times,* August 27, 1991.

77. Ibid.

78. *New York Times,* October 18, 1991.

79. *New York Times,* December 10, 1991.

*Chapter 13*

# TRANSFORMATION OR COLLAPSE I: CONTROL OVER THE CENTER

The crucial question is whether Russia is in the process of transformation to a democratic or dictatorial political system or whether it is destined to collapse into a new time of troubles, with a vacuum of power at the center and anarchy sweeping the country. Any effective government must, at a minimum, be able to protect the country from external aggression, provide internal order, and create the conditions necessary for citizens to provide for themselves and their families. Russians traditionally fear centralism and autocracy, but they fear the consequences of anarchy and chaos more. The danger of a return to a Hobbesian state of nature haunts Russians who fear it may be the only alternative to autocratic government. Like the Bolsheviks, the present regime has attempted a fundamental alteration in the nature of both the economic and political systems. The Bolshevik revolution had both the advantage and disadvantage of being a genuine revolution in the sense that the institutions and personnel of the old regime were totally discredited and swept aside. It had to begin at the beginning and create new institutions. The collapse of the Soviet system was fundamentally different.

The failure of the coup led to the collapse of the Communist Party and the loss of the outer empire, the republics of the Soviet Union. Yeltsin, the first democratically elected president in Russian history, "won his fantastic grudge match with . . . Gorbachev, and used . . . [the] coup to pull the state out from underneath him."[1] Gorbachev resigned as president on December 25. Yeltsin immediately moved into the Kremlin, taking over his offices and much of his power. The Soviet Union was officially dissolved on December 31, 1991. Yeltsin had the advantage of enormous popularity and a euphoria at the end of communism, but there were also a sense of humiliation at the loss of empire and a bewilderment at the sudden collapse.[2] Moreover, a national consensus on the future was lacking. It was questionable whether Yeltsin could institutionalize his popularity and create a consensus in favor of political democracy and economic reform. Unlike previous rulers, he was unable to gather his own team to carry out his policies.

The caving in of the Soviet Empire did not sweep aside the old institutions and personnel. The work of creating new social, political, and economic systems would have to be undertaken while the old systems were lingering on. The regime was faced with the problem of instituting change amid continuity. The beneficiaries of the old regime, the *nomenklatura*, use their preferred positions to seize advantageous positions in the new by privatizing state property that they previously managed. All those who have something to gain from the preservation of the old regime dig in their heels and do what they can to prevent change.

## THE POLITICAL STRUCTURE

An important limitation on the power of Yeltsin to act is the fact that he has had to operate within the scope of the Soviet-era constitution. Although it was amended more than 300 times since mid-1991, its second article still proclaims, "All power to the soviets." The Congress is defined as the "supreme form of state power." Only the Congress can legally dissolve itself or approve a new constitution. The legitimacy of the constitution itself was in question. At the end of February 1993, Yeltsin declared, "I did not swear my oath to such a constitution."[3] Yeltsin stakes his legitimacy on the people, on the fact that he is the first democratically elected leader in a thousand years of Russian history. His claim to a popular mandate was reinforced by the April 1993 referendum in which he won a clear majority, but the Congress argued that this vote conferred no legal powers on Yeltsin and represented only about 35 percent of the eligible voters. Congress stakes its legitimacy on the constitution. Until a new constitution can be drafted and approved, Russia struggles on with no agreed-upon source of legitimacy, with no agreement on the justification of the right to rule. In August 1991, Yeltsin had such overwhelming popularity that he would have been able to dictate the basic principles of a new constitutional order, but the old structures remained. The April 25, 1993, referendum demonstrated public impatience with the legislature and support of presidential powers, strengthening Yeltsin's ability to push for a new constitution. However, fundamental disagreement on the constitutional structure was not resolved by the voters. Yeltsin wants a strong presidential system with a weak legislature. The legislature wants a European-style parliamentary system, with the president relegated to a largely ceremonial role. Although the hand-picked delegates of the Constitutional Assembly called by Yeltsin in the summer of 1993 approved Yeltsin's draft of a new constitution, the Congress insists that it alone is empowered to change the constitution.

Yeltsin's office of the presidency had been grafted onto the preexisting political structure. Under the patched-together system, the president is not in charge of day-to-day management: this is the job of the prime minister, who is nominated by the president but confirmed by the Supreme Soviet. The president can veto a law passed by the Supreme Soviet, but his veto can be overturned by a simple majority. He can declare martial law, but the Supreme Soviet must confirm it within twenty-four hours. Despite the fact that the president does not have the power to dissolve the parliament, political advisers to Yeltsin now argue that he should have dissolved it and called a new election after the failed coup. Because of his extraordinary popularity at the time, he could have done so and avoided being saddled with a parliament opposed to the main lines of his policy.[4] Yeltsin's advisers argued that the parliament lacks legitimacy because it was elected while the Soviet system still existed. But the problem is that Yeltsin, too, was elected under the old regime. The questions in the April 1993 referendum calling for new elections for the legislature and the presidency both failed to get the required majority of all eligible voters. Although Yeltsin was strengthened by the referendum while the legislature was weakened, all institutions still face a crisis of legitimacy.

Much of the power of Yeltsin's presidency was derived from emergency powers granted by the Russian Congress of People's Deputies in November 1991 that formally expired on December 1, 1992. After Yeltsin continued to issue decrees, the Congress voted in March 1993 to remove these powers. Under these special powers, Yeltsin could appoint all ministers except the prime minister without parliamentary approval. His use of decree power to push his policies led opponents to call him "Tsar Boris," but these decrees had force only as long as there was no law on the subject. Those faced with a decree to which they objected often failed to implement it in the hope that a law would soon supersede it. One consequence was that Yeltsin, like Gorbachev before him, found many of his decrees ignored.[5]

Rutskoi, a former air force colonel and Afghan war hero, was elected vice president on a joint ticket with Yeltsin in June 1991. As a supporter of Yeltsin, Rutskoi helped organize the defense of the White House in August 1991. A moderate conservative, he is a strong critic of shock therapy, which he labeled "economic genocide." He prefers a mixed economy with strong social protection. Rutskoi strongly backs the interests of Russians living in former Soviet republics. He opposed Yeltsin's call for a referendum and broke decisively with Yeltsin at the end of March 1993, when Yeltsin declared emergency rule. He is one of the most influential and popular leaders in Russia and the clearest alternative to Yeltsin.[6]

Yeltsin served as his own prime minister at first. Then, in order to put himself in a position above politics, able to criticize other actors and mediate among them, Yeltsin appointed Yegor Gaidar as acting prime minister in June 1992. The government is primarily responsible for the economy, although the central bank, which is legally responsible to parliament, conducts monetary policy on behalf of the government. It is not the prime minister but the president who nominates members of the government. The cabinet includes the ministers of defense and security, but they report to the prime minister only on questions of finance and procedure. On questions of defense and security they report directly to the president.[7] After the December Congress of People's Deputies, Gaidar was replaced by the more conservative Viktor Chernomyrdin. In March, in an effort to draw a wedge between the president and the prime minister and to bring the government under legislative direction, the Congress made concessions to the Cabinet. The government was given power to initiate legislation. It was agreed that several key financial officials, including the heads of the Central Bank, the Federal Property Fund, and the Pension Fund, would sit on the Cabinet, but they would remain responsible to parliament.[8] Chernomyrdin and the Cabinet nevertheless remained loyal to Yeltsin.

The parliament was chosen in a multicandidate election in the spring of 1990, six weeks after the end of the Communist Party monopoly. Under the system then in effect, voters elected a thousand-person-plus Congress of People's Deputies to set broad lines of policy. The Congress, which was to meet at least twice a year, named a 252-member bicameral standing legislature, the Supreme Soviet. The Congress originally provided the political base for Yeltsin by electing him its chairman by a slim margin. Although at the time of the election 86 percent were Communist Party members, many were from the reform wing and were not chosen as party representatives. Most were supporters of Yeltsin.[9] With the dissolution of the Communist Party, they emerged with no party loyalties, consistent positions, or party discipline. Instead, they formed a broad array of loose alliances and endlessly shifting factions. Frequently attacked by economic reformers as a bastion of old *apparatchiki* and directors from the military-industrial complex, the parliament was the focus of democratic resistance to the coup in 1991. By 1992, however, Russian politics was characterized by endless battles between the executive and the legislature. Many deputies were suspicious of reform, ignorant of democratic procedures, noisy and often crude, and disdainful of intellectuals. Although less friendly to the United States than Yeltsin's supporters, most were not anti-American. Only 20 percent of deputies regularly supported Yeltsin, 35 percent were hard-line nationalists, and the rest, called the "swamp," vacillated.[10]

After Yeltsin was elected president in June 1991, he backed Ruslan Khasbulatov as speaker of the parliament, the position he was vacating. During Yeltsin's heroic stand against the coup, Khasbulatov stood by his side. Khasbulatov, a Chechen who had no major Communist Party background, now lives in Brezhnev's former apartment and has appropriated much of the old Central Committee staff. The unpopularity of Yeltsin's economic policies soon inspired Khasbulatov to attack those changes. As speaker, he has the power to approve funds for foreign junkets, apartments, and other perks. He soon turned the position into a power base. Parliament's control over the Central Bank gives him significant power and has enabled him to work at cross-purposes with the government. He took advantage of the disorganization of parliament to manipulate procedures and ram votes through.[11] Although he has been accused frequently of grabbing for Yeltsin's powers, the lack of constitutional clarity as to the division of powers makes it inevitable that institutions will engage in a struggle for power.

Yeltsin tried to get around what he perceived as parliamentary obstructionism by creating an extra-governmental agency, the Security Council, empowered to supervise defense, security, the police, and foreign policy. The council, which meets almost daily, can make decisions on anything that affects Russia's vital interests, which gives it wide scope. In late November 1992, the six voting members included four reformers, but Yuri Skokov, named chief of staff, was a former defense factory director and opposed radical economic reform.[12] In February 1993, Yeltsin created an Interdepartmental Security Council Foreign Policy Commission, controlled by Skokov, to coordinate the activities of all ministries responsible for external security.[13] In May, Yeltsin dismissed Skokov.

The Russian Constitutional Court, chaired by Valery Zorkin, is the first independent judiciary in Russian history. Unlike the rest of the court system, the Constitutional Court is not under the Ministry of Justice. Established by the Russian legislature in July 1991 at Yeltsin's urging, the court was charged with protecting the constitutional order and strengthening the rule of law. Although the special law established a court of fifteen justices to be elected by the Congress, the Congress was able to gather only a simple majority to approve thirteen justices in October 1991. The justices, who serve until mandatory retirement at age sixty-five, are not permitted to engage in political activity. In what was hailed as an important step toward establishing the rule of law, the court issued a balanced decision when it had to judge the constitutionality of Yeltsin's ban on the Communist Party and the seizure of the party's assets. It ruled against his plan to merge the KGB and the Interior Ministry and ruled that his ban on the National Salvation Front was illegal. Since the court was charged with upholding the constitution that Yeltsin declared he was no longer bound by, a clash between the two was inevitable.[14]

## POLITICAL PARTIES

The timing of the coup and the collapse of Soviet government were too much of a surprise for Yeltsin and his supporters to be able to plan and prepare for the future. The dissolution of the Communist Party left a vacuum, but there were no organized political parties prepared to fill that vacuum and provide the power base necessary to support the leadership. Yeltsin's supporters were skilled in criticizing power, but unpracticed in using power. A functioning multiparty democracy requires real political parties with branches in cities and towns and villages across the country, with stable memberships, structure, and discipline. In contrast, Russia's parties are often called "taxicab" parties because there is room for only three to four people who hop in and out for purposes of their own while the party drives around in circles.[15] Three broad groupings can be discerned.

## The Democrats

Like Charles de Gaulle, Yeltsin initially wanted to establish himself above parties, as a republican king.[16] Democratic Russia, the loose bloc of liberals and reformers that brought Yeltsin to power, was a potent force in 1991, but it soon dwindled and fragmented. Its members had little in common except their opposition to communism and support of Yeltsin. Once Yeltsin was in power, differences came to the fore. Although all supported a transition to a free market, they differed in emphasis. Many liberal and intellectuals abandoned Yeltsin, while others sought to push their own economic advantage. On the eve of the Seventh Congress of People's Deputies in December 1992, Yeltsin called on his supporters to set up a "presidential party" based on Democratic Russia to back reform. Many of its more radical adherents lost their enthusiasm for Yeltsin after what they perceived as his betrayal of Gaidar at the Congress. With its loss of popularity and support, it was questionable whether it could be fashioned into a party able to provide Yeltsin with an adequate political base. The remnant of Democratic Russia is joined on the democratic wing of parliament by a coalition of forty or so groups called Democratic Choice, an alliance formed to support radical economic reform. The Radical Democrats, primarily younger liberals, are an important party in the bloc.[17] The Democrats' greatest support comes from the young, urban, self-employed who have everything to gain from a free market system. The popular endorsement of Yeltsin and his economic policies in the April referendum should serve to galvanize the reformers, who are now confident that they can win in a free election.

## The Center

Civic Union, which controls the largest bloc of seats in parliament, represents the center ground of politics. Its leaders call for a gradual transition to a market economy and support government intervention to halt the decline in industrial production.[18] It was launched on June 21, 1992, by three influential politicians: Rutskoi, the vice president; Arkady Volsky, the chairman of an organization of industrial managers; and Travkin, the leader of the country's largest and best-organized political party.

Travkin's Russian Democratic Party broke with Democratic Russia in early 1992 and found itself isolated. Although with 50,000 activists it was Russia's largest party, it was too small to have any real influence on politics on its own. Rutskoi's People's Party of Free Russia, formed out of the reformist wing of the Russian Communist Party, has good organization and a great deal of local power. Volsky is chairman of the Union of Entrepreneurs of Russia, a lobby for managers of state enterprises whose members account for two-thirds of Russia's industrial output. He organized a party called Renewal and then proposed that Travkin and Rutskoi join him in a bloc. Renewal provided Civic Union with funds and three powerful government ministers.[19] Anders Aslund, the Swedish economic adviser to the government, says, "It is the clever Mr. Volsky who dictates Civic Union policies."[20]

### The Reactionaries

Angry communists and right-wing nationalists are still a visible presence, even in Moscow and St. Petersburg. Reds and Browns have demonstrated to oppose higher prices, denounce the collapse of the Soviet Union, and protest Yeltsin's sell-out to the West. The Reds are communist and neocommunist groups demanding the restoration of the Soviet Union and the reversal of economic reforms. They include the Working Peoples Socialist Party, the Communist Party, and the Russian Communist Workers Party. After the ban on the Communist Party was lifted, it organized a demonstration of 20,000 on the streets of Moscow on February 23, 1993. The Browns are right-wing nationalists who share their antipathy for democracy but support private property. The communist far Left and the nationalist far Right make common cause in their nostalgia for strength and order. They share a sense of wounded nationalism and hostility to liberal democracy and open societies. Some have called for restoration of the boundaries of the Soviet Union, by force if necessary. They opposed support of the United States on Iraq and have called for support of Serbia.[21]

The National Salvation Front, a new alliance of communists, fascists, and extreme nationalists, met on October 24, 1992, to demand an end to the "plundering of Moscow by the Jews" and the ousting of "the capitalist louts" in charge of the government. Paramilitary guards in black shirts and jackboots flanked the crowd. Three days later, Yeltsin banned the National Salvation Front on the ground that it had called for the overthrow of the government by illegal means and that it was a danger to civil order. The front ignored the decree, and its leaders demonstratively visited Saddam Hussein, whom they regard as a maligned ally.[22] The Constitutional Court ruled that Yeltsin's ban was illegal.

Russian Unity is a coalition of tough communists and nationalists who oppose Yeltsin. Their goals include restoring socialism and re-creating a powerful state. Its major factions include the "Russia" Party led by Sergei Baburin, a former law professor and a vehement critic of Yeltsin; Civic Society (not to be confused with Civic Union); Fatherland, which includes several high-ranking military and KGB officers; the Agrarian Union, which represents state farm officials; and Communists of Russia, one of several communist groups. Many deputies in Russian Unity are also in the National Salvation Front.[23] On February 10, 1993, a member of Baburin's Russia Party was elected to run one of the two chambers of the Supreme Soviet.[24]

There is some worry that the Red-Brown groups might be a kernel for fascism, winning the support of Russians frustrated by a collapsing economy and rising social disorder. But the creation of Civic Union has strengthened democratic forces by providing a viable in-system alternative that attracts respectable elements dissatisfied with government policy.[25]

Although there are no legal restrictions on parties, until now there has been little incentive for politicians to join one since ministers need not be party members. Civic Union has already announced that it will hold its government ministers accountable to the party that put them there. Their effort to make ministerial careers dependent upon party loyalty is an important step in the development of political parties.[26] Elections will be a catalyst toward the formation of a three-coalition or three-party system.

## LAWLESSNESS

"In a society long accustomed to predictability . . . many ordinary Russians have an ominous sense of life spinning out of control. Crime, corruption, wild inflation and general lawlessness have left many feeling helpless, hopeless and bewildered."[27] With the disintegration of central authority, many Russians fear a Hobbesian war of all against all. Increasing numbers are calling for a strong hand, a Hobbesian sovereign, to restore order.

The crime rate has moved steadily higher: the 1991 rate was up 18 percent; the 1992 rate was up another 30 percent.[28] Every new entrepreneur is visited by armed racketeers specializing in extortion who threaten devastating consequences if their security services are refused. Organized gangs armed with machine guns, hand grenades, and hand-held rocket launchers present a serious challenge to authority. Gang violence is now common. Car hijackings, open prostitution, arms and drug traffic, kidnappings, shoot-outs, mysterious fires, and armed robbery are increasing. Taxi drivers kidnap and brutalize fares; passengers on trains are robbed. As the major financial and tourist center, Moscow attracts people from all over the former Soviet Union. Some come fleeing ethnic violence or seeking employment. The police force claims that half the crime in Moscow is the work of outsiders, and 80 percent of these are Caucasians. But organized gangs are not confined to Moscow. Almost every major city has seen a rise in crime. Security officials uncovered 2,600 separate organized crime groups, of which nearly 300 are large syndicates. These are engaged in systematic smuggling operations.

Vodka is worsening the crime rate and aggravating absenteeism and lost production. Although the production of vodka remains a state monopoly that accounts for more than 10 percent of government revenues, the sale of vodka is no longer a state monopoly. It can now be bought twenty-four hours a day. It is sold in private kiosks along with cigarettes, perfume, and cosmetics. Renewed drinking is considered the main reason male life expectancy is falling again.[29]

Bribery has become part of the cost of doing business. Entrepreneurs offer bribes to obtain export licenses, preferential credits, low prices on the purchase of state property, and special conditions for setting up businesses. The concept of conflict of interest is unknown to politicians, who openly market their influence. Yeltsin has said that nearly 40 percent of the new businessmen and two-thirds of Russia's commercial structures had ties to the criminal world. Many Russian factories, instead of manufacturing goods, resell their raw material allocations at inflated prices. Much of this material is smuggled across the thousands of miles of unprotected borders. Customs officials believe secret military airfields are being used for smuggling operations. According to Yeltsin, officials at the Defense Ministry were stealing entire ammunition depots. Shady Western firms have moved in for quick profits. Huge sums are diverted from Russia into Western bank accounts, trading companies, and joint ventures. The Russian Security Ministry reported confiscating 9 million tons of metal that was being smuggled out of the country. One-third of Russian oil and half of the nickel that reaches the West arrive illegally. Oil and precious metals are bought for rubles and then illegally resold overseas for hard currency, which is stashed abroad. Some Western oil companies have bypassed the central government and made direct deals with oil-producing associations. Others obtain oil after it has left Russia. Much of the illegal traffic in raw materials is funneled through the Baltic states—Latvia and Estonia have become major exporters of nonferrous metals, which they do not produce. The outflow of funds is equal to or greater than the new Western aid received by Russia in 1992. The International Institute of Finance estimates that $17 billion in hard currency left Russia in 1991 and 1992, at least one-quarter of the hard currency earned from Russia's exports. Yeltsin has accused institutions at the highest reaches of government of sabotaging reforms for personal profit.[30]

## THE POLITICAL STRUGGLE

Although the crucial question of Russian politics is whether effective rule can be maintained over the center and the periphery, the battles have been fought over who should rule, the president or the legislature. In the process, the effectiveness of governance has weakened. Although antagonism between the president and the legislature had been building for some time, the seventh Congress of People's Deputies on December 1, 1992, was the opening scene of a major power struggle between Yeltsin and the legislature.

The outcome of the December Congress was a stalemate, but the evident lack of a parliamentary culture eroded the legitimacy of all parties to the conflict. The third day of the Congress saw a scuffle at the podium, forcing the speaker to cut short the session. Rumors spread that Yeltsin might disband the Congress and hold new elections. The Congress of 1,041 deputies defeated a proposal by hard-line members to consider Yeltsin's impeachment but also refused to endorse Yeltsin's request for full control over economic policy. It fell only a few votes short of the two-thirds necessary to adopt amendments to dilute Yeltsin's control over the government and give new powers to parliament.[31]

When it became clear that Gaidar's confirmation as prime minister was in trouble, Yeltsin made a deal with Civic Union in exchange for critical votes for Gaidar. The legislators, however, held a secret ballot, undermining whatever control faction leaders might have over individual deputies. They voted against Gaidar, 467 for and 486 against. Gaidar's supporters were outraged.[32]

The next day, Yeltsin strode into the chamber, declared he could no longer work with hard-line lawmakers, and demanded a nationwide referendum to decide who ruled, the president or the Congress. He called on his supporters to walk out with him but only 150 left and only a few thousand took to the street in his support. Enough deputies were left for the Congress to continue. Supported by Vice President Rutskoi, it passed an amendment that would have stripped the president of his powers if he attempted to dissolve the Congress. The stage was set for a risky struggle of power between the legislature and the president.[33]

Valery Zorkin, the chief justice of the Constitutional Court, intervened and a compromise was reached. In consequence, Chernomyrdin replaced Gaidar as prime minister. Gaidar's supporters believed that Yeltsin had betrayed them. They attacked Chernomyrdin and his supporters as hardcore reactionaries. Andrei Kozyrev, the foreign minister, dramatized the possible outcome by giving a startling cold war speech at a meeting of the Conference on Security and Cooperation in Europe.[34] The most important concession Yeltsin won was Congress's agreement that a referendum would be held on April 11 on the basic principles of a new constitution.

Despite warnings of dire consequences, Yeltsin approved a Cabinet put together by Chernomyrdin that was, with a few exceptions, a replica of the Gaidar government. Deputy prime minister Alexander Shokhin, in charge of foreign economic relations; Anatoly Chubais, head of the privatization program; and economics minister Andrei Nechaev were all retained. The Cabinet was strengthened by the addition of Boris Fyodorov, a liberal economic reformer, as deputy prime minister with responsibility for economic reform. Fyodorov had worked for the European Bank for Reconstruction and Development and the World Bank. His inclusion in the Cabinet was strong evidence that economic reform would be continued. Even Andrei Kozyrev was retained.[35]

Chernomyrdin tried to steer a middle course, seeking to curb excessive credits while also preventing massive unemployment and increasing poverty. He supports reform, but is a gradualist rather than a shock therapist. He and his government emerged as strong supporters of Yeltsin in his struggle with the legislature.

The constitutional referendum soon appeared to be risky. Khazbulatov began campaigning against the referendum almost immediately. Regional leaders warned that a constitutional referendum might encourage movements for increased local autonomy. Zorkin, the chief justice, fearing that a referendum might set off unintended consequences, opposed it. Khasbulatov and Yeltsin began jockeying for support of regional leaders, promising increasing concessions to local autonomy. Yeltsin warned that he would be prepared to take "extreme measures."[36]

The Russian parliament voted to hold an emergency session of the Congress to determine whether there should be a national referendum in April. The stage was set for an intensified struggle for power. In an effort to bolster Yeltsin's position, President Bill Clinton agreed to schedule a summit meeting in Vancouver for April 3–4, offered an increase in direct American aid, and called for an early meeting of the G-7 to consider new economic aid to Russia.[37] On the eve of the session, Yeltsin informally requested Western political support if he were to assume emergency powers, declare a state of emergency, and suspend parliament. Attempting to intimidate the Congress, Yeltsin again warned that he was prepared to take "extreme measures" if a satisfactory agreement was not reached. This was dramatized by a secretive meeting with military leaders.[38]

The Congress met in an atmosphere of confrontation, seemingly intent on humiliating Yeltsin. Deputies heaped scorn on Yeltsin, market economic reforms, Western aid, and "democrats." When the deputies approved a resolution ending the president's decree powers, Yeltsin stormed out. With Yeltsin's chair empty, the Congress canceled the referendum, repudiating the December compromise. Although he lacked the legal right to call a referendum on his own, Yeltsin declared that he would hold a plebiscite on April 25 to decide who would rule the country.[39]

On March 20, in a dramatic, televised address, Yeltsin declared that he was assuming virtually unlimited emergency powers to rule by decree and called for a vote of confidence in the president and vice president on April 25. At the same time, he declared, Russians would vote on the draft of a new constitution and a draft law on elections to a new parliament. Until then, no decisions by the legislature or any other organ would have any legal force. Yeltsin identified his opposition as a communist-led conspiracy of former *apparatchiki*. Vice President Rutskoi and Zorkin declared the actions unconstitutional. Khasbulatov attacked Yeltsin's move as a neototalitarian threat and summoned an emergency session of the Supreme Soviet. The Supreme Soviet declared Yeltsin's measures an attack on the constitutional basis of Russian statehood and called on the Constitutional Court to rule on their legality.[40]

On March 23, the Constitutional Court, without hearing arguments from lawyers or having any briefs before it, ruled that Yeltsin's assumption of special powers was in violation of the constitution. No formal decrees had yet been published, so the court's decision was based on Yeltsin's television speech. The decision did not question Yeltsin's right to hold a referendum, nor did it mention impeachment. Supporters of Yeltsin immediately attacked the constitutionality of the court's decision, especially since Zorkin had expressed his views publicly before the court even met. The belief in the impartiality of the court was severely damaged.[41] The Supreme Soviet summoned a full Congress to consider the ouster of Yeltsin.

When Yeltsin's decree was published the following day, it retained the demand for nationwide votes of confidence, a new constitution, and new electoral laws but omitted any mention of special powers. Since none of the measures the court had found unconstitutional were retained, Zorkin and Khasbulatov were put in an uncomfortable situation.[42]

By the time the Congress met, perhaps fearful of unleashing civil unrest, the chief protagonists became increasingly conciliatory. Khasbulatov was unsure if he could muster the 689 votes needed to oust Yeltsin. In a nationwide television appeal on the eve of the Congress, Khasbulatov attacked Yeltsin but declared that he was opposed to impeachment. Zorkin proposed new elections for a new bicameral parliament to replace the Congress and warned that impeachment could have catastrophic results. Khasbulatov steered the Congress away from efforts at impeachment, and Yeltsin was conciliatory. He admitted that there had been some mistakes in economic policy and fired his economics minister, Nechaev. However, he promoted Fyodorov to finance minister, ensuring the continuance of radical reform. An effort by hard-liners to put Yeltsin's ouster on the agenda failed to gain a simple majority.[43]

Khasbulatov and Yeltsin announced they had struck an overnight compromise that called for early elections for both the parliament and the president in early November and replacement of the Congress by a bicameral legislature. Rather than solving the impasse, the backstage maneuvering angered the legislature, which called for the ouster of both Khasbulatov and Yeltsin. Yeltsin announced he would not abide by the Congress's ruling and went into the streets, where 50,000 supporters had turned out. In secret ballots, the legislators voted 558 to 339 to reject the motion to dismiss Khasbulatov. The move to remove Yeltsin fell just 72 votes short of the required two-thirds majority. Only 268 deputies opposed his ouster.[44]

The next day the Congress agreed to hold a referendum on April 25 in which voters were to be asked four questions: if they had confidence in Yeltsin; if they approved of the government's economic and social policies; if they supported early elections for the president; and if they supported early elections for the Congress. The second question was an invitation to the voters suffering from a drastic decline in their living standards to reject Yeltsin's economic reforms. Under the rules passed by the Congress, the question dealing with confidence in the president would require approval by a majority of all 106 million registered voters, an impossible condition. On April 21, the Constitutional Court ruled that the first two questions were not constitutional issues and therefore needed only a simple majority of votes cast. It ruled that the last two questions were constitutional issues and would require approval from a majority of all eligible voters.[45]

The stage was set for continued confrontation. During the campaign, Yeltsin went on the offensive, making populist economic promises and attacking the legislature, the Central Bank, the Constitutional Court, and the vice president. Since Rutskoi was the only opposition figure with sufficient credibility to challenge Yeltsin, he took the lead in the campaign, accusing the government of corruption. The referendum was a clear psychological victory for Yeltsin. Not only did a majority of the voters support Yeltsin, but they even endorsed his economic policies. Yeltsin emerged stronger and parliament slightly weaker, but the vote did not end the power struggle.

A vote against Yeltsin would have strengthened opponents of democracy, but the voters did not necessarily endorse political democracy. Much of the support for Yeltsin came from voters attracted to a strong leader and an iron hand. Plebiscites do not strengthen respect for procedural democracy, nor should we be heartened by the spectacle of a strong leader appealing directly to the people, ruling by decree, refusing to be bound by the constitution, and demonizing his opponents. Neither should we be surprised that the political culture was not transformed in under two years. Sergei Schmemann notes that the struggles between Yeltsin and the legislature "were the convulsions of a system in profound transformation" and adds, "But despite the extraordinary passions, there was a curious lack of panic or violence."[46]

## NOTES

1. *New York Times*, August 9, 1992, 3.

2. Martin Malia maintains that for the magnitude of the loss of power and prestige, the reaction was mild, particularly in comparison to France after the loss of Algeria and America after the "loss" of China. See Martin Malia, "Apocalypse Not," *The New Republic* 208 (22 February 1993): 24.

3. *New York Times*, March 1, 1993.

4. "A Survey of Russia," *The Economist*, December 5, 1992, 17; *The Economist*, January 23, 1993, 52.

5. "A Survey of Russia," 18.

6. Katrina vanden Heuvel, "Russia's Veep," *The Nation* 256 (April 12, 1993): 472–73.

7. "A Survey of Russia," 18.

8. *New York Times*, March 14, 15, 1993.

9. *New York Times*, October 25, 1992.

10. "A Survey of Russia," 17; *New York Times*, October 25, 1992; March 13, 14, 1993.

11. *New York Times*, October 25; November 29, 1992.

12. *The Economist*, August 1, 1992, 40–41; August 15, 1992, 42; September 12, 1992, 53; October 31, 1992, 48; "A Survey of Russia" 18–19.

13. *The Economist*, March, 13, 1993, 52–53.

14. *New York Times*, March 22, 23, 1993.

15. "A Survey of Russia," 20.

16. For the reference to de Gaulle, see John Weightman, "Fatal Attraction," *The New York Review of Books*, February 11, 1993, 10.

17. *New York Times*, November 15, 29; December 12, 1992; "A Survey of Russia," 20; *The Economist*, December 5, 12, 1992.

18. *New York Times*, August 2; November 15, 1992.

19. *The Economist*, June 27, 1992, 59–60; *New York Times*, March 22, 1993.

20. Anders Aslund, "Go Faster on Russian Reform," *New York Times*, December 7, 1992, 15.

21. *New York Times*, January 13, 20; February 24; March 16, 18; May 5; June 8; July 9, 1992; *The Economist*, February 29, 1992, 55; (Cleveland) *Plain Dealer*, November 12, 1992.

22. *Time Magazine*, July 7, 1992, 41; *New York Times*, October 28, 29, 30; November 15, 1992; *The Economist*, October 31, 1992, 48.

23. *New York Times*, November 29, 1992.

24. *The Economist*, February 13, 1993, 51.

25. "A Survey of Russia," 20.

26. Ibid.

27. (Cleveland) *Plain Dealer*, January 16, 1993.

28. On the crime problem, see *New York Times*, August 30; October 20; November 29, 1992; (Cleveland) *Plain Dealer*, February 13, 1993; Andrew Kopkind, "From Russia with Love and Squalor," *The Nation* 256 (January 18, 1993): 44–62.

29. *New York Times*, October 23, 1992.

30. *New York Times*, August 30; November 29, 1992; (Cleveland) *Plain Dealer*, February 13, 1993; *Washington Post National Weekly Edition*, February 15–21, 1993; March 1–7, 1993.

31. *New York Times*, December 2, 6, 1992; *Washington Post*, December 2, 1992.

32. *New York Times*, December 9, 10, 13, 1992.

33. (Cleveland) *Plain Dealer*, December 11, 12, 1992; *New York Times*, December 13, 1992; *The Economist*, December 19, 1992, 46–47.

34. *New York Times*, December 15, 1992; *The Economist*, December 19, 1992, 15, 47.

35. *The Economist*, December 19, 1992, 15; December 26, 1992, 62; January 9, 1993, 42; *New York Times*, December 24, 1992.

36. *The Economist*, February 13, 1993, 50–51; *New York Times*, March 6, 1993.

37. *New York Times*, March 12, 1993.

38. *New York Times*, March 10, 1993.

39. *New York Times*, March 14, 1993.

40. *New York Times*, March 21, 24, 1993.

41. *New York Times*, March 24, March 1993; *The Economist*, March 27, 1993.

42. *Washington Post*, March 25, 1993; *New York Times*, March 25, 26, 1993.

43. *New York Times*, March 26, 27, 28, 1993; (Cleveland) *Plain Dealer*, March 27, 1993.

44. *Washington Post*, March 29, 1993.

45. *New York Times*, March 30; April 16, 1993; (Cleveland) *Plain Dealer*, April 22, 1993.

46. *New York Times*, March 30, 1993.

*Chapter 14*

# TRANSFORMATION OR COLLAPSE II: THE ECONOMY

Despite Russia's lack of experience with capitalism and its deeply entrenched system of centralized planning, Yeltsin was convinced that Russia needed to embark on "shock therapy." Western economic advisers recommended the immediate elimination of all elements of state socialism. Yeltsin spoke of the need for tough monetary and financial policies, budget cuts, privatization, price liberalization, tax reform, and a stronger ruble. In an interview published on December 14, 1992, Yeltsin promised to stabilize the economy in a year.[1] The term *shock therapy* seemed to imply a short period of intense suffering followed by quick results. Marshall Goldman points out, however, that shock therapy has "always been followed by enormous political and social aftershocks."[2]

Rather than considering economic restructuring as a means to create the social and economic base necessary to foster democratic pluralism or even as a means to raise living standards, economic reformers made the transformation to free markets an end in itself. To achieve this end, they were willing to sacrifice the standard of living of Russians and endanger fragile democratic institutions. For most Russians, support for the transformation to free markets was not ideologically grounded but based rather on the belief that it would increase their material well-being. They wanted an end to scarcity, lines, and shoddy goods. They had seen a deterioration in living standards during the Gorbachev era and looked forward to improvement. They were unprepared for the inflation, unemployment, and decline in living standards that accompanied the attempt at a rapid transition. Yeltsin and the radical economists failed to understand the political dimensions of economic reform and made no effort to sell the austerity program to the public. They brushed politics aside as an impediment put in their path by backers of the military-industrial establishment and their supporters in the legislature.

A team of young reformers took over under Gaidar, who was appointed minister of finance, later acting prime minister. On January 2, price controls were lifted on 90 percent of goods. Prices rose by an average of 250 percent the next day.[3] The fact that Russians did not come out into the streets in protest was a sign that they had faith in Yeltsin and his reform team and that they believed that the pain would shortly lead to significant economic improvement. The freeing of prices was based on the assumption that higher prices would encourage increased production. However, rather than responding by increasing supplies, which would in time lower prices, monopolist producers curtailed production, shifted to a more expensive assortment of output, stockpiled production in anticipation of even higher prices in the future, and even shut down production facilities.[4] Khasbulatov called for Yeltsin's resignation for enacting an "uncontrolled, anarchic" economic reform. Yeltsin himself expressed outrage at rising food prices and vowed to crack down on trading monopolies and "mafia-like structures."[5] However, after the G-7 announced a $24 billion package of aid on April 1, Yeltsin announced that the economy was on track and under control.[6] The elimination of most price supports, a tight monetary policy, and defense cuts lowered the budget deficit from 20 percent of the gross domestic product (GDP) in 1991 to 5 percent in the first quarter of 1992.[7]

The tight monetary policy introduced under shock therapy soon threatened a wave of bankruptcies because firms were unable to get credit to pay wages and suppliers. Women were pressured to use up their three-year maternity leaves or retire on maternity benefits. Workers were offered long vacations at half pay or shorter workweeks at reduced pay. In regions where the only employment was in the military-industrial complex, there was genuine fear of the future.[8]

In the second quarter, therefore, the government issued credit to enterprises equal to about 20 percent of that quarter's GDP. Pumping this much money into the economy resulted in increased inflation. Ruble-printing presses were unable to keep up, causing a severe shortage of cash. Russia's money supply fell by 75 percent in real terms. About 14 percent of factories and enterprises ran out of money and often could not pay workers. The problem was compounded by the fact that while cash is used for wages and in stores, transactions between enterprises are made by debiting and crediting bank accounts. These two circuits are separate—enterprises cannot convert bank deposits into cash. As a consequence, the cash shortage hit consumer demand, but industrial enterprises were unaffected. To avoid cutting output, they began to lend and borrow among themselves at a faster rate.[9] The value of debts exploded. Standing at 39 billion rubles as of January 1, 1992, they reached 3.2 trillion in mid-June, more than all the money then in circulation.[10] Stabilization was also threatened by uncontrolled spending by local governments and issuance of credit to independent countries of the former Soviet Union that remained in the ruble zone. Russia's payment system was in chaos.

Jeffrey Sachs, Anders Aslund, and other Western economic advisers to the Russian government insisted that shock therapy was the proper policy—they blamed economic problems on failure to implement shock therapy fully. Russia's domestic oil price was about one-fifth of world prices even after an increase in May. The failure to free energy prices, they argued, encouraged waste and distorted the relative prices of millions of other goods. Further, state shops were not allowed to charge a markup of more than 25 percent, and many local authorities were still subsidizing producers, wholesalers, and retailers to keep their prices down. This then reduced incentives for firms to increase supplies of new goods. At the wholesale level, state orders continued to account for up to 40 percent of the output of some goods, and between one-quarter and one-half of agricultural produce was supposed to be sold to the government. The advisers argued that the complex system of export quotas, taxes, and multiple exchange rates was responsible for a fall in exports. A trade surplus of $10 billion in 1991 turned into a deficit in the first quarter of 1992. For them, the cure for the problems was more shock therapy.[11]

Despite the fact that the goal of the first stage of reform, economic stabilization, had not been achieved, the reformers introduced the ambitious second stage of economic reform on July 1. This included a single floating exchange rate for the ruble.[12] The intent was to move toward ruble convertibility, which was essential to make pricing meaningful in terms of world prices, to enable Russia to increase trade in world markets, and to ensure foreign investors that they could repatriate their profits. The second stage meant new rules for exports and imports, a bankruptcy law, and a privatization plan. As David Mason points out, a workable market system necessitates the breakup of state monopolies into independent units that will respond to supply and demand. While the inefficient should be allowed to go out of business, most of the rest should be sold. But privatization is linked to the establishment of a commercial banking system and creation of stock markets. If government subsidies are to be eliminated, loans and credits must be obtainable from commercial sources. The lack of private capital therefore presaged enormous difficulties.[13]

After the former chairman of the Soviet state bank, Viktor Gerashchenko, was appointed head of the Russian Central Bank in July, he froze and netted out the interfirm debts. Gerashchenko's subsequent actions outraged the economic reformers. Since the Central Bank was responsible to the legislature, the Cabinet and the president had no control over his actions. What he did was to ease monetary policy. He issued credits to industries, commercial banks that lend to industries, the government itself to cover its budget deficit, and independent former Soviet republics who used rubles for their currency. Since the interest rate on credits was below the inflation rate, borrowing was encouraged. Accounts were simply credited with sums of money, which could be spent, thereby increasing the amount in circulation.[14] During the third quarter of 1992 the Central Bank increased its lending by 42 percent a month, setting off fears of hyperinflation.[15] The inability of Russian Cabinets to control the bank prevented any coherent monetary and fiscal policy.

By the beginning of August, there was a growing sense that Gaidar's policies were failing. Prices were soaring, output was falling, and real wages were halved. Privatization was marginal, disorganized, and riddled with corruption. New entrepreneurs were choked with taxes and had to pay bribes, usurious interest rates, and protection money. State managers were appropriating state property and "privatizing" it, exporting raw materials, importing Western goods, and investing profits abroad. The G-7 industrialized nations promised an immediate $1 billion credit from the International Monetary Fund (IMF), and the World Bank announced a $600 million loan. But additional funds would require Russia to shrink its budget deficit from 17 percent of the GDP to 5 percent and limit monthly inflation to a maximum of 9 percent by the end of the year.[16] Yeltsin faced the same problem Gorbachev had earlier. Rather than giving aid as a way of making reform possible, international agencies promised aid as a reward. But no leader dared to take the measures needed to produce the results that could bring them the reward.

The problem was that making factories produce or fold would force millions out of work. Credit issued by the Central Bank to keep them afloat paid for wages and raw materials, but it was equivalent to printing money. More and more money was poured into an economy producing fewer and fewer goods. Inflation in September was three times higher than the June rate. Enterprises stockpiled production, assuming they could sell it later for higher prices. Prices began to climb by 20 percent a month.

The then $70 billion hard currency debt total for the former Soviet Union was a severe drain on government resources, hurting the country's credit-worthiness. Commercial banks were alarmed at Russia's worsening balance of payments. Uncertainties caused by delay in rescheduling old Soviet debt were stifling trade and undermining the confidence of foreign investors in Russia. Russia needed to use its foreign exchange for essential imports, not debt service.[17]

Shock therapy called for privatization of enterprises to create a free market. More than 14,000 small businesses were privatized in 1992. This was only 11 percent of the total number of small businesses compared with a target of 60 percent, but one-fifth of Russia's workers were employed in the private sector. More than half the stores in Moscow, St. Petersburg, and Nizhni Novgorod were private.[18] Russia announced plans to privatize more than 6,000 large- and medium-sized companies in 1993, the largest privatization ever undertaken. Firms were required to choose one of two schemes of privatization. Under the first option, they could give employees nonvoting shares worth 25 percent of the company's capital at no charge, plus an option to buy a further 10 percent of voting shares at a 30 percent discount. Top managers would get an option on 5 percent of the voting shares, and the remaining 60 percent would be sold to outsiders. Under the second option, workers and managers together could buy 51 percent of a firm's assets at 1.7 times its book value as of January 1992, and the remainder would be sold to the public. Firms chose the two methods in about equal proportions.[19]

On October 1, the government began issuing vouchers worth 10,000 rubles to every man, woman, and child. Vouchers could be sold for cash. They sold way below face value, but the price rose from under 4,000 rubles to 7,000 when the date of the first auction was announced. Enough people sold their vouchers to create a liquid market in the commodity exchanges and even in street kiosks. December 9 was the first time ordinary Russians could buy shares in a state-owned enterprise—The Bolshevik Biscuit Factory.[20]

The government began in January trying to sell hundreds of firms in fourteen regions, with an emphasis on speed. The intent was to move as rapidly as possible to create a situation that could not be reversed if conservatives should come to power. All companies, except those specifically identified as hopeless by the governors of the fourteen regions, were to be auctioned as is, leaving it up to new owners to restructure them. The International Finance Corporation, an arm of the World Bank, assisted local governments.[21] By early April, 700 firms had been privatized and auctions were proceeding rapidly.

No regulatory system was established to control trading in vouchers or shares. Unfortunately, and perhaps inevitably, unscrupulous businessmen soon moved in to take advantage of citizens' inexperience. In St. Petersburg, unregulated companies induced the unwary to invest their vouchers and money in fraudulent get-rich-quick schemes. Promoters of the investment funds then fled. Anger was high and directed against the government. Even greater problems are predicted in the wholesale end of Russia's new securities markets. There are 300 licensed investment funds and over 100 stock exchanges. *The Economist* points out, "Big profits combined with so little regulation are an irresistible temptation for any swindler."[22]

By the end of 1992, critics of shock therapy had become increasingly vocal. The ruble, which had been at 180 rubles to the dollar at the beginning of 1992, was down to 450 to the dollar at the end of 1992.[23] The budget deficit increased from 1.5 percent of GDP to 15 percent, and the economy had been unable to attract foreign investments and integrate Russia into the world economy.[24] Inflation had wiped out the savings of all except the new syndicates of officials and businessmen who had put their money into hard currency and stashed it abroad. Productivity had plunged by 24 percent in 1992, compared with the 8 percent drop in 1991.[25] Although state enterprises were being privatized, new factories were not being created to replace old factories that would be closed down as unprofitable. The average wage bought only three-fifths of what it could buy before the freeing of prices on January 1.[26] About one-third of the population lived below the poverty line. Consumer spending was down to one-half of the previous year's figures in real terms. Infant mortality was up, the birthrate was down, and diphtheria and cholera were spreading.[27] For the first time since World War II, the birthrate fell below the death rate.[28] Higher prices, by lowering demand, had increased the supply of goods in stores. But surely the hope of the Russian people had been that they would be able to buy more, not that shelves would be stocked because people could not afford goods.

Much of the controversy centered not on the issue of whether a transition should be made to free markets but on how that transition should be achieved, at what speed, and at whose expense. Ignoring the experience of most of Western Europe, supporters of shock therapy argued that there was no third way between a centralized state-monopolistic economy and a totally unfettered market.

Since the greatest fear of the radical reformers is hyperinflation, defined as 50 percent a month, they preach resistance to budget deficits and insist on the necessity of putting the squeeze on monetary growth.[29] *The Economist* maintains that Russian industry is too big and that too many resources that could be put to better use are tied up in inefficient industry. Military-industrial output accounted for 20 percent of industrial employment and 20 percent of output. If all the raw materials that Russia uses were sold abroad, Russia would earn twice as much as its present total GDP. Russian industry is thus subtracting, not adding, value to the raw material it consumes. Therefore, they argue, reform ought to cause a slump. It ought to drive inefficient firms out of business so the resources can be put to better use. They advocate improving living standards by selling raw materials and later creating new firms that can use the resources more efficiently. They support a policy of deindustrialization.[30]

Critics are unwilling to contemplate transformation into a Third World economy dependent on small shops and raw material exports. They argue that stopping the fall in production is primary and combatting inflation is secondary. Civic Union, which presses for a slower, more managed transition to a free economy, calls for state support for large industries as they try to convert to private corporations. They insist that although reformers speak of halting subsidies to state-owned dinosaurs and letting them die out, in fact even potentially successful industries are threatened by tight credit. Shutting down huge industries could impoverish whole regions of the country.[31]

Civic Union seeks protection against unemployment and maintenance of safety nets. It supports an activist government intervening in the economy to maintain full employment, increase productivity, and protect strategic industries.[32] Russia produces high-quality arms and can sell them abroad for hard currency. Russians are unlikely to give up this market as long as the United States continues to sell arms abroad.[33]

Large-scale foreign economic and financial aid necessary for the transformation to a market economy was not forthcoming. Although the G-7 announced a $24 billion aid package for Russia on April 1, 1992, only about one-half was ever delivered. A $6 billion ruble stabilization fund contingent on harsh austerity measures was never established since Russia was unable to bring monetary and budget policies under control. Of the $4.5 billion from the IMF, World Bank, and European Bank for Reconstruction and Development, IMF provided only $1 billion. The core of the package was an $11 billion commitment for credits, of which only about $8 billion were received. They were distributed not in the form of cash but as food, industrial equipment, and other goods purchased by Russia from the lending countries on commercial terms. Because Russia was unable to obtain commercial loans for these purchases, the credits were beneficial. But many Russians viewed them as business arrangements enabling the lending countries to find markets for their goods. Much of the credit was a repackaging of old arrangements, including a $3.5 billion credit from the United States to buy grain, primarily for livestock. Other credits were given to Russian industries, but it was not until the summer that the Russian government required the industries to repay the foreign credits and interest themselves. The credits to Russia increased the country's debt without providing long-term solutions.[34]

The West used the promise of loans to pressure the Russian government into pursuing a stringent monetary policy and attempting a rapid and large-scale reorganization of the entire economy. It did this despite the absence of banks, insurance companies, commercial law, and other essential elements of the infrastructure. Parliament resisted the tight money and budget balancing insisted upon by IMF. The Central Bank refused to rein in the money supply. In consequence, negotiations with IMF were suspended.[35] Peter Reddaway says the Russians put "too many eggs in the wobbly basket of western aid."[36]

After it became clear that Yeltsin's future and the future of economic reform were in jeopardy, the West moved to strengthen him politically. At Vancouver, in a political gesture of support for Yeltsin, the United States came up with an aid package of $1.6 billion in money already approved by Congress. Japan promised Russia $1.8 billion in bilateral assistance. A two-day emergency meeting of G-7 foreign and finance ministers on April 14–15 produced conditional promises of $49 billion, including $28.4 billion in loans and $15 billion in debt relief. Most of the aid will pass through international lending institutions. Six billion dollars of the total was the IMF ruble stabilization fund set up in 1992 that was never used because Russia was unable to meet the terms. A new IMF loan program of $3 billion was established to ease transition to a market economy. Half was to be disbursed as soon as Moscow committed itself to economic change. The other half was to be sent after initial progress in getting inflation under control. "Standby" IMF loans of $4.1 billion are conditional on a comprehensive macroeconomic stabilization program, but conditions are less strict than for the 1992 stabilization fund. Ten billion dollars is in loans and guarantees for exports to Russian enterprises to help Russia purchase equipment to expand its exports, particularly oil, gas, and minerals. President Clinton made a new commitment of $1.8 billion in direct aid, which would require Congressional approval.[37] He agreed to review restrictive legislation that denies Russia most-favored nation trading status.[38]

Fyodorov, the finance minister, pledged to reduce the monthly inflation rate from over 20 percent a month to under 5 percent by Christmas.[39] Political pressures, however, made it far from certain that Moscow would be able to meet the terms for much of the assistance. Yeltsin courted public support for the referendum by raising wages, increasing spending, issuing cheap government credits for industries, and indexing savings. He reversed an increase in gas prices and rents and promised higher student stipends, compensation to pensioners for savings lost to inflation, and more benefits for coal miners. Chernomyrdin promised new credits for the energy industry and for farmers, criticized the privatization of state-owned businesses, and insisted on the continued need for price controls and state planning and distribution.[40]

Despite misgivings, inflation slowed to about 16 percent a month, and the ruble began to stabilize at about 1,000 to the dollar.[41] To help shore up the economy, the IMF agreed on June 30 to extend a $1.5 billion loan to Russia. The World Bank approved a $660 million loan for development of the Russian oil industry and several million dollars for medicine and other needed imports. Russia instituted austerity measures, cutting back spending, raising energy prices, and reducing subsidies to state-owned enterprises. The Central Bank raised interest rates and pledged to pull back on increases in the money supply. In response to the Russian efforts, leaders at the G-7 meeting in July agreed to provide an immediate $3 billion in aid in loans, grants, and export credits over an eighteen month period. Although this was mostly a reallocation of funds already committed, it was welcomed by Yeltsin.[42]

Mild optimism about the economy soon dissipated. Before recessing on July 23, the parliament refused to pass the government's draft budget and approved a series of measures that, if implemented, would increase the budget deficit to 25 percent of Russia's GDP. It also cancelled a presidential decree on privatization.[43]

Although the actions by parliament threatened Russia's austerity measures, it was the Central Bank that jolted faith in the system. On July 24, while Yeltsin was on vacation and Fyodorov, the finance minister, was in America, the Central Bank announced that all rubles issued before 1993 would be taken out of circulation before the beginning of the year. Confiscatory limits were placed on the number of old rubles that could be exchanged. The purpose was to slow inflation and tighten control over the money supply. The move would have caused enormous difficulties for businesses, both legal and illegal. Former Soviet republics using the ruble and others who held rubles for trade with Russia would have been seriously affected. The Central Bank estimated that 20 percent of Russia's money supply consisted of older notes held by former republics. Although they endorsed the goals of slowing inflation and tightening control over the money supply, Jeffrey Sachs and other Western economists argued that the move, taken without consultation with Yeltsin, Fyodorov, or the IMF, could erode support for economic reform. The fear was that the move would cause Russians to lose faith in their currency and lead them to spend rubles, thereby triggering further inflation. When Yeltsin returned to Moscow on July 26, he first issued a decree guaranteeing that mass privatization could continue.[44] Since Chernomyrdin, his prime minister, supported the Central Bank, Yelstin did not rescind the currency measure, but eased limits on the number of rubles that could be exchanged. After popular anger became evident, Khasbulatov, who had originally supported the measure, denounced it. On July 28, the parliament abolished all limits on the number of old rubles that could be exchanged. Parliament thus managed to gain popular support, while the government was blamed for the fiasco. The incident shook the confidence of Russia's citizens and the West in the government's ability to stabilize the economy.[45]

The fragility of the Russian economy is exacerbated not only by the rivalry between the legislature and the presidency, but by the division within the government itself. Although Fyodorov and other senior members of the finance ministry opposed the Central Bank's move, it was supported by Chernomyrdin and most members of the government. There is growing concern that the government will be unable to lower the budget deficit and cut inflation sufficiently by the end of 1993 to qualify for the second installment of $1.5 billion in loans from the IMF and accelerated loans of approximately $2 billion from the World Bank.[46]

Yeltsin's highest priority had been the rapid transformation of the economy through shock therapy. Russian citizens were incredibly patient, understanding that short-term pain might be necessary before improvement could be expected. Their endorsement of Yeltsin's economic reforms in the April referendum surprised most observers. The vote provided support for continued privatization and economic reform. Yeltsin and his supporters need to be careful not to lose sight of the fact that the citizenry in a democracy judge economic policy by its ability to sustain and improve their standard of living. During the campaign, Yeltsin showed flexibility in modifying the prescriptions of shock therapy in order to gain political support. To govern effectively, he may need to support further departures from the advice of Western economists. The danger is that since Yeltsin and the West insisted that democracy required a market economy, failure of the economic transformation could endanger democracy.

## NOTES

1. *New York Times*, December 15, 1991.

2. Marshall I. Goldman, "Yeltsin's Reforms: Gorbachev II?" *Foreign Policy* 88 (Fall 1992): 81.

3. "A Survey of Russia," *The Economist*, December 5, 1992, 5.

4. *Rossiiskaya gazeta* January 17, 1992, in *Current Digest of the Post-Soviet Press* (CDPSP) 44 (February 12, 1992): 1.

5. *New York Times*, January 14, 15, 16, 17, 1992.

6. *Rossiiskaya gazeta*, April 8, 1992, in *CDPSP* 44 (April 12, 1992): 5.

7. *The Economist*, July 4, 1992, 64.

8. *New York Times*, May 28, 1992.

9. *The Economist*, July 4, 1992, 64.

10. "Survey of Russia," 6.

11. *The Economist*, July 4, 1992, 64. Anders Aslund is the Director of the Stockholm Institute of East European Economics.

12. *New York Times*, July 1, 2, 1992.

13. David S. Mason, *Revolution in East-Central Europe* (Boulder, Colo.: Westview Press, 1992), 90–91.

14. *New York Times*, April 11, 1993.

15. *New York Times*, November 29, 1992; *The Economist*, January 30, 1993, 75–76.

16. *New York Times*, August 2, 9, 1992; *The Economist*, August 15, 1992, 13, 42.

17. Jeffrey Sachs and David Lipton, "Russia's Monetary Madness," *Washington Post National Weekly Edition*, October 5–11, 1992, 24.

18. *The Economist*, November 28, 1992, 16–17, 69–70.

19. Ibid., 69–70.

20. *The Economist*, December 12, 1992, 56; *New York Times*, December 14, 1992.

21. *The Economist*, January 16, 1993, 66–67.

22. *The Economist*, February 27, 1993, 84; (Cleveland) *Plain Dealer*, March 3, 1993.

23. In April, the ruble hit 800 to the dollar. At that rate, it values average industrial wages at thirty dollars a month. See *The Economist*, April 10, 1993, 51. The ruble fell to 1,072 to the dollar on June 3. See *New York Times*, June 4, 1993.

24. "Survey of Russia," 6.

25. *The Economist* January 9, 1993, 62.

26. Peter Reddaway, "Russia Comes Apart," *New York Times*, January 10, 1993, 23.

27. *New York Times*, November 29, 1992.

28. David M. Kotz, "The Cure That Could Kill," *The Nation* 256 (April 19, 1993): 515.

29. Anders Aslund, "Go Faster on Russian Reform," *New York Times*, December 7, 1992, 15.

30. "Survey of Russia," 10–11.

31. David M. Kotz, "No More Radical Reform," *New York Times*, December 15, 1992, 16; John Greenwald, "Why It Still Doesn't Work," *Time Magazine*, December 7, 1992, 60–61.

32. The usual criteria for identifying strategic industries include potentially high profits, social gains, and military usefulness in possible future conflicts.

33. John Edwin Mroz, "Russia and Eastern Europe: Will the West Let Them Fail?" *Foreign Affairs* 72 (1992/93): 54. He reports that after the United States pressured Russia not to sell arms to Taiwan, it turned around and did so itself.

34. *New York Times*, April 1, 4, 1993.

35. *New York Times*, December 22, 1992.

36. Reddaway, "Russia Comes Apart," 23.

37. *New York Times*, April 16, 1993; *The Economist*, April 17, 1993, 50.

38. *New York Times*, April 5, 1993; *The Economist*, April 10, 1993, 52.

39. *New York Times*, April 11, 1993.

40. *New York Times*, April 9, 1993; (Cleveland) *Plain Dealer*, April 15, 1993.

41. *New York Times*, July 28, 1993.

42. *New York Times*, July 1, 3, 10, 1993.

43. *The Economist*, July 24, 1993, 50; July 31, 1993, 50; *New York Times*, July 26, 1993.

44. Although parliament suspended Yeltsin's decree on August 6, the government said it would ignore parliament. See *New York Times*, August 7, 1993.

45. *New York Times*, July 25, 26, 27, 28; August 7, 1993; *The Economist*, July 31, 1993, 16–17, 41–42.

46. *New York Times*, August 7, 1993.

*Chapter 15*

# TRANSFORMATION OR COLLAPSE III

"If we don't find some way that the different ethnic groups can live together in a country, how many countries will we have?" Warren Christopher, in speaking these words before the Senate Foreign Relations Committee at his confirmation hearings was referring to a worldwide phenomenon.[1] The breakup of the Soviet Union is an example of the process of disintegration, but we have no assurance that the process will end at this point. Russia, like the former Soviet Union, is a multinational federation. Under the Soviet system, federalism did not apply to the centralized party that held the system together. Gorbachev's transfer of power from the party to the state left the Soviet Union subject to centrifugal forces. The Russian Federation has no centralized power structure to hold the system together. Parts of the federation are drifting out of the control of the center. If the leadership of Russia uses force to stem the disintegration, the fragile structure of democracy may give way to xenophobic nationalism, as has occurred in Yugoslavia.

## THE "NEAR ABROAD"

In the aftermath of the failed coup of August 1991, the Soviet Union was replaced by a tenuous Commonwealth of Independent States (CIS). Many Russians find it difficult to accept that former republics are independent foreign states. Politicians often refer to them as the "near abroad" to differentiate between them and the rest of the world. Paul Goble points out that the Russian state began to absorb other peoples before the Russian people had ever consolidated themselves as a nation. Because the boundaries of the people and the state were never clear, Russians have found it difficult to accept the loss of any part of their territory. Not only sentiment but real geopolitical interests are at stake. The empire provided Russia with strategic ports, access to raw materials, transportation and communication, and factories whose production was not duplicated by plants in Russia.

Russian national interest dictates that outside powers be denied access to regions that might be used to threaten Russia itself.[2] Furthermore, most Russians feel that Russia has an obligation to protect the 25 million Russians still living in the fourteen non-Russian republics, where they are now often treated as second-class citizens. There is deep concern over the fate of 400,000 Russians who have fled to Russia from other republics. Although communists and nationalists have exploited the situation for political purposes, resentment is not limited to extremists.

Some Russians see the CIS not as the final stage in the dissolution of the Soviet Union but as a step toward a reconstituted federation. The CIS, though, is more shadow than substance. It includes ten of the former republics of the Soviet Union as members and Azerbaijan as an observer—only the three Baltic states and Georgia are unaffiliated. A CIS Council of Heads of State and a Council of Heads of Government were formed, and agreement was reached to place strategic forces under unified command. Members have agreed on terms for commonwealth peacekeeping: force will be sent only if requested and if peace is already in place. Six of the republics have signed a collective security treaty promising to aid each other in case of military need. Any decision to send peacekeepers is to be made collectively, and command of peacekeeping operations was handed over to the commonwealth's armed forces.[3] The joint military command was dissolved in mid-June 1993.

The ten heads of the CIS met at a summit meeting in Minsk on January 22, 1993, to consider a new commonwealth charter, but Ukraine announced in advance that it would not sign. Leaders at the summit prepared two documents: a charter calling for greater integration and a memorandum calling for looser cooperation. They all agreed to sign the memorandum but allowed members more time to consider the charter. Ukraine, Moldova, and Turkmenistan feared that the charter, which would more closely coordinate defense and economic powers, could lead to an attempt to create new federal structures. Leonid Kravchuk, the Ukrainian president, declared that he would "not allow the Commonwealth of Independent States to be turned into a supranational body subject to international law."[4] The other seven leaders signed the charter,which will come into effect only after ratification by their national parliaments.

At the end of February 1993, Yeltsin called for international organizations, including the United Nations, to grant Russia special powers as "the guarantor of peace and stability in regions of the former USSR." Yeltsin asserted that stopping such armed conflicts was "Russia's vital interest."[5] Ukraine and Georgia saw this as resurgence of Russian imperialism.

### Ukraine

It is especially difficult for Russians to accept the permanence of Ukrainian independence. Not only was Ukraine part of the Slavic core, but more than 11 million Russians live in Ukraine. Relations with Ukraine have been strained over numerous issues—the most contentious have been the disposition of the Black Sea fleet, the status of the Crimea, and control of nuclear weapons.

Although it was agreed that strategic forces would be put under control of the commonwealth, Ukraine argued that the Black Sea fleet was not part of strategic forces since none of its ships carried weapons of mass destruction. It then moved to take over the Black Sea fleet. This struck a severe blow at Russian pride, since the Black Sea fleet has a symbolic role in Russian history.[6] Although the fleet is a collection of 325 badly repaired and outdated ships and submarines, the two sides exchanged threats until an agreement was reached in August 1992 on provisions to divide the Black Sea fleet by 1995.[7] When more than two hundred ships hoisted the Russian navy's St. Andrews flag in June 1993, Ukrainians were infuriated. Russia and Ukraine issued a joint communiqué agreeing again to divide the fleet by 1995.[8]

Once the issue of the Black Sea fleet was raised, it was inevitable that the Crimean question would arise. Not only had the Crimea historically been part of Russia, but it had important naval ports and a Russian ethnic majority. The Ukrainian parliament gave extensive home rule to the Crimea in an effort to stave off an independence move. However, in May 1992 the Crimean parliament voted to declare conditional independence from Ukraine and proposed to confirm the decision through a referendum. The referendum was postponed indefinitely after Ukraine granted autonomy to the Crimea.[9] After the Russian parliament asserted Russian control over the Crimean port of Sevastopol, the headquarters of the Black Sea fleet, tensions increased. The UN declared that Sevastopol belonged to Ukraine. Yeltsin and Kravchuk again agreed to split the fleet, with the precise division to be decided by a bilateral commission before 1995. Russia is to be allowed to use the port of Sevastopol, and the 70,000 members of the fleet are to receive dual citizenship.[10]

The breakup of the Soviet Union left nuclear weapons in four republics—Russia, Ukraine, Belarus, and Kazakhstan. The weapons, maintained by Russians, were technically under the unified command of the CIS and tied into an electronic network built by the Soviets to control all weapons from Moscow. The secret codes and procedures needed to order a launch—the nuclear button—are in the hands of the Russian president and the commonwealth military commander. In May 1992, representatives of the four republics and the United States agreed in the Lisbon Accords that under START I, the Strategic Arms Reduction Treaty of July 1991, the three non-Russian republics would give up the nuclear arms stationed on their territories and adhere to the 1970 Nuclear Nonproliferation Treaty. Belarus ratified START I and pledged to adhere to the nonproliferation treaty. It agreed to send all nuclear-tipped SS-25 mobile missiles to Russia for dismantling. Kazakhstan ratified START but has not yet adhered to the nonproliferation treaty.

Ukraine has had second thoughts. It has insisted that the 176 strategic missiles and 37 bomber aircraft with more than 1,500 warheads on its soil are Ukrainian property. Although it is happy to turn over 130 old missiles, many with leaking fuel systems, it has balked at transferring the more modern missiles to Moscow for dismantling unless it gets financial compensation from the West and security guarantees against a revanchist Russia. Ukrainian political leaders indicated they might ratify START I but not join the nonproliferation treaty. After the Russian parliament declared Sevastopol a Russian city in June 1993, Ukrainian nationalists increased the pressure to retain nuclear weapons. When the CIS joint military command dissolved in mid-June and its commander resigned to become Yeltsin's security adviser, Russian forces were left in control of the nuclear arms. This increased Ukrainian reluctance to turn the missiles over to Russia. In an effort to reach a resolution, the United States proposed placing nuclear warheads based in Ukraine under the control of an international commission pending their elimination.[11] The Ukrainian position is crucial because the United States and Russia have stated that they will not implement START I until Ukraine ratifies the accord and signs the nonproliferation treaty. START II is dependent on implementation of START I. Although it has denied it is trying to become a nuclear power, Ukraine could possess the world's third largest nuclear arsenal. This could set off a nuclear arms race between Russia and Ukraine.[12]

Other relations between Russia and Ukraine have suffered. In 1992, Russia exported 25 percent less oil to Ukraine, while Ukraine exported only about 40 percent of the usual amount of sugar to Russia. Russian-Ukrainian relations have been strained by disputes over what price Russians will charge for oil and gas and how much they will supply. Although the price Russia charges is 30–50 percent below world market prices, Ukraine is in arrears by 572 billion rubles or $523 million. Ukrainians are convinced the disputes are part of a Russian campaign to undermine their independence. In November 1992, in an effort to better control its monetary policy, Russia forced Ukraine to leave the ruble zone. The result was a precipitous fall in Ukrainian currency, the coupon, which was considerably weaker than the ruble. In the first quarter of 1993, inflation was 314 percent—more than three times the Russian rate. The new prime minister, Leonid Kuchma, attempted to hold the deficit down by cutting back on both subsidies and the welfare system. The government refused to bail out unprofitable firms and used strikebreakers against workers demanding pay increases. Opposition to these moves was strongest in Russified eastern Ukraine, where heavy industry and coal mines are concentrated. Russians in eastern Ukraine demanded increased autonomy for predominantly Russian regions and recognition of two official languages. Loss of government subsidies encouraged separatist ambitions. In June 1993 a wave of strikes swept from the Donbas coal fields through eastern Ukraine. Nationalists in Russia defend the interests of their fellow Russians in Ukraine. Some are not reconciled to the permanent independence of Ukraine.[13]

### Belarus

Belarus has changed little since the collapse of the Soviet Union. Its Communist Party has been reestablished and several government leaders are expected to rejoin it. It has retained Soviet-style central planning. Price controls still cover more than half the economy—sugar, flour, and vodka are rationed. The fall in production has been held to only 10 percent, half of Russia's, and the 1992 budget deficit was only 4.6 percent of GDP. Although Belarus, like other former Soviet republics, was forced out of the ruble zone, it supports a strong Commonwealth of Independent States and close relations with Russia.[14]

### Moldova

In Moldova, where 14 percent of the population is ethnically Russian, approximately 800 people were killed, and 4,000 others were displaced from their homes because of fighting in 1992. Russians and Ukrainians, who make up a majority of the population in the Trans-Dniester region, proclaimed an independent Dniester republic in 1990.[15] After ten people were killed in fighting between Moldovan police and separatists in early April 1992, Kozyrev, the Russian foreign minister, called for intervention on behalf of the Russian inhabitants. Yeltsin transferred the Soviet Fourteenth Army to Russian jurisdiction, interposed it between the Dniester guards and Moldovan forces, and stated that it would aid the Dniester Russians if they were attacked by Moldova. Moldova threatened to seek assistance from Romania if the Fourteenth Army intervened on behalf of the Dniester Russians. Ethnic fighting escalated.

After a Moldovan attack in Dniester toward the end of June 1992, the Dniester republic appealed for Russian help. Russians accused Moldova of genocide. Yeltsin approved use of force in self-defense, and the Fourteenth Army waded in. Fighting finally subsided in August after Russia and Moldova signed an agreement that established a trilateral peacekeeping force of Russian, Moldovan, and Dniester forces and called for the withdrawal of the Fourteenth Army.[16] The commander of the Fourteenth Army has said his units will not leave until the political status of Trans-Dniester is settled.[17]

### The Baltics

Because Lithuania did not feel threatened by the 20 percent of the population that was ethnically non-Lithuanian, it granted automatic citizenship rights after independence. The situation in Estonia and Latvia was different. Only 62 percent of the population of Estonia is ethnic Estonian, and ethnic Latvians are a bare majority in Latvia. Estonia granted citizenship only to those residents and their descendants who had lived in the republic during its independence period. Latvian and Estonian citizenship laws require residency and a language test that few Russians will be able to pass. Most of the residents in Russian-speaking Narva, Estonia's second largest city, work in huge Soviet-built factories that depended on Russia for raw materials and orders. Large numbers have been laid off and some factories shut down. Since only citizens can vote or serve in government, Narva residents are disenfranchised. Russians cannot claim minority rights, and noncitizens cannot own property. In mid-June 1993, the Estonian parliament approved a law requiring noncitizens who had not filed for citizenship to apply for a residency permit within two years or leave the country. Russian residents demonstrated in protest. After Yeltsin denounced the law as a form of ethnic cleansing and after Western expressions of disapproval, Estonia's president returned the law for reconsideration. A modified version was adopted July 12. Noncitizens lawfully employed in civilian jobs, pensioners, and others collecting state benefits will not be expelled. Soldiers, criminals, and foreign spies must leave. Tight quotas will be imposed on the number of Russians who can win naturalization. There is enormous anxiety among Russians who have nowhere else to go.[18]

All three Baltic states were overwhelmed by economic crisis. Although shops are filled with Western goods, few can afford to buy them. There have been sharp declines in industrial and agricultural production. Since they are not in the CIS, Russia has charged them the world-market prices for oil. Few buildings had heat or hot water over the long winter. The volume of trade with Russia and other areas of the former Soviet Union fell drastically. In a presidential election in Lithuania in February 1993 and in parliamentary elections in November 1992, Brazaukas and his Democratic Labor Party of reform-minded former communists were victorious. Brazaukas wants to slow the pace of privatization and stop the breakup of collective farms into small unprofitable private holdings. He has moved to improve relations with Russia.[19]

Estonia took a different path and cut subsidies to industries, allowed prices to rise freely, kept wages down, and prohibited the Central Bank from printing new money. Trade was reoriented toward Finland and Scandinavia. Inflation dropped sharply, to only 1.7 percent a month in May 1993. Purchasing power also dropped.[20]

Troop withdrawal is a major issue. Only Lithuania has negotiated an agreement with Russia, but Russia has agreed in principle to troop removal from all three Baltic states. However, Russia cites difficulties of timing, issues of compensation, and problems of disposition of military bases and materials. At the beginning of October 1992 all three Baltic states asked the UN General Assembly to persuade Russia to remove the 80,000 remaining Russian troops, more than half of which were in Latvia. In response, Russia announced that it was temporarily suspending troop withdrawal in the Baltics because there was no place for the men to live in Russia and because the rights of Russian-speaking minorities were being violated. Withdrawals resumed, but again, at the end of March 1993, Russia announced that a housing shortage left it no choice but to temporarily halt the pullout of its remaining 50,000 troops in the Baltics.[21] Subsequently, however, Russia withdrew its troops from Lithuania at the end of August.

Baltic nationalists want the departure of Russians, whom they see as a potential fifth column. Russians, who have nowhere else to go, complain of blatant discrimination but have not created an organized resistance movement. Yeltsin, on November 6, 1992, asked the UN to take measures to help end human rights violations against ethnic Russians in the Baltics.[22] Yeltsin's opponents blame him for not doing enough to protect the rights of Russians in the Baltics.

## Georgia

Fighting between Georgian troops and Abkhazian separatists broke out after the Abkhazian parliament declared independence in July 1992.[23] Georgian troops entered in August, allegedly to rout supporters of Gamsakhurdia, the ousted Georgian president, and recaptured Sukhumi, the principal city. Muslim militias on the Russian side of the border lined up with the Abkhazians. More than 1,000 people were killed. Shevardnadze accused Russia of collaborating with the separatists and demanded that Russian troops leave Georgia. Tension increased when Georgia announced its intention to seize all former Soviet military equipment in Georgia, part of which was with the Russian army.[24] A cease-fire was reached in September.

Toward the end of March 1993, two Russian warplanes attacked Georgian howitzer and mortar positions at the same time that Abkhazian forces shelled Sukhumi. Shevardnadze asserted that thousands of Russian mercenaries and regular army men were directly involved in military hostilities. Russia, which has military airfields and thousands of troops along Abkhazia's Black Sea coast, denied the charges, insisting that Russian troops in Abkhazia were neutral but on high alert to repel any attacks against Russian military facilities. The Russian Defense Ministry maintained the air raid was in response to Georgia's artillery bombing of a Russian military laboratory near Sukhumi, which is reported to be a monitoring station for nuclear explosions. Russia declared a no-fly zone around the laboratory and stated it would fire in self-defense. At the end of the first week in April, the warring sides agreed to disengage. Russian defense minister Pavel Grachev stated that Russian army units would remain in Georgia until 1995.[25] On July 1, Abkhazian rebels advanced toward Sukhumi. Shevardnadze declared martial law. After a month of fighting in which about 1,000 people were killed, Russia, Abkhazia, and Georgia agreed to a cease-fire plan under which Georgian troops were to withdraw from Abkhazia and be replaced by Russian troops and ninety UN observers.[26]

Ossetia has been a second area of Russian-Georgian confrontation. The 162,000 Ossetians in Georgia seek independence or unification with North Ossetia just over the Russian border. Fighting between Georgians and Ossetians broke out in 1989. Thousands of refugees began pouring into North Ossetia in mid-June 1992, and South Ossetia officially asked to be annexed by Russia. Russian armed forces were being drawn into the conflict. Shevardnadze appealed to the UN and other regional organizations to prevent aggression against Georgia.[27] On June 24, 1992, Yeltsin and Shevardnadze agreed to enforce a cease-fire in the Georgian-Ossetian conflict.[28] In July, a Russian-Georgian-South Ossetian peace force was deployed to South Ossetia. Since then, the region has been quiet. If Russia, which has no interest in this barren, mountainous area, decides to pull out, fighting is likely to begin again.[29]

### Armenia and Azerbaijan

Neither side appears willing to compromise in the war over Nagorno-Karabakh that has cost about 3,000 lives since it began in 1988. Because they are better organized than the Azeris and inherited more equipment from the Soviet army, the Armenians have done better in the fighting. In 1992, Armenian Karabakh forces gained control of Nagorno-Karabakh and punched a land corridor through, linking it to Armenia. Nagorno-Karabakh declared independence after 99 percent of voters supported it in a referendum. Peace talks took place under the auspices of the Conference on Security and Cooperation in Europe (CSCE). Turkey and Russia also sought to mediate. But in early April 1993, Armenian forces launched an attack in northwestern Azerbaijan and opened a second corridor from Armenia into Nagorno-Karabakh. Armenians then attacked towns and villages in southwestern Azerbaijan along the Iranian border, occupying a almost one-tenth of Azerbaijani territory. About 100,000 refugees streamed down from the mountains that were the scene of the fighting. The offensive in the southwest was an attempt to seal off Nakhichevan, a part of Azerbaijan surrounded by Armenia, Turkey, and Iran, which had been receiving food and energy supplies from Iran and Turkey. The Azeris accused Russia's Seventh Army, stationed in Armenia, of siding with the Armenians.[30]

In June 1992, Abulfez Elchibey, who headed a broad noncommunist coalition, was elected president of Azerbaijan with 60 percent of the vote. Defeats in the war over Nagorno-Karabakh, corruption, and a disintegrating economy weakened the popularity of the coalition. Surat Husseinov, a warlord, marched on Baku in early June 1993. Elchibey asked Heidar Aliyev, a former communist leader who had served on the Politburo, to mediate. Elchibey then went into exile, leaving Aliyev as head of parliament and acting president. Aliyev named Husseinov his prime minister and head of all security forces. Armenian Karabakh forces launched a major offensive into Azerbaijan. Husseinov vowed to retake all lands lost to Nagorno-Karabakh and to reestablish control over it. CSCE continues its efforts to end the conflict and the United States is now playing a leading role in seeking an end to the war.[31]

Armenia is now facing disaster as a consequence of an Azerbaijani blockade of landlocked Armenia's main rail and road supply lines. At the end of January 1992 Armenia's last source of energy, a gas pipeline running through Georgia, was blown up. Temporary repairs allowed the restoration of some power but the pipeline was again blown up in April after the Armenian offensive. In retaliation for Armenia's attack in Azerbaijan, Turkey closed its borders to overland relief for Armenia. The country is disintegrating with little or no heat, electricity, or running water and a desperate shortage of food.[32]

## Central Asia

Since about 9 million Russians live in Central Asia, Russia does not believe it can just stand by and do nothing while the region is swept up in chaos. Hundreds of thousands of Russians have fled.

Kazakhstan has avoided ethnic violence, but the potential is present. Russians are now 38 percent of the population, almost equal to the Kazakh portion; Ukrainians, ethnic Germans, and Belarussians make up most of the rest. Most Russians live in the north while the agricultural south is mostly Kazakh. The capital, Alma-Ata, is about two-thirds Russian. Russians built the major cities and industries, and Russian remains the primary language of business and industry. Although the Kazakh elite is Russified, there is a growth of Kazakh nationalism. Increasing numbers of Kazakhs are being appointed to government positions. Protests by Russian speakers in July 1992 persuaded Nazarbaev, the president of Kazakhstan, to amend the new constitution to prohibit discrimination against residents who did not speak Kazakh and to postpone switching all official business to Kazakh. Although future presidents must have a good working knowledge of the Kazakh language, they do not have to be ethnically Kazakh. The compromise led to picketing of the Kazakh parliament by Kazakh nationalists. Kazakhstan produced one-third of the grain in the Soviet Union and contains 90 percent of the former Soviet Union's chrome, 60 percent of its silver, and other valuable minerals. In addition, it contains about 25 billion barrels of recoverable oil reserves. The country is attracting an increasing number of Western and Asian business executives. Nazarbaev has urged renewed political and economic union with Russia in a core group within the CIS, and endorses a joint commonwealth peacekeeping force.[33]

In Tajikistan, 10,000 Russian troops are caught up in the middle of a civil war that is both ideological and ethnic.[34] Territorial and tribal rivalries are intertwined with the forces of communism and fundamentalism. A loose coalition of Islamic fundamentalists and "democrats" faces a rival force of communists. The communist forces are supported by people from the wealthier lowlands, while the fundamentalists are supported by people from the more impoverished and religious regions. Arms flow in from Afghanistan, and gunmen roam the countryside.

Russians have become increasingly concerned about the fate of Russians in Tajikistan and about the flood of Russian refugees. One-quarter of the Russian-speaking population, 90,000 people, fled in 1992 alone. When, in early September, the communist leader Rakhmon Nabiyev was forced out of power, Russia became worried about Iranian influence and intervention by Tajiks from Afghanistan. Uzbekistan, Kazakhstan, and Kirgizstan feared that the spread of Islamic fundamentalism would bring chaos and civil war to the whole of Central Asia.

In December, resurgent communist armies began a counteroffensive, allegedly with the help of Uzbekistan. A militia of at least 5,000 men under Sangak Safarov, a tough ex-convict and chieftain, played a major role in driving the Islamic opposition forces from Dushanbe. More than 25,000 people were killed and about 500,000 displaced since 1991. At least half the cotton and grain crops were lost, factories ceased to operate, and farms were destroyed. In early February 1993, Russia offered to help build a new Tajik army and to restore Russian antiaircraft defenses along the frontier. Russian troops attempted to guard the Tajik-Afghan border across which guns and gunmen have been streaming.[35] Armed bands of Islamic forces took to the mountains east of Dushanbe, and other bands formed in Afghanistan where they received uniforms, weapons, and training. Yeltsin declared that the Tajik-Afghan border was "in effect Russia's." Russia sent in 10,000 reinforcements bringing the total number of troops on the Tajikistan southern border to 15,000. Russian warplanes bombed rebel positions east of Dushanbe. In an effort to end the bloodshed, Yeltsin urged reorganization of the Tajik government to reflect all ethnic and clan interests.[36]

In reaction to the warfare in Tajikistan and fearing the spread of Islamic fundamentalism, President Islam Karimov of neighboring Uzbekistan has cracked down on dissent. Karimov, who led Uzbekistan under the Soviets and won election in December 1991, is concerned to maintain political stability in a period of economic transition. To prevent an influx of refugees, he closed the border with Tajikistan. Uzbek leaders are nervous that the 1.5 million Tajiks in the Uzbekistan population of about 19.9 million may be sympathetic to fundamentalism. All religious-based parties, including the Islamic Renaissance Party, have been banned. The crackdown has been extended to Karimov's secular democratic opponents. The leaders of Birlik, the main opposition movement, have been beaten, arrested, and intimidated. Erk, or Freedom, the registered opposition party, has had its bank accounts and cars seized, its newspaper closed, and its building requisitioned.[37] Since 1985, 800,000 people, mostly Russians, have left Uzbekistan.

Turkmenistan has maintained similarly tight controls, persecuting dissenters, imposing censorship, and outlawing opposition parties. The Russified former communist leader was elected president in June 1992 in an uncontested election in which he received 99.5 percent of the vote. Turkmenistan has been labeled a second Kuwait because of its relative prosperity and vast reserves of natural gas. The government subsidizes rent and food while water, gas, and electricity are free. Each citizen is entitled to receive five hectares of land. Niyazov is determined to maintain political stability, to encourage foreign investment, to persuade skilled Russians to remain, and to avoid ethnic hostilities.[38]

## THE RUSSIAN FEDERATION

Although 82 percent of the 150 million people in the Russian Federation, the core of the old Soviet Union, are ethnic Russians, it includes 130 nationalities and ethnic groups in 88 "subjects" of which 20 have republic status. Local authorities attempt to gather increasing power from an enfeebled Moscow, much as the republics of the Soviet Union drew power from the center.

The Russian Federation has five tiers of government: federal, republican, regional, city, and district. Ethnically based republics have their own constitutions and substantial self-governing powers. Although 27 million non-Russians live in the 20 republics, Russians are actually the majority in 9 and account for 30 percent or more in another 8. In April 1992, eighteen of the twenty republics signed a Federation Treaty that gives the central government responsibility for defense, long-distance communication, and basic science while the republics are responsible for local social services and most privatization. The two levels are jointly responsible for development of natural resources. Chechnya in effect seceded, and Tatarstan did not sign the Federation Treaty. Other republics signed with significant reservations.[39]

The new draft constitution is vague about whether all eighty-eight "subjects" have equal rights. The twenty republics have their own languages, citizenship requirements, and constitutions, but, in economic terms, the republics and the sixty-eight regions are treated equally. This has satisfied neither. Only eight of the twenty ethnic republic leaders initialed the draft. Since Tatarstan negotiated bilateral agreements with the federal government, other republics are demanding the same right. Regional leaders, of whom one-third declined to initial the draft, resent the fact that their taxes are subsidizing the republics. They want more economic control over their resources.[40]

There has been a decisive shift in power from the center to the republics and regions. Almost all social services, including hospitals, schools, transportation, and rent subsidies, are under regional control. This has produced tremendous strain on the budgets of local governments as new spending obligations rise faster than the money necessary to support them. Almost all of their revenue comes from fixed shares of federal taxes. Some regions are tempted to solve their budget problems by withholding taxes due to the central government. This could create a situation similar to what occurred in the Soviet Union in 1991 when Russia bankrupted the central government by withholding taxes. However, the Soviet republics controlled all taxes. In contrast, locally gathered taxes account for one-third of Russia's taxes, so the danger is somewhat less.[41]

Interests of different regions are often antagonistic. The interests of raw material–producing regions like Siberia clash with those of the industrial centers in the Urals. Large cities are usually dominated by reformers while communists control rural areas. Regions are reforming at different speeds. While Moscow and St. Petersburg sold nearly half their shops to the private sector in the first half of 1992, the ethnic republics privatized almost nothing. Local reform leaders like Boris Nemtsov of Nizhny Novgorod argue that reform can succeed only if regional power is increased, but most local governments have chosen to control, not liberalize, their economies. Many push outright protectionism. In Tyumen, Russia's largest oil-exporting region, oil producers need an export license. Nearly one-third of Russia's cities still control most local food prices. Tatarstan issues special coupons for local food purchases. Local governments often require factories and farms to sell them a portion of their output, which the governments then barter for goods from other localities. Farmers often refuse to sell grain to the central government. Krasnodar, which includes some of the richest farmland in Russia, suspended shipments of grain to other parts of Russia.[42]

The feud between Yeltsin and his rivals in the legislature has had reverberations at the local level, where local governors tend to support Yeltsin while the local soviets support the legislature. The strongest opposition to Yeltsin's demand for stronger executive power came from the ethnic republics.

## Siberia and the Far East

Siberia accounts for three-quarters of Russia's landmass and more than half of its raw material wealth and export-earning capacity. When energy prices are freed, investment in Siberian mines and oil fields is likely to increase. As the large industries of European Russia fold, the country's economic center is likely to shift to Siberia. Siberian deputies from the Russian parliament and regional parliament have demanded steps to decolonize Siberia. The heads of Siberia's local governments formed a group called Siberian Accord, which demands greater power over foreign economic relations, taxation, and the development of natural resources.[43] Yeltsin has promised to invest a large proportion of American assistance in Siberia.

Sakha, formerly Yakutia, a huge Siberian republic of 3.1 million square miles, accounts for 99 percent of Russia's diamond production and one-fourth of the world's. The diamond industry earned Russia about $1.4 billion a year through hard-currency exports. There is also vast wealth in gold, silver, oil, gas, and coal. The Yakuts, a Turkic people who account for one-third of the population, have seen few benefits. There are unpaved roads, wooden huts with outside facilities, and no running water except when the snow melts in the spring. In 1990, Yakutia issued a declaration of sovereignty and changed the name of the republic to Sakha, the ancient Yakut name. The 1991 constitution claims primacy for local laws. Yakutia has won the right to keep 20 percent of the diamonds and other minerals it produces plus 45 percent of the hard-currency earnings from foreign diamond sales. It has raised average salaries to twice the Russian level and created a multi-billion ruble social security fund. After bitter battles in the Russian parliament, a new joint stockholding company in which Russia and Yakutia are equal partners is being formed to control the entire diamond industry. Although these changes will affect Russia economically, relations with the largely communist leadership of Yakutia are good.[44]

Administrative districts are determined to fight for the same powers granted republics. The Tyumen district of Western Siberia produces 70 percent of the country's oil and 90 percent of its gas but has the lowest standard of living of any Russian district. Leaders are demanding a larger share of the earnings from raw material exports.Tyumen has won the right to keep the earnings from 10 percent of local oil and gas exports. The governor wants the right to grant exploration licenses and is calling on Western firms to enter agreements directly with Tyumen, bypassing the central government.[45]

Despite talk of Siberian independence, the small population and economic importance of the area make it highly unlikely that independence could become a reality. But the region will be able to retain a greater proportion of the wealth it produces.

## The Caucasus

Since the collapse of the Soviet Union, the Caucasus has reverted to a violent cauldron of more than fifty ethnic groups. Each of the string of backward autonomous republics on the northern slopes of the Caucasus has its own history, language, and grievances. They have set up roadblocks "manned by vigilantes with Kalashnikovs."[46] Special units of Russian internal troops have tried to control illegal transportation of weapons across the borders.

The 800,000 Chechens, who declared independence from Russia in November 1991, are led by a former Soviet strategic bomber pilot, Dzhokar Dudayev. He has threatened to send his supporters to blow up nuclear power stations in Russia if Moscow tries to overthrow him. Moscow sent troops but pulled them back under pressure from Chechen forces. After his inauguration as president in December 1991, Dudayev made state visits to

Saudi Arabia and Turkey, kicked out the Russian military garrison in the capital city of Grozny, and provided sanctuary for Gamsakhurdia, the deposed president of Georgia. Chechen volunteers have been fighting alongside the Abkhazians, thus straining Russia's relations with Georgia. The Chechen "Mafia," which runs the oil and arms trade, has long been considered the most ruthless and well organized in the former Soviet Union. Slavs have been fleeing. The city of Grozy, with a Slavic population of 72 percent, is especially hard hit. Their departure left administrative chaos. Although there are more imported cars per person in Grozny than in any other ex-Soviet city, basic services have broken down. It is without water much of the time, and the telephone system collapsed. Its oil wealth has enabled it to survive a Russian economic blockade.[47]

After the Chechen majority of what had been Chechen-Ingushetia declared independence from Moscow, the Russian parliament decided that the Ingush were entitled to their own autonomous republic. After the Ingush were allowed to return from exile in 1957, much of their land remained in the hands of Ossetians. Now the Ingush assumed the way was open to border changes. In late October 1992, Ingush commandos mounted raids in an effort to regain control of a district in North Ossetia that they had held until Stalin deported thousands of Ingush to Kazakhstan in 1944. Well-armed Ossetian soldiers attacked and devastated Ingush villages. In a few days in early November, all Ingush in North Ossetia—some 50,000 people—were driven from their homes, which were looted and burned. Russia imposed a state of emergency on North Ossetia, and Ingushetia and Russian troops tried to seal North Ossetia's borders to prevent the Ingush in Chechnya from joining in the fighting. Some Russian troops reportedly participated in the killing of Ingush civilians. When, on November 10, Russian troops moved into the capital of Ingushetia, General Dudayev declared this a violation of Chechen territory and threatened to take action. Russian troops soon became embroiled with Chechen forces, but an agreement on disengagement was reached and Russia reaffirmed the neutrality of its soldiers.[48]

Since the Caucasian republics border on other states and have a combined population of only 6.5 million, their secession would not much affect Russia's future. In fact, many Russians believe that the control of the area is not worth the effort. Russian nationalists feel nothing in common with the peoples of the Caucasus, whom they look upon as lawless savages.

### The Middle Volga

The middle Volga is a vital concern of the Russian government since it controls transportation links between European Russia and Siberia and access to western Siberian oil fields. Tatarstan, a republic of 3.8 million people, produces nearly a fourth of all Russia's crude oil and grows enough food to feed itself and export to other areas of Russia. A Russian army division is stationed in Kazan, the capital, and many of Tatarstan's factories are involved in military production.[49] It held a referendum in April 1992 in which 61 percent of those who voted favored independence. It has not signed the Federation Treaty and has adopted a constitution declaring the supremacy of Tatarstan's laws on its territory. Echoing the calls of Tatar nationalists of the 1920s, at the end of 1992 the Tatar parliament called for creation of a Volga confederation. Such a move, if successful, would give Tatarstan a border with Kazakhstan. A successful declaration of independence would increase the danger that neighboring Bashkortostan and others would follow, cutting Russia in half. If that occurred, Russia could lose control over Siberia.[50]

In an effort to gain the support of Tatarstan in their battle with the legislature, Yeltsin and Chernomyrdin agreed in January 1993 to draw up a treaty to grant Tatarstan more power than that allowed to other republics under the Federation Treaty.[51] Tatarstan agreed to participate in the April referendum, supplying Yeltsin with some needed votes, but made it clear that it expected increased regional authority from Yeltsin in return.[52] Tatarstan is negotiating twelve bilateral agreements with the federal government. The three signed in June 1993 divided responsibility for defense plants in Tatarstan, divided other property, and gave Tatarstan control of its own customs service.[53]

Neighboring Bashkortostan owes its status as a republic to the Bashkirs, a Muslim Turkic people who constitute 22 percent of the republic's population of 4 million. Forty percent are Russian and 28 percent Tatar. It has its own constitution and laws. It signed the Federation Treaty on condition that it receive special concessions, including exclusive control of all property on its territory. Like other republics, it has developed policies that diverge from Moscow's. Since it is a major center of Russia's petrochemical industry, it is able to finance social benefits such as free kindergartens. Basic food is subsidized, and there is state-supported health insurance. There have been little privatization of firms and strong opposition to any attempt to privatize land. Negotiations with Moscow have centered on the division of state-owned assets between the republic and Moscow and on taxes paid to Moscow.[54]

### Other Republics and Regions

Movements for increased autonomy or independence are not restricted to those areas just covered. Buryatia, Tuva, and other republics along the Mongolian border are gradually slipping from Moscow's control.[55] Even the Finns in Karelia, to the east of Finland, want autonomy. They and the Karelians and Vepsy, two related ethnic groups that together make up less than 20 percent of Karelia's population, have met to demand legal recognition by Russia. Many want the area returned to Finland, although Finns in Finland have shown no desire to take over the poor republic. About 8,000 have moved to Finland, which wants to discourage any further immigration by the 100,000 Finns in the former Soviet Union.[56]

In an effort to build political support, Yeltsin issued a decree in mid-March 1993 making significant concessions to the Cossack communities, known as Hosts. There are about 7 million Cossacks in Russia and 2 million outside Russia's borders. The decree, which is being challenged by the parliament in the Constitutional Court, established purely Cossack units in the army, border guards, and militia with traditional Cossack ranks, uniforms, and insignia. It also reestablished the right of Cossack Hosts to land and self-government. The Cossacks of the Don region confronted local authorities, demanding recognition of their territorial autonomy. Cossack troops surrounded the Rostov government building and threatened local officials. Although the crisis was overcome, recognition of military formations not controlled by Moscow could weaken control by the center.[57]

## DISINTEGRATION?

"Laws are not being observed . . . there is a power crisis and economic reforms are not conclusive."[58] More than 16,000 local laws are opposed to the laws of the central government. Not only republics, but regions and even villages, have declared they are not subject to any laws of the center that contradict their own.

Yeltsin attacked the legitimacy of the parliament because it was elected under Soviet rule, but in doing so he put the legitimacy of the entire political system in jeopardy because he, too, was elected under Soviet rule. As fighting between the executive and legislative branches intensified, central government control over the country weakened. Both Yeltsin and the parliament have spent their energies in political jockeying, seeking to gain political advantage over each other; and in the process they have undermined hope of a national consensus on fundamental principles of governance. As the referendum approached, competition for the support of republics and regions led to increasing concessions, further weakening the power of the center. There is little respect for the central government, because the people see no benefit from its actions.

Sergei Stankevich, a Yeltsin adviser, has warned: "Russian people do not have any other country. The dismemberment of Russia cannot be accomplished peacefully. That is a road to chaos and civil war."[59] What seems more likely is that for the next several years, power will continue to drift from the center to the regions and republics. Rather than confronting them, the center will make increasing concessions to placate them and maintain at least a semblance of loyalty. But the center will be increasingly dependent upon the regional and republic governments for enforcement of laws and decrees. Some border areas may fall away permanently—those on the Mongolian border or in the Caucasus. But Tatarstan and Bashkortostan are more likely to push for increasing autonomy while avoiding the direct confrontation that could push Russia to act forcibly.

## NOTES

1. *New York Times*, February 7, 1993.

2. Paul Goble, "Russia and Its Neighbors," *Foreign Policy* 90 (Spring 1993): 79–84.

3. *The Economist*, November 14, 1992, 59–60.

4. *New York Times*, January 3, 1993.

5. *New York Times*, March 1, 1993.

6. *Izvestia*, January 4, 1992, in *Current Digest of the Post Soviet Press (CDPSP)* 44 (February 5, 1992): 13.

7. *New York Times*, July 22, 1993.

8. *New York Times*, June 18, 1993.

9. *Nezavismaya gazeta*, May 23, 1992, in *CDPSP* 44 (June 24, 1992): 1–2.

10. *New York Times*, July 10, 22, 1993.

11. *New York Times*, June 18, 1993.

12. Michael Mandelbaum, "By a Thread," *The New Republic* 208 (April 5, 1993): 18–23; *The Economist*, April 3, 1993, 52; *New York Times*, March 31; April 8, 1993; (Cleveland) *Plain Dealer*, April 6, 7, 1993.

13. *New York Times*, November 6, 1992; June 12, 16, 20, 1993; *The Economist*, February 13, 1993, 56; March 13, 1993, 56–57.

14. *The Economist*, February 20, 1993, 49.

15. *New York Times*, February 7, 1993.

16. *Izvestia*, July 22, 1992, in *CDPSP* 44 (August 19, 1992): 20–21.

17. *New York Times*, March 1, 1993.

18. *The Economist*, September 26, 1992, 18; July 31, 1993, 45; *New York Times*, November 22, 1992; June 26, 1993.

19. *The Economist*, November 21, 1992, 63.

20. (Cleveland) *Plain Dealer*, June 23, 1993.

21. *New York Times* October 4, 21, 31; November 22, 1992; March 30, 1993.

22. *New York Times*, November 8, 1992.

23. Abkhazia's population is 45 percent Georgian, 17 percent Abkhazian, and 30 percent Russian or Armenian.

24. *New York Times*, October 7, 8, 1992; *The Economist*, January 30, 1993, 47–48.

25. *New York Times*, March 18, 20, 21, 1993; (Cleveland) *Plain Dealer*, April 3, 8, 1993.

26. *New York Times*, July 6, 7, 27, 28, 1993; *The Economist*, July 24, 1993, 55; August 14, 1993, 48.

27. *Izvestia*, June 15, 20, 1992, in *CDPSP* 44 (July 15, 1992): 16–17.

28. *Nezavismaya gazeta*, June 26, 1992, in *CDPSP* 44 (July 22, 1992): 6.

29. *The Economist*, November 14, 1992, 59–60; January 30, 1993, 48.

30. (Cleveland) *Plain Dealer*, February 27, 1993: *New York Times* April 2, 5, 7, 12, 1993; *The Economist*, April 10, 1993, 58.

31. *New York Times*, June 19, 21, 22, 23, 24, 25, 29, 30; July 6, 9; August 2, 1993.

32. Margaret Shapiro, " 'Welcome to Hell' in Armenia," *Washington Post National Weekly Edition*, February 8–14, 1993, 12; *New York Times*, April 11, 1993; *The Economist*, April 10, 1993, 58.

33. *The Economist*, August 8, 1992, 29–30; *New York Times,* March 2; August 8, 1993.

34. *New York Times*, September 30; October 18, 1992; February 7, 21, 1993; *The Economist*, November 14, 1992, 60; (Cleveland) *Plain Dealer*, February 17, 1993.

35. *New York Times*, March 1, 1993.

36. *Financial Times*, May 12, 1993; *New York Times*, July 19, 20; August 8, 1993; *The Economist*, July 24, 1993, 38; August 7, 1993, 36.

37. *New York Times*, February 13, 15, 1993.

38. Jeri Laber, "The Dictatorship Returns," *New York Review of Books*, July 15, 1993, 42–44.

39. *The Economist*, September 5, 1992, 53; "A Survey of Russia," *The Economist*, December 5, 1992, 24–26.

40. *New York Times*, July 13, 1993; *The Economist*, July 17, 1993, 47.

41. "Survey of Russia," 24–25; *The Economist*, September 5, 1992, 53–54.

42. "Survey of Russia," 24; *The Economist*, September 5, 1992, 53–54.

43. *Izvestia*, March 30, 1992, and *Rossiiskaya gazeta*, April 2, 1992, 2, in *CDPSP* 44 (April 29, 1992): 9–10.

44. *New York Times*, November 1, 1992.

45. *The Economist*, November 21, 1992, 64.

46. *Washington Post National Weekly Edition*, November 2–8, 1992, 15–16.

47. Ibid.: *Izvestia*, July 9, 1992, in *CDPSP* 44 (August 5, 1992): 27.

48. *New York Times*, November 2, 11, 1992; (Cleveland) *Plain Dealer*, November 16, 1992; *The Economist*, November 28, 1992, 58. The approximately 100,000 Ingush in Ingushetia, Chechnya, and North Ossetia are predominantly Muslim while the approximately 400,000 Ossetians in North and South Ossetia are predominantly Orthodox Christians.

49. (Cleveland) *Plain Dealer*, April 7, 1993.

50. *The Economist*, January 30, 1993, 47; Peter Reddaway, "Russia Comes Apart," *New York Times*, January 10, 1993, 23.

51. *The Economist*, January 30, 1993, 47.

52. (Cleveland) *Plain Dealer*, April 7, 1993.

53. *The Economist*, July 17, 1993, 47.

54. *New York Times*, March 28, 1993.

55. *The Economist*, January 30, 1993, 47.

56. *The Economist*, January 9, 1993, 42.

57. (Cleveland) *Plain Dealer*, April 7, 1993.

58. *The Economist*, January 30, 1993, 47.

59. Dmitri Simes, "What Clinton Must Do to Aid Democracy in Russia," *Washington Post Weekly Edition*, February 8–14, 1993, 24.

## Chapter 16

# PROSPECTS FOR DEMOCRATIC TRANSFORMATION

The euphoria with which many Russians greeted the collapse of the Soviet Union has long since disappeared. It was, of course, unrealistic for anyone to believe that it would be easy for Russia to transform itself from a powerful empire into a nation-state while simultaneously restructuring its economic system and moving from an arthritic autocracy to a dynamic democratic system. Russia has never separated nation-building from expansion; it has never had a free market economy; it has never experienced political democracy. The task was not merely to recover a system that had been stifled by the imposition of communism but rather to create new economic and political institutions that had never before existed except in nascent form.

There was no consensus on democratic values. The Soviet Union had collapsed, but not everyone was reconciled to its disappearance. Russia was confronted with a struggle between remnants of the old regime and those seeking to create a new one. The political actors have had to learn the nature of democratic politics as they govern. The military-industrial elite, the *apparatchiki*, and the old *nomenklatura* have little sympathy with Western democracy, individual rights, and political pluralism. Military leaders are more committed to order than to democracy. Workers and peasants are more concerned with unemployment, soaring prices, and loss of economic security. Many who supported Yeltsin did so not because they supported democracy but because they yearned for a strong leader. Parties and movements that call themselves democratic and fought communism are not necessarily committed to Western-style democracy, and when they are, there is little understanding of its basic principles.

The democrats were more committed to economic transformation than to political democracy. Shock therapy, imposed from the top down, produced a falling standard of living, near hyperinflation, a severely falling ruble, plunging production, deindustrialization, and declining exports.

Old factories and whole industries are threatened with closings, but no new factories are taking their place. Savings were wiped out, while wages and pensions failed to keep pace with rising consumer prices.

Corruption, bribery, and *nomenklatura* privilege helped undermine the legitimacy of the Soviet system. But corruption and bribery have increased, while the *nomenklatura* and former black marketeers are seen as the prime beneficiaries of privatization and free market reforms. The growth of a new class who flaunt their wealth in conditions of poverty has created frustration and resentment that can easily spill over into ethnic hatred and xenophobic nationalism. The task of economic construction is overwhelming and cannot be accomplished in a short time. The implied promise of shock therapy, that it would produce quick results after a short period of intense suffering, has been betrayed by the economic misery. A more gradual transition to a market economy and preservation of a safety net may be more suitable to Russian conditions and ultimately more successful. Western economic aid is necessary not to reward achievement but to assist Russians in making the transition.

The democratic reformers are the country's best hope, but they have no practical experience in government and no realization of the problems encountered in the real world of politics. Rather than seeking to understand politics and the interplay of interests, they see all opposition as a nefarious plot to restore the old communist regime. When they attack men like Chernomyrdin, accusing him of trying to restore communism, they undermine their own credibility. Calling themselves democrats and supporting free market economics, civil liberties, and human rights, they fail to understand the relationship among pluralism, loyal opposition, and democracy. Instead they demand agreement, not only with their goal of a free market economy but also with methods of achieving it, the speed at which it must be attained, and its exact contours. The success of democracy requires the formation of a governing party or coalition with a coherent program and ability to control its deputies and ministers, and the formation of a loyal opposition that shares the overall goal but differs in emphasis, speed, and method. It requires not only the toleration of organized alternative views and criticism but acceptance of the right of the opposition to come to power through elections.

Russians have experienced a government dominated by inexperienced economic reformers and a parliament full of talkers. Under Gorbachev, the deadening unanimity of the Soviet era legislatures was broken, and open criticism and confrontation became the norm. Gorbachev came to complain of the lack of a "parliamentary culture." The Russian legislature has opposed Yeltsin without being able to offer an alternative program. It is more concerned with protecting its own power and privilege than with enacting workable policies. The constant confrontation between the legislature and the president, who took increasingly to rule by edict rather than by law, has served to undermine the legitimacy of all branches of government. The weakening of authority at the center has given rise to criminal gangs and Mafia-type organizations often based on ethnicity. Not only is there no rule of law, but the habit of obedience to the law is being undermined. Bribery was endemic to the Soviet system, but ordinary citizens knew whom to bribe and how much and what to expect in return. Now there are gunfights in the streets, protection rackets, and no assurance of physical safety. The center is gradually losing control over the periphery, especially in the nationality-based republics of the Russian Federation.

The Russian people, at least a majority of those who voted, endorsed Yeltsin and his economic policies in the April 1993 referendum. Much of his support may well have come from those attracted to authoritarianism and a strong hand, rather than from supporters of democracy. The power struggle between Yeltsin and his opponents was not solved by the referendum. Much will depend on whether Yeltsin uses the results of the referendum to strengthen democracy, civil liberties, human rights, and the rule of law, or whether he uses it to create a demogagogic dictatorship that demonizes his opponents.

On September 21, Yeltsin disbanded parliament and called for elections on December 11–12 for a new bicameral legislature. Acknowledging that he had no constitutional authority to dissolve parliament, Yeltsin declared that the constitution was outmoded and useless and proclaimed himself the guarantor of security. Yeltsin could have let the lame duck legislature simply sit; instead, Yeltsin cut the tenuous remaining ties to constitutionality and threw down the gauntlet to the legislature.

In response, the legislature moved to a higher level of confrontation, voting to remove Yeltsin from power and naming Rutskoi acting president. The Constitutional Court ruled that Yeltsin's decree had violated the constitution. On September 24–25, military detachments were moved to the White House and the building was surrounded by barbed wire.

Yeltsin controlled reporting of the crisis and took over all parliamentary newspapers, radios, and television programs. He set presidential elections for June 12, six months after parliamentary elections, and refused to compromise by agreeing to joint elections. Electricity, telephone services, and city water to the White House were cut off. The legislators' access to the outside world was increasingly tenuous. Rutskoi believed he would prevail that military divisions would support the parliament, regions would come to his assistance, and the populace would support his cause. Rabid nationalists and communists demonstrated in support of parliament. Riot police and protesters clashed. Legislators were warned to leave the parliament building and turn in their weapons.

Serious violence first broke out on October 2 when proparliamentary demonstrators threw rocks and firebombs at police, who subsequently fled. The next day, protestors marched on the White House. When they broke through the security cordon at the parliament building, deputies were convinced that a popular uprising was occurring. In response to a call from

Rutskoi and Khasbulatov, the mob took over the mayor's office and moved on to attack Ostankina, the main television station, killing 62 and wounding about 400. Parliamentary leaders now called for their followers to storm the Kremlin. Any talk of compromise was dead.

Yeltsin, who had been strangely quiet, now arrived in Moscow. Armored personnel carriers moved toward Moscow center. The following morning, they took up positions around the White House and shooting broke out. At 10 A.M., huge battle tanks slammed a shell into Khasbulatov's office, which was set on fire. Shelling continued and more fires broke out. At shortly after 6 P.M., Rutskoi and Khasbulatov surrendered and were taken to prision. The White House was in flames.

Yeltsin banned opposition organizations and newspapers, censored mainstream papers, fired opponents, and purged regional councils. Censorship was lifted on October 7, but suspension of opposition newspapers remained in effect. Yeltsin retained control over state television and radio. He forced Zorkin to resign and then suspended the Constitutional Court. The chief prosecutor was fired. Six organizations, including the National Salvation Front and the Communist Worker's Party, were banned outright. Others were suspended. Suspension of the 600,000 member Communist Party and Rutskoi's People's Party of Free Russia was lifted on October 19.

Elections were again scheduled for December 11–12. The new parliament, Yeltsin decreed, would consist of two houses: The Federation Council, an upper house, would have 2 representatives directly elected from each of Russia's 88 regions and republics. The 450-member State Duma, the lower house, would have half its members elected directly in constituencies and half elected from party lists. To run candidates in the elections, parties had to collect 100,000 signatures from at least 7 regions. Rival reform and antireform political parties and alliances formed quickly around well-known political figures. The new constitution, which will define the role of the new parliament, was to be voted on the same day. Yeltsin claimed the right to appoint and fire regional governors. He called on regional soviets to disband; new smaller dumas were to be chosen at the December election.

Although Yeltsin was victorious, his image as the defender of democracy has been badly tarnished. He is in debt to the military, and the slender reed of constitutionality has been broken. The December elections have become the only hope for restoring legitimacy.

# SELECTED BIBLIOGRAPHY

Abraham, Richard. *Alexander Kerensky, The First Love of the Revolution*. New York: Columbia University Press, 1988.

Alexeyeva, Ludmilla. *Soviet Dissent*. Middletown, Conn.: Wesleyan University Press, 1987.

Alstadt, Audrey L. *The Azerbaijani Turks: Power and Identity Under Russian Rule*. Stanford, Calif.: Hoover Institution Press, 1992.

Anderson, Thornton. *Masters of Russian Marxism*. Englewood Cliffs, N.J.: Prentice-Hall, 1963.

Arendt, Hannah. *The Origins of Totalitarianism*. New York: Harcourt Brace Jovanovich, 1966.

Aslund, Anders. *Gorbachev's Struggle for Economic Reform*. 2d ed. Ithaca, N.Y.: Cornell University Press, 1991.

Azrael, Jeremy R. *Managerial Power and Soviet Politics*. Cambridge: Harvard University Press, 1966.

Baradat, Leon P. *Soviet Political Society*. Englewood Cliffs, N.J.: Prentice-Hall, 1992.

Barghoorn, Frederick C., and Thomas F. Remington. *Politics in the USSR*. 3d ed. Boston: Little, Brown, 1986.

Benn, David Wedgwood. *From Glasnost to Freedom of Speech*. London: Pinter, 1992.

————. *Persuasion and Soviet Politics*. Oxford: Blackwell, 1989.

Berdyaev, Nicolas. *The Origin of Russian Communism*. London: Geoffrey Bles, 1937.

Bergson, Abraham, ed. *Soviet Economic Growth*. Evanston, Ill.: Row, Peterson, 1953.

Berlin, Isaiah. *Karl Marx: His Life and Environment*. New York: Oxford University Press, 1959.

Bialer, Seweryn. *Stalin's Successors*. Cambridge: Cambridge University Press, 1980.

————, ed. *Politics, Society and Nationality Inside Gorbachev's Russia*. Boulder, Colo.: Westview Press, 1989.

Bienen, Henry, and Mansur Sunyaev. "Adjustment and Reform in Russia." *SAIS Review* 13 (Winter-Spring 1993): 29–44.

Billington, James. *The Icon and the Axe*. New York: Alfred A. Knopf, 1966.

Bremmer, Ian, and Ray Taras, eds. *Nations and Politics in the Soviet Successor States*. Cambridge: Cambridge University Press, 1993.

Breslauer, George. *Khrushchev and Brezhnev as Leaders*. London: Allen and Unwin, 1982.

Brown, Archie. "Andropov: Discipline and Reform." *Problems of Communism* 32 (January-February 1983): 18–31.
———. "Gorbachev: New Man in the Kremlin." *Problems of Communism* 34 (May-June 1985): 1–23.
———. *Political Leadership in the Soviet Union*. London: Macmillan, 1989.
Brumberg, Abraham. "Not So Free at Last." *New York Review of Books*, 22 October 1992, 56–64.
———, ed. *Chronicle of a Revolution*. New York: Pantheon, 1990.
———, ed. *Russia Under Khrushchev*, New York: Praeger, 1962.
Brzezinski, Zbigniew. *The Grand Failure*. New York: Collier, 1990.
———. *Ideology and Power in Soviet Politics*. NewYork: Praeger, 1962.
———. *The Permanent Purge*. Cambridge: Harvard University Press, 1956.
———. "Post-Communist Nationalism." *Foreign Affairs* 68 (Winter 1989/90): 1–25.
———. "The Soviet Political System: Transformation or Degeneration?" *Problems of Communism* 15 (January-February 1966): 1–15.
Bunce, Valerie, and Philip G. Roeder. "The Effects of Leadership Succession in the Soviet Union." *American Political Science Review* 80 (March 1986): 215–40.
Carew Hunt, R. N. *The Theory and Practice of Communism*. Baltimore, Md.: Penguin, 1963.
Carr, E. H. *A History of Soviet Russia*. New York: Macmillan, 1950.
Carter, Stephen K. *Russian Nationalism*. New York: St. Martin's Press, 1990.
Chamberlin, William Henry. *The Russian Enigma*. New York: Charles Scribner, 1943.
———. *The Russian Revolution*. New York: Grosset and Dunlap, 1965.
Clark, William A. *Crime and Punishment in Soviet Officialdom*. Armonk, N.Y.: M. E. Sharpe, 1993.
Clarkson, Jesse D. *A History of Russia*. Rev. ed. New York: Random House, 1969.
Cohen, Stephen F. *Sovieticus: American Perceptions and Soviet Realities*. New York: W. W. Norton, 1986.
Cohen, Stephen F., and Katrina vanden Heuvel. *Voices of Glasnost*. New York: W. W. Norton, 1989.
Cohen, Stephen F., Alexander Rabinowitch, and Robert Sharlet, eds. *The Soviet Union Since Stalin*. Bloomington: Indiana University Press, 1980.
Colton, Timothy J. *The Dilemma of Reform in the Soviet Union*. New York: Council on Foreign Relations, 1984.
Colton, Timothy J., and Robert Legvold. *After the Soviet Union*. New York: W. W. Norton, 1992.
Conquest, Robert. *The Great Terror*. New York: Macmillan, 1968.
———. *The Harvest of Sorrow*. New York: Oxford University Press, 1986.
———. *Power and Policy in the USSR*. New York: Macmillan, 1961.
———. *Russia After Khrushchev*. New York: Praeger, 1965.
———. *The Soviet Police System*. London: Bodley Head,1968.
———. *Stalin and the Kirov Murder*. New York: Oxford University Press, 1989.
Cornell, Richard, ed. *The Soviet Political System*. Englewood Cliffs, N.J.: Prentice-Hall, 1970.
Cullen, Robert. "A Reporter at Large: Roots." *The New Yorker*, April 15, 1991, 55–76.
———. "A Reporter at Large: Siberia." *The New Yorker*, July 27, 1992, 34–52.
Curtiss, John S. *The Russian Revolution of 1917*. Princeton: Van Nostrand, 1957.

Dallin, Alexander, and George Breslauer. *Political Terror in Communist Systems.* Stanford, Calif.: Stanford University Press, 1970.

Dallin, Alexander, and Gail Lapidus, eds. *The Soviet System in Crisis.* Boulder, Colo.: Westview Press, 1991.

Dallin, Alexander, and Alan Westin, eds. *Politics in the Soviet Union.* New York: Harcourt, Brace and World, 1966.

Davies, R. W. *The Socialist Offensive.* London: Macmillan, 1980.

DeBardeleben, Joan. *Soviet Politics in Transition.* Lexington, Mass.: D. C. Heath, 1992.

Denber, Rachel, ed. *The Soviet Nationality Reader.* Boulder, Colo.: Westview Press, 1992.

d'Encausse, Helene Carrere. *Decline of an Empire.* New York: Harper Colophon Books, 1981.

Deutscher, Isaac. *The Prophet Armed.* New York: Vintage, 1965.

————. *The Prophet Unarmed.* New York: Vintage, 1965.

————. *Russia: What Next?* New York: Oxford University Press, 1953.

————. *Stalin: A Political Biography.* 2d ed. New York: Oxford University Press, 1967.

Diuk, Nadia, and Adrian Karatnycky, *New Nations Rising.* New York: John Wiley, 1993.

Doder, Dusko, and Louise Branson. *Gorbachev: Heretic in the Kremlin.* New York: Viking, 1990.

Draper, Theodore. "Who Killed Soviet Communism?" *New York Review of Books,* June 11, 1992, 7–16.

Eberstadt, Nick. "The Health Crisis in the USSR." *New York Review of Books,* February 19, 1981.

Fainsod, Merle. *How Russia Is Ruled.* Rev. ed. Cambridge: Harvard University Press, 1963.

Fischer, Louis. *The Soviets in World Affairs.* New York: Vintage, 1960.

Friedrich, Carl J., and Zbigniew K. Brzezinski. *Totalitarian Dictatorship and Autocracy.* 2d ed. New York: Praeger, 1966.

Friedrich, Carl J., Michael Curtis, and Benjamin Barber, eds. *Totalitarianism in Perspective: Three Views.* New York: Praeger, 1969.

Garthoff, Raymond L. *Soviet Military Policy.* London: Faber and Faber, 1966.

Goble, Paul. "Ethnic Politics in the USSR." *Problems of Communism* 38: (July-August 1989): 1–15.

————. "Russia and Its Neighbors." *Foreign Policy,* no. 90 (Spring 1993): 79–88.

Goldman, Marshall I. *The Soviet Economy: Myth and Reality.* Englewood Cliffs, N.J.: Prentice-Hall, 1968.

————. *USSR in Crisis.* New York: W. W. Norton, 1983.

————. *What Went Wrong with Perestroika.* New York: W. W. Norton, 1991.

————. "Yeltsin's Reforms: Gorbachev II?" *Foreign Policy,* no. 88 (Fall 1992): 76–90.

Gooding, John. "Gorbachev and Democracy." *Soviet Studies* 42 (April 1990): 195–231.

Gorbachev, Mikhail. *The August Coup.* New York: HarperCollins, 1991.

————. *Perestroika.* New York: Perennial Library, 1988.

Green, Barbara B. "Moscow and Tallinn Under Gorbachev." *The Gamut* 28 (Winter 1989).

————. "Soviet Politics and Interest Groups." *Current History* 51 (October 1966): 213–17, 246.

Grossman, Gregory. "The 'Second Economy' of the USSR." *Problems of Communism* 26 (September-October 1977): 25–40.

Gustafson, Thane. "Gorbachev's Gamble." *Problems of Communism* 36 (July-August 1987): 1–20.

Gustafson, Thane, and Dawn Mann. "Gorbachev's First Year: Building Power and Authority." *Problems of Communism* 36 (May-June 1986): 1–19.

Gwertzman, Bernard, and Michael Kaufman, eds. *The Decline and Fall of the Soviet Empire.* New York: New York Times Company, 1992.

Hahn, Jeffrey W. "Power to the Soviets?" *Problems of Communism* 38 (January-February 1989): 34–46.

Haimson, Leopold. *The Russian Marxists and the Origins of Bolshevism.* Cambridge: Harvard University Press, 1955.

Hajda, Lubomyr, and Mark Beissinger, eds. *The Nationalities Factor in Soviet Politics and Society.* Boulder, Colo.: Westview Press, 1990.

Heeger, Gerald A. *The Politics of Underdevelopment.* New York: St. Martin's Press, 1974.

Hendel, Samuel, ed. *The Soviet Crucible.* 5th ed. North Scituate, Mass.: Duxbury Press, 1980.

Hewett, Edward A. *Reforming the Soviet Economy.* Washington D.C.: Brookings Institution, 1988.

Hill, Ronald J. "The CPSU: From Monolith to Pluralist?" *Soviet Studies* 43 (1991): 217–35.

Hingley, Ronald. *Russia: A Concise History.* Rev. ed. London: Thames and Hudson, 1991.

———. *The Tsars, 1533–1917.* New York: Macmillan, 1968.

Hoffmann, Erik P., and Robbin F. Laird. *The Soviet Polity in the Modern Era.* New York: Aldine, 1984.

Hosking, Geoffrey. "The Roots of Dissolution." *New York Review of Books,* January 16, 1992, 34–38.

Hough, Jerry F. *Soviet Leadership in Transition.* Washington, D.C.: Brookings Institution, 1980.

———. *The Soviet Union and Social Science Theory.* Cambridge: Harvard University Press, 1977.

———. "Understanding Gorbachev: The Importance of Politics." *Soviet Economy* 7 (1991): 166–84.

Huber, Robert T., and Donald R. Kelley. *Perestroika-Era Politics.* Armonk, N.Y.: M. E. Sharpe, 1991.

Ignatieff, Michael. "In the New Republics." *New York Review of Books,* November 21, 1991, 30–32.

Johnson, Priscilla. *Khrushchev and the Arts: The Politics of Soviet Culture 1962–1964.* Cambridge: Harvard University Press, 1965.

Jones, Anthony, Walter D. Connor, and David E. Powell, eds. *Soviet Social Problems.* Boulder, Colo.: Westview Press, 1991.

Kaiser, Robert. *Russia: The People and the Power.* New York: Washington Square Press, 1984.

———. *Why Gorbachev Happened.* New York: Touchstone, 1992.

Kelley, Donald R., ed. *Soviet Politics in the Brezhnev Era.* New York: Praeger, 1980.

Kennan, George F. *The Decision to Intervene.* Princeton, N.J.: Princeton University Press, 1958.

Knight, Amy. *The KGB: Police and Politics in the Soviet Union.* Boston: Unwin Hyman, 1988.

Kopkind, Andrew. "From Russia with Love and Squalor." *The Nation* 256 (January 18, 1993): 44–62.

Kornai, Janos. *The Road to a Free Economy.* New York: W. W. Norton, 1990.

Kotz, David M. "The Cure That Could Kill." *The Nation* 256 (April 19, 1993): 514–516.

Laber, Jeri. "The Dictatorship Returns." *New York Review of Books*, July 15, 1993, 42–44.

Lane, David. *Soviet Society Under Perestroika.* Rev. ed. New York: Rutledge, 1992.

Lapidus, Gail W., and Victor Zaslavsky, eds., with Philip Goldman. *From Union to Commonwealth: Nationalism and Separatism in the Soviet Republics.* Cambridge: Cambridge University Press, 1992.

Laqueur, Walter. *Stalin: The Glasnost Revelations.* New York: Scribner's, 1990.

Leggett, George. *The Cheka: Lenin's Political Police.* New York: Oxford University Press, 1981.

Lenin, V. I. *What Is to Be Done?* New York: International, 1929.

Lewin, Moshe. *The Gorbachev Phenomenon.* Berkeley: University of California Press, 1988.

———. *Russian Peasants and Soviet Power.* London: Allen and Unwin, 1968.

Linden, Carl A. *Khrushchev and the Soviet Leadership.* Baltimore: Johns Hopkins University Press, 1966.

McAuley, Mary. *Soviet Politics 1917–1991.* New York: Oxford University Press, 1992.

Macrides, Roy. *Contemporary Political Ideologies.* Cambridge, Mass.: Winthrop, 1980.

Mandelbaum, Michael. "By a Thread." *The New Republic* 208 (April 5, 1993): 18–23.

Medvedev, Roy. *Let History Judge.* New York: Alfred A. Knopf, 1972.

Medvedev, Zhores. *The Legacy of Chernobyl.* New York: W. W. Norton, 1990.

Mickiewicz, Ellen. *Split Signals.* New York: Oxford University Press, 1988.

Millar, James R., ed. *Politics, Work, and Daily Life in the USSR.* New York: Cambridge University Press, 1987.

Moore, Barrington, Jr. *Social Origins of Dictatorship and Democracy.* Boston: Beacon Press, 1966.

Moskoff, William. *Hard Times: Impoverishment and Protest in the Perestroika Years.* Armonk, N.Y.: M. E. Sharpe, 1993.

Motyl, Alexander J. *Will the Non-Russians Rebel: State, Ethnicity, and Stability in the USSR.* Ithaca, N.Y.: Cornell University Press, 1987.

Nahaylo, Bohdan, and Victor Swoboda. *Soviet Disunion: A History of the Nationalities Problem in the USSR.* New York: Free Press, 1990.

Newhouse, John. "Profile: Chronicling the Chaos." *The New Yorker*, December 31, 1990, 38–72.

Nove, Alec. *An Economic History of the U.S.S.R.* Middlesex, England: Penguin Books, 1972.

———. *Glasnost in Action.* Boston: Unwin Hyman, 1989.

———. *The Soviet Economic System.* 3d ed. Winchester, Mass.: Allen and Unwin, 1983.

Organski, A.F.K. *The Stages of Political Development.* New York: Alfred A. Knopf, 1965.

Orlov, Alexander. *The Secret History of Stalin's Crimes*. New York: Random House, 1953.

Pankhurst, Jerry G., and Michael Paul Sacks, eds. *Contemporary Soviet Society: Sociological Perspectives*. New York: Praeger, 1980.

Pethybridge, Roger. *A Key to Soviet Politics*. New York: Praeger, 1962.

Pipes, Richard. *The Formation of the Soviet Union*. Cambridge: Harvard University Press, 1954.

————. *The Russian Revolution*. New York: Alfred A. Knopf, 1990.

————. *Russia Under the Old Regime*. New York: Scribner, 1974.

Reddaway, Peter. "Russia on the Brink." *New York Review of Books*, January 28, 1993, 30–35.

Reed, John. *Ten Days that Shook the World*. New York: Vintage, 1960.

Remington, Thomas F. *The Truth of Authority, Ideology and Communication in the Soviet Union*. Pittsburgh: University of Pittsburgh Press, 1988.

Remnick, David. "Dead Souls." *New York Review of Books*, December 19, 1991, 72–81.

———— *Lenin's Tomb: The Last Days of the Soviet Empire*. New York: Random House, 1993.

Reshetar, John S. *The Ukrainian Revolution, 1917–1920*. Princeton, N.J.: Princeton University Press, 1952.

Roeder, Philip G. "Soviet Federalism and Ethnic Mobilization." *World Politics* 23 (January 1991): 196–233.

Roth, David F., Paul V. Warwick, and David W. Paul. *Comparative Politics: Diverse States in an Interdependent World*. New York: Harper and Row, 1989.

Saivetz, Carol, and Anthony T. Jones, eds. *The Emergence of Pluralism in the Soviet Union*. Boulder, Colo.: Westview Press, 1992.

Sakwa, Richard. *Gorbachev and His Reforms 1985–1990*. New York: Prentice-Hall, 1990.

Schapiro, Leonard. *The Communist Party of the Soviet Union*. New York: Vintage, 1964.

————. *The Origin of Communist Autocracy*. Cambridge: Harvard University Press, 1955.

Sedaitis, Judith, and Jim Butterfield, eds. *Perestroika from Below*. Boulder, Colo.: Westview Press, 1991.

Sharlet, Robert. *Soviet Constitutional Crisis*. Armonk, N.Y.: M. E. Sharpe, 1992.

Shipler, David K. *Russia: Broken Idols, Solemn Dreams*. New York: Penguin Books, 1989.

Shmelev, Nikolai, and Vladimir Popov. *Revitalizing the Soviet Economy*. New York: Doubleday, 1989.

Shub, Anatole. *The New Russian Tragedy*. New York: W. W. Norton, 1969.

Shub, David. *Lenin*. Middlesex, England: Penguin Books, 1966.

Smith, Gordon. *Soviet Politics*. 2d ed. New York: St. Martin's Press, 1992.

Smith, Graham, ed. *The Nationalities Question in the Soviet Union*. New York: Longman, 1990.

Smith, Hedrick. *The New Russians*. New York: Avon Books, 1991.

Solzhenitsyn, Alexander. *The Gulag Archipelago*. Trans. Thomas P. Whitney. New York: Harper and Row, 1973.

Talmon, J. L. *The Origins of Totalitarian Democracy*. New York: Praeger, n.d.

Teague, Elizabeth, and Dawn Mann. "Gorbachev's Dual Role." *Problems of Communism* 39 (January-February 1990): 1–14.

Ticktin, Hillel. *The Origins of the Crisis in the USSR*. Armonk, N.Y.: M. E. Sharpe, 1992.

Tolz, Vera. *The USSR's Emerging Party System*. New York: Praeger, 1990.

Trotsky, Leon. *The History of the Russian Revolution*. Ann Arbor: University of Michigan Press, 1965.

Tucker, Robert C. *Political Culture and Leadership in Soviet Russia*. New York: Norton, 1987.

————, ed. *Stalinism: Essays in Historical Interpretation*. New York: W. W. Norton, 1977.

Ulam, Adam. *The Bolsheviks*. New York: Macmillan, 1965.

————. *Stalin: The Man and His Era*. New York: Viking Press, 1973.

Vernadsky, George. *A History of Russia*. 6th ed. New Haven, Conn.: Yale University Press, 1969.

White, Stephen. *Gorbachev and After*. Cambridge: Cambridge University Press, 1991.

White, Stephen, Alex Pravda, and Zvi Gitelman, eds. *Developments in Soviet & Post-Soviet Politics*. Durham, N.C.: Duke University Press, 1992.

Wilson, Edmund. *To the Finland Station*. New York: Farrar, Straus, and Giroux, 1972.

Wolfe, Bertram D. *Three Who Made a Revolution*. Rev. ed. New York: Dell, 1964.

Wolin, Simon, and Robert M. Slusser. *The Soviet Secret Police*. New York: Praeger, 1957.

Wren, Melvin C. *The Course of Russian History*. 3d ed. New York: Macmillan, 1968.

Wright, Arthur. "The Soviet Economy." *Current History* 51 (October 1966): 218–25, 240–41.

Wright, Robin. "Report from Turkestan." *The New Yorker*, April 8, 1992, 53–75.

Yeltsin, Boris. *Against the Grain*. New York: Summit Books, 1990.

# INDEX

**About the Author**

BARBARA B. GREEN is Professor of Political Science at Cleveland State University, where she has held many administrative posts including Vice Provost, Interim Vice President for Academic Affairs, and Director of the General Education Program. Dr. Green has been a Visiting Professor at Ljubljana University and an associate with the Russian Research Center at Harvard. She has also been a faculty member at Wellesley College. Her present academic specialization is Russian and Central/Eastern European politics.

# DATE DUE

| | | | |
|---|---|---|---|
| NO¹2 '98 | | | |
| OC19 '99 | | | |
| NO29 '99 | | | |
| OC23 '00 | | | |
| AP19 '04 | | | |
| | | | |
| | | | |
| | | | |
| | | | |
| | | | |
| | | | |
| | | | |
| | | | |
| | | | |
| | | | |
| | | | |
| | | | |
| | | | |

DEMCO 38-297